"REDEMPTION" OF
AHASUERUS

BARUCH GITLIS

"REDEMPTION" OF AHASUERUS

The "Eternal Jew" in Nazi Film

Translated from the Hebrew by Dr. Norman Berdichevsky

HOLMFIRTH BOOKS
Astoria, New York

Cover design: Yehuda Salomon

Gitlis, Baruch
"Redemption" of Ahasuerus
Special Edition
Printed simultaneously in the U.S.A. and Israel

ISBN 965–414–001–2

CONTENT

Forward	9
Introduction	11
Preface	15

PART 1 PROPAGANDA — 19
1. The Art of Propaganda — 21
2. Film as an Instrument of Propaganda — 33
3. Art and Propaganda in Nazi Germany — 39
4. Ideology and Propaganda — 71
5. Propaganda and Stereotype in the Anti-semitic Film — 88

PART 2 THE NAZI ANTI-SEMITIC FILM — 107
1. Preliminary Anti-semitic Films — 109
2. *The Eternal Jew* the *Mein Kampf* of the Anti-semitic Nazi Cinema — 113
3. *Jud Süss*-Propaganda through entertainment — 143
4. *The Rothschilds* — 159
5. Summary and final word — 164

Appendices — 169
1. Appendix A *The Eternal Jew* — 171
2. Appendix B *Jew süss* — 187

Footnotes — 257
Recommended Film Bibliography in English and German — 267
Index — 272

'But bethink ye that one thing can redeem
you from the curse that burdens you: the
redemption of Ahasuerus: Destruction'

Richard Wagner
Judaism in Music

FOREWORD

Since its original formulation centuries ago, the Christian legend of the Wandering Jew, condemned for having rejected Christ on the way to the cross, has continued to exert a powerful influence. At first, the legend had only indirect connections with the Jews. It spoke of Cartaphilus, a porter in the service of Pontius Pilate who impiously struck Jesus on the back and mockingly said: "Go quicker, Jesus, go quicker; Why do you loiter?" Jesus, looking back at him said: "I am going, and you will wait till I return."

The legend has changed and details were added with the passage of time. A thirteenth century chronicle of Bolognese origin tells of Ahasuerus, a Jew by birth and native of Jerusalem, who was a shoemaker and had been present at the Crucifixion. According to the legend, when Jesus tried to rest a while on his way to martyrdom, Ahasuerus drove him along wickedly in order to impress his fellow Jews with these words "Go, go thou tempter and seducer, to receive what you have earned." Jesus is said to have replied: "I go, and you will wait for me until I come again." *(Ignoti Monachi Cistercencis S. Mariae de Feviarra Chronica...ed. A. Gandenzi, 1888.)*

Ahasuerus, then a cant name for Jew, through the familiarity it achieved in Purim plays, became the most common appellation of the Wandering Jew in later literature, though in French he is frequently called Issac Laquedem (a corruption of the Hebrew for Isaac the Old, or Isaac from the East). According to a German legend, this Ahasuerus was the Eternal Jew, an evil and insidious creature who infected the German People with cholera and syphilis.

In the Nazi cinema of hate, Ahasuerus, the Eternal Jew, became a fully fledged personification of the Jewish people, who had insinuated themselves into positions of power in order to destroy Germany and the German people.

INTRODUCTION

The origins of this book stem from a series of lectures I gave at the University of Tel Aviv and on the campus of Bar Ilan University in Ramat Gan, Israel, on the theme: The Propagation of Anti-Semitism in the 20th Century. In such an interdisciplinary theme, I dealt of course with the Nazi cinema of hate.

The view that the object of the cinema is solely to serve as a form of mass entertainment is regarded today as obsolete and simplistic. Even less sophisticated viewers understand today that films represent ideological and political positions, and that the cinema does not stand in the splendid isolation of innocence.

History has proven that from the very beginnings of its development, the cinema served clear ideological tendencies. At the same time that it is a tool of artistic expression and art form, the cinema also embodies something much more than just an attraction for the masses.

The cinema has always had the power not only to entertain, but also to teach, educate, convince, awaken, sell, incite, and perhaps even the power to cure afflictions or hypnotize (in the abstract sense of these concepts), a power that has the capacity "To root out and to pull down, to destroy and to throw down, to build and to plant," (Jeremiah 1:10). When this power was discovered, it was immediately exploited by educators, clerics, sociologists, psychologists, soldiers, politicians, presidents and of course, dictators.

The main thrust of this book is an examination of film propaganda and its practical realization in the anti-Semitic Nazi cinema.

Several of the films that were produced by the Nazi dictatorship still serve as the most outstanding examples of propaganda films. In this capacity they portray principles of propaganda which are characteristic and typical of totalitarian regimes. One must not, however, lose sight of the fact that wherever governments participated in the production of films in general, propaganda films did not lag far behind. As means of communication improved, so too did the importance of the cinema as a propaganda tool.

In an analysis of Nazi anti-Semitic propaganda films one must examine the special rhetoric of the cinema. The Nazis followed Aristotle who defined rhetoric as an art revealing and utilizing all available means of influence. This book places the Aristotelian definition in a cinematic context, and concentrates on the special qualities of the cinema which contributed to mass persuasion.

In this connection, the factors and reasons which led to the choice of the film as a propaganda/documentary genre are explored, and a detailed diagnosis is made of how the film *The Eternal Jew,* which can be called the *Mein Kampf* of the Nazi anti-Semitic cinema, uses the basic elements of this genre. Of course the anti-Semitic feature films, and especially *Jew Süss,* are explored as instruments for the achievement of ideological and political goals.

Since the book deals with the propagandistic rhetoric of the Nazi films, it takes on an interpretive ideological coloration. Its chapters are arranged according to a division by ideas rather than the chronological order of events – the usual framework of historical research. Even though this is not a historical research study in the accepted use of the term, it is a research in history examining certain matters according to their historical context. Among other things it looks at the Nazi films as "folk films." The question then arises: do these films reflect the mentality of the German people in a more comprehensive way than other forms of art, and do they represent a collective thought pattern and character of the German people? The answer is not simple.

It is obvious that as films they reflect popular motifs whose producers assumed that they were satisfying the popular will of the viewers. In that case does this "popular will" point to "a German who is evil from birth?"

It is not proper, of course, to speak of inherently evil Germans just as there are no such Jews. One must rather point to the power of a corrupt education of national traditions brought about by the special circumstances of German history.

Therefore, this book explores the theological, philosophical, and historial roots of German nationalism and anti-Semitism, which became the pillars of Nazi propaganda and found their special expression in films.

In this connection one could find the propagandist portrayal of the Jewish stereotype before the Nazis came to power. The propagandistic portrayal of the Jew in these films are analysed from the standpoint of the producers' anti-Semitic ideas and stereotyped biases. The Jewish stereotype was not created in Germany, but it was in Nazi Germany that it was portrayed for the first time in a consistent way, and in a concentrated form by the technical and qualitative means of the cinematic medium. In this way the cinema contributed to making the image of the Eternal Jew, which many Germans had only pictured in their imagination, into something concrete and alive on the screen with the use of propaganda. It became something almost tangible, making palpable the danger lurking on the doorstep of every German home.

12

An analysis of anti-Semitic Nazi propaganda cannot be carried out without an examination of the major theories of propaganda. Therefore, the approaches and definitions of social scientists and communication experts are reviewed. This is essential for understanding the concept of film propaganda as it was applied by totalitarian regimes, and to better insulate any civilized individual of the twentieth century from easily falling victim to its malignant aspects.

Although the main thrust of this book is an examination of film propaganda and its practical realization in the anti-Semitic Nazi cinema, it is not intended for film circles alone. The cinema developed from a minor and unimportant entertainment attraction to the most popular art form among the means of communication in the 20th century, and has become a part of our lives in the process.

Through the anti-Semitic films they produced, the Nazis attempted to exclude the Jew from society while in our time the film medium seeks to involve us in world events along with television, video cassettes, the computer and satellites, and influences our opinions and way of life.

Thus it is my hope that this book will lead to a greater consciousness and understanding of the power of films as a means of propaganda, and to a familiarity with the danger of its use by scoundrels.

It is appropriate here to express my appreciation to all those who have had a hand in contributing to this book in its final form. First and foremost I wish to thank Prof. Moshe Lazar, who closely followed my research during the last decade and helped me all along the way and whose advice was invaluable. Without him I would not have finished this book. I owe a debt of gratitude to the late Alfred Weichselbaum who helped me considerably during the period of research.

I also wish to gratefully thank Dr. Theo Fürstenau, the director of the German Institute of Film Art who granted me his time and shared with me his wide ranging views; Prof. Morton Zarkoff, for his patience, support and encouragement; Prof. Wolfram Von Hanwher, whose contacts in Europe opened many doors to me.

I am indebted to Reuben (Robbi) Wax who is particularly knowledgeable in the history of Germany and who helped me with the translation of texts and terminology in German and to Yoram (Rami) Tal who helped me with the editing of the Hebrew edition; my friend Jacob Saar whose professional advice helped me in the choice of photographs, and to Benny Bloch who helped me during my stay in Germany in retrieving German documents in which I had an interest.

I owe special thanks to the members of the The German Institute for Film Art through whose courtesy the illustrations for the book were submitted to me; to Dr. Norman Berdichevsky of the University of Tel

13

Aviv for his translation from Hebrew to English and editorial advice; to Yehuda Salomon for the graphic lay-out and to the staff of the Harry Karren Israeli Institute for the Analysis of Propaganda in Herzliya which placed at my disposal several of the films mentioned in the book and helped me with the coordination of research.

PREFACE

As was her custom each morning, the aged Martha Feuchtwanger refreshed her eyes with a view of the blue waters of the Pacific Ocean spread out before the third floor balcony of her villa. She concentrated her sight on a distant point on the horizon while in her mind arose a memory of a story from her rich and adventurous past at the side of her deceased husband, Leon, author of the novel *The Jew Süss.*

Suddenly the ringing of the telephone abruptly cut the flow of memories.

With an agility not typical of people her age, she hurried to her office one floor below. She sunk into one of the heavy armchairs in a room decorated with antique furniture, and listened to her secretary's voice over the telephone.

"A Swiss merchant wants to contact you immediately," said the secretary in a voice shaking with excitement. "In his hand he's holding the only negative in the world of the Nazi film *Jew Süss.*"

Martha reacted passively. "According to him, there are many other anxious takers ready to jump at a bargain but he prefers to sell it to you for $80,000," said the secretary in a secretive and choked voice. The secretary waited for an answer which was delayed in coming.

Martha smiled bitterly to herself. She muttered: "Anti-Semitism is still top-selling merchandise with plenty of people willing to pay a high price for it." She let out a sigh which her secretary took as a sign that the proposition was being weighed, but this was not the case.

The widow was familiar with the various transformations of the Nazi film *Jew Süss* and was not unaware of the trade in copies of the film. Even the attempt to sell a copy of the film to the brother of the king of Saudi Arabia, Ibn-Saud, who gave President Roosevelt a quick lesson on "The Jewish Problem," when they met, was also known to her.

"I don't have the slightest interest in it," declared Martha to the astonishment of her secretary. "If this Swiss dealer calls again, please slam the phone down on him," she ordered.

She then returned to the balcony of her house in the prestigious California community of Pacific Palisade, and looked out at the calm ocean. The incident brought her back to the dark days of October 1938.

In Germany that October was also known, among other things, as the time of the "Baarova scandal." The German Minister of Propaganda, Dr. Joseph Goebbels had cast his eyes upon Lida Baarova, a captivating novice Czech actress. The bedroom of the ruthless Minister of the world of the screen, was the surest way to a glittering screen career but his relations with Lida Baarova had burst through its four walls and become common knowledge.

His jealous wife, Magda, complained to the Führer about her husband who was then summoned by Hitler and warned that he would be removed from the government. Later, Lida Baarova told that Goebbels' answer to Hitler was, "I don't care if I go to Japan and sell neckties." However, in time Goebbles complied. He succeeded in remaining in his post and satisfying the will of the Führer in the conduct of Nazi propaganda. He stopped meeting with his actress lover.

However, due to the considerable occupation of German film personnel with the Minister and his love affair, their attention was diverted from a letter which they received during that month of October 1938. The letter was signed by the Minister of Propaganda himself. In it, he requested that they produce anti-Semitic films. Although there were no practical suggestions in this letter, those who received it were well aware of Goebbels' long term desire to see Marlowe's *The Jew of Malta*, and Shakespeare's The *Merchant of Venice* put on the screen.

The Minister's wish also reached far away Württemberg where the German author Ludwig Metzger lived at that time. From as early as 1921, Metzger had tirelessly labored to interest the German film companies in producing a film about a Jew named Süss Oppenheimer who had been active at the court of the Duke Karl Alexander of Württemberg.

The enormous success of the novel *The Jew Süss* by Feuchtwanger, which was published in 1925, increased Metzger's enthusiasm. When news of Goebbel's letter came to his attention, he decided to cease pounding on the doors of the film companies, and turned directly to the Ministry of Propaganda.

His appeal was accepted in Berlin as "a bull's eye, exactly what the doctor had ordered" and instructions were immediately given for production of the most notorious and poisonous film of the time, *Jew Süss*. The task was placed upon the director Veit Harlan who fulfilled the will of his masters to the last degree and produced an exemplary anti-Semitic film.

After the Second World War, Harlan was put on trial and accused of crimes against humanity. The principal accusation dealt with the notorious film, *Jew Süss*. He defended himself by claiming that he hadn't wished to produce the film at all. In his conversations with Goebbels, he referred to the script as "dramatized *Stürmer*," comparing it to the infamous Nazi anti-Semitic newspaper, edited by Goebbels' colleague, Julius Streicher.

Harlan even claimed that he was willing to be sent to the front rather than direct the film, but Goebbels' reply was: "If you won't direct the film, you will be considered a deserter and be condemned to execution by a firing squad, because all the staff of the German film industry are soldiers." But the scene which was revealed before the eyes of Harlan's judges was entirely different. They watched a screening of the film and observed a torrent of poison, hate, and distortion emanating from the direction, one dimensional acting, and the arrogant dialogue. Harlan had exploited to the maximum all artistic leeway in the service of anti-Semitic propaganda. The art which he prided himself in, coincided exactly with the "art" to which Goebbels had aspired.

During the trial however, the director who had pleaded for his life, changed his statement of the case, and acknowledged that he had presented the Jewish question in an artistic way and revealed a true picture of reality rather than a distortion.

At the same time as Harlan's trial was being held, Hans Frietsche was put on trial. He had been responsible for Nazi propaganda on the radio. The radio personality, like the film director, had been directly under Goebbels. The court ruled that, although his broadcasts bore a clear negative propagandistic character, there was no possibility to accuse him from a legal standpoint of participation in acts of murder.

Both Frietsche and Harlan wee acquitted based on this argument. The director of the film *Jew Süss* promised in public to destroy the negatives of the film in his possession. He even confirmed later that he had done so. But remarkably, since 1954, copies of the film began to appear frequently all across the world. An invisible hand, or perhaps not so invisible, began to distribute the film. The first copies were discovered in Egypt and Lebanon in Arabic language versions.

The aged Martha Feuchtwanger looked at the blue ocean waters. The sun began to rise and skip over the few waves. Peace and tranquility reigned all around, and there was not a hint that anti-Semitic propaganda continued to poison hearts in a world which had risen from the ruins of World War II and the ashes of the Holocaust.

17

PART 1
PROPAGANDA

1

THE ART OF PROPAGANDA

The Concept

Like air, propaganda is all around us. But unlike air, propaganda is generally thought of as a noxious element which poisons the social atmosphere. To say of a given presentation that it is propaganda is at once to dismiss or at least question its veracity and good faith. Ironically, the term, as originally coined in the sixteenth century, was the short form of the phrase *Congregatio de propaganda fide,* i.e. the one true faith as embodied in the Catholic Church.[1]

To this end, Pope Gregory XV, in 1622, established the College of Propaganda, consisting of a committee of cardinals to supervise the foreign missions of the church and the training of priests for these missions. Significantly, this was done at a time when Protestantism was making serious inroads among the church's faithful. Propaganda, as practiced from the seventeenth century up through the nineteenth, was the propagation or dissemination of dogma – originally religious, and then, from the French Revolution on, political dogma. One of the first to discern, clearly articulate, and to foresee the portentous implications of this tendency, was the English statesman, Edmund Burke. He wrote that it was difficult to predict the direction and speed of dissemination of the French anti-clerical sentiments throughout Europe, but that the church everywhere was on the defensive and had reached a low ebb. He attributed this largely to the power of the press which had increased its influence and audience many times over.

> The writers of these papers...are like a battery in which the stroke of any one ball produces no great effect, but the amount of continual repetition is decisive. Let us only suffer any person to tell us his story, morning and evening, but for one twelvemonth, and he will become our master.[2]

Despite, or perhaps because of, its ubiquity and influence, there is little agreement among social scientists and media specialists as to how to approach the concept of propaganda and how the term propaganda is to be defined.

The Popular Approach

The transformation of propaganda into an integral part of twentieth century politics brought in its wake a variety of approaches dealing with the term and its significance. The most widespread approach is the popular one which found its expression in books dealing with advertisements, public relations campaigns, and the supposedly scientific publications of the American Institute of Propaganda Analysis, which no longer exists. Many of the researchers who belong to the popular approach have themselves created the "handbag of lies" of the twentieth century, declaring that truth is not relevant. What is relevant is the question posed by Lewis Mumford: "Is there anybody who wants to believe it?"

Of course, history is full of examples in which lies were turned into truths that millions of people all over the world preferred to believe in and regard as valuable possessions. As a consequence, several of the popularizers even added oil to the fire by enlarging upon the negative connotation ascribed to the term propaganda. Others took an opposite view, and emphasized the importance of propaganda as a positive tool of political power and psychological warfare.

One of these is the English gentleman, John Hargrave, who wrote a book entitled *Words Win Wars*. This short work which has the subtitle: *Propaganda: The Strongest Weapon of All*, exemplifies the widespread exaggeration in popular literature regarding the power of propaganda. In this way it is represented as an all-powerful force, not at all "aristocratic," but definitely capable of replacing the bullet and the rifle, and triumphing in every war. Hargrave's exaggerated notion of the power of propaganda is expressed in the title. He defines propaganda as follows:

> The power that makes the trigger finger hesitate, or obey, is more powerful than armed force. It is the power of the Word: the word of Persuasion, the word of Command... Words build empires, and destroy them. Words bring people together and break them apart. Words carry all knowledge and foolishness.[3]

It is permissible to pardon these exaggerations in a popular work, the object of which was to direct the consciousness of a nation in the midst of war towards a fact which the author defines as follows:

> In modern war, not to use propaganda is treason. Not to use it skillfully is to court disaster.[4]

There is no doubt that during the war many people in Great Britain agreed with him.

But what about peacetime? Most people are simply not aware that propaganda exists and thrives in technologically advanced societies in times of peace. It resembles the air around us, of which we are not aware, but must have in order to breathe. Most people are therefore easy prey to propaganda because they associate it with lies, and assume that what is "true" cannot be propaganda.

It is a characteristic of modern sophisticated propaganda to operate with many different subjective or partial "truths" such as half-truths, limited truth, truth out of context, etc. It is the lack of a capacity to distinguish these distortions of truth that leads to the creation and implicit acceptance of many myths surrounding propaganda with which we shall now deal.

Propaganda is Associated Only with Totalitarian Regimes

The most apparent myth about propaganda ties it to the well-known totalitarian regimes, the communists in the Soviet Union, the Fascists in Italy, and above all, the Nazis in Germany. The explanation for this, is anchored in totalitarian thought, which seeks total rule over the life of the individual without hindrance, and acknowledges the superiority of the state and nation over any other consideration.

Totalitarian rulers in modern times have always cynically claimed that they seized power "in the name of the people," or were "called upon" by the masses to save them from danger. Those who did not shrink from calling the regime a dictatorship, embellished it with some form of legitimacy rather than the simple rule of a group or clique.

But all this has been to no avail, and failed to alter the dictatorial image in societies where freedom of thought and expression, rather than blind obedience, are still valued. The totalitarian regimes, in spite of their acrobatic semantics, are viewed as ruling in opposition to the freely expressed desires of the people. In public opinion the term propaganda is associated with oppressive regimes and coercion, dictatorship, fascism, communism, and violence against expression of thought and belief. All of these terms bear a negative connotation.

This association rests on a concrete historical foundation and is confirmed by no less an expert than Joesph Goebbels, outstanding student of German literature at the University of Heidelberg, chief editor of two newspapers who later became the Nazi Minister of Propaganda and Enlightenment.

Goebbels, the talented and fanatical speaker whom Hitler regarded as his heir, conducted propaganda catering to the most primitive instincts of the masses and in so doing paved the way to power for National Socialism. "We created the Third Reich with propaganda," wrote Goebbles in his

23

diary that was published in 1948, and reveals his conscious recognition of the criminal character of the Nazi regime. The virtuosity and cynicism of the Nazi propaganda machine was such that it succeeded in spreading absurd lies that no apparently sane individual would believe, yet they were assimilated by the nation which produced Kant, the philosopher of rational thought.

Although the historical examples speak for themselves, it is impossible to disregard the fact that propaganda exists in every mass society whatever the nature of the political regime. An interesting detail is that Nazi propaganda, in the form of the propaganda of a political organization, sprouted and flowered in a democratic regime, that of the Weimar Republic. The 25-point Nazi Party program of February 24, 1923 was composed by Gotfred Feder, declaring that a Jew could not be a part of the German people (*Volk*) or a citizen of the German state. It was published immediately after the promulgation of the constitution of the Weimar Republic.

The consolidation of the Nazi Party as the dominant power in Germany began in 1932 during the last democratic elections and in the wake of a propaganda campaign polluted by anti-Semitic motifs which were undoubtedly effective. This does not mean, of course, that the Nazis preferred to campaign under a democratic system. We have only to rely once again on the testimony of that master of words, Dr. Joseph Goebbels.

"We, the national socialists have never taken pride in representing democratic beliefs. But we openly declared that we used democratic means in order to achieve power. After achieving this power, we would ruthlessly deny all those means which had been granted to us when we were in the opposition."[5]

As is well known, the first institution Hitler eliminated was the parliament (the Reichstag). However, as long as he was outside the regime, Hitler used the parliament and parliamentary methods. This was part of the tactics of Nazi propaganda, to use all means if they served the end. It follows from this that the poisonous propaganda of the Nazis was, from the beginning, conducted within a democratic system which was known, accepted, and exploited at its weakest links.

From this it further follows that the root of evil is not propaganda itself as a process, but rather its content and the monopoly over its use. The connection between propaganda and absolutist regimes does not therefore reflect the entire picture.

It is universally recognized that in a democratic society, information is a kind of commodity and various sources of information are in competition with each other. In a totalitarian regime information is a monopoly of the

24

regime. Thus, the news simply becomes the official and selectively chosen pronouncements of the regime.

Consumers desire to obtain reliable information, but where there is a monopoly, indoctrination rather than information is all that can legally be acquired. In order to illuminate these differences, a monopoly of knowledge can be compared to the advertising field. In this way knowledge can be defined as something people are willing to pay for, and advertising, as what the advertiser pays for to bring a message to the attention of the consumers. The case of a monopoly in a totalitarian regime closely resembles advertising with the regime fulfilling the role of the advertiser.

The paradox is that in a democratic regime, the citizen's need for propaganda increases. Why? Modern mass society is characterized by a rapid expansion of education and enlightenment. This has brought about a situation in which the citizens of a democratic regime are no longer willing to act on the basis of commands and orders, but rather through their own conviction. As a result of urbanization and modern technology, the individual has lost many interpersonal contacts that used to provide him with information at frequent intervals.

Since the fundamental strength of democracy rests on the active participation of the citizen in the political process, even more than in the past, the citizen must have access to information in order to arrive at decisions of the political process, requiring a rational choice between alternatives. Modern life is full of situations in which we are called upon to decide what to buy, where to invest money, and of course, what political choice to make.

In contrast, however, to what philosophers might think, the need to decide is not a pleasure. It is rather a task performed under pressure. The increase in difficult problems facing a modern state leads to a situation in which even the most enlightened citizen is unable to absorb all the information relevant to a particular issue, and then to weigh all the alternatives. The citizen does not wish to appear unknowledgable about issues, and must therefore rely on partial information.

It is precisely here that propaganda enters the picture, supplying information to the citizens. This may be accurate, partially accurate, distorted, or false, all depending upon his self-interest. Whether the propagandist or "lobbyist" does a service or a disservice to his customer depends on the specific issues and interests involved.

The Myth of Propaganda's Unlimited Capabilities

Another myth is that propaganda enjoys unlimited power in modern society. According to this myth, propaganda is an unstoppable multi-armed octopus with tentacles extending everywhere. It is equipped with electronic devices able to exert unhindered control over the mind, and brings us close to the fulfillment of the terrible prophecy of the future totalitarian society pictured in George Orwell's famous novel, *1984.*

Vance Packard, in his book, *The Hidden Persuaders,* discussed the threat of mind-control by the use of propaganda to play on our subconscious. In effect we are unable to resist this form of propaganda because we are not even aware of it. Packard writes:

> The motivational analyst and symbol manipulators pooling their talents and with millions of dollars at their disposal, are a fascinating, and at times, disturbing team... In their operations beneath the surface of American life, [they are] starting to acquire a power of persuasion that is becoming a matter of justifiable public scrutiny and concern. [6]

Who then can save us from the movie theater owner who screens a subliminal slogan "Drink Coca-Cola" at a speed faster than the eye can register but which is absorbed by the brain at a lower level of consciousness. Of course our concerns and fears would be magnified many times if a political ideology could be sold as readily as the famous beverage. The power of our emotions to influence the mind is so strong that many fear a return to the primeval days of the Garden of Eden when the first naive human beings were seduced by the wiles of the serpent.

Our anxiety is even deepened when manipulators appear who glorify in their ability to influence our behavior by scientific means. Research on the power of communications is still in its infancy. While there is evidence regarding the ability of the media to influence us, this is mainly in the form of results after the fact. Research of advertising's ability to sell products as a result of commercial messages is also scanty in spite of many exaggerated claims.

The accepted statistics tell us that only one in ten new products distributed in the market fulfill the expectations of an American advertising and marketing campaign. From this it appears that the principle still directing advertising campaings is the pragmatic one: "What works works and what influences influences." [7] On this particular point we must not forget that modern man is much more sophisticated, and just as he is open to coercive propaganda, he is also capable to developing an awareness and resistance to it. In the light of all this, mass society must not be regarded only as a collection of isolated individuals, a nation of sheep easily sacrificed on the altar of propaganda. Instead we find a varied public, the majority of whom possess cultural and humane impulses as well as a large degree of sophistication and awareness.

The Myth That Changing Opinions is the Goal of Propaganda

Another myth is that propaganda's main objective is to change opinions. This is not correct. In many cases the purpose of propaganda is to strengthen already existing views and work to prevent them from being altered. In such cases the situation of the propagandist is easier and his chances of success are greater.

Modern man has a tendency to interpret various events through a system of opinions and values which have been formulated as a result of his life experiences, education, culture, and other factors. This system (or ideology) helps one to interpret events quickly without the need for much information. In other words, any event or confrontation is immediately placed within the context of an existing ideology enabling the individual to reach an immediate opinion.

Why is the propagandist's work easy in such a situation? It is because the individual is already predisposed to interpreting the event. The propagandist finds a receptive audience ready to absorb his message. In the case of unclear events, the propagandist helps his audience by providing a framework that assigns events to an existing set of cubby holes, thus strengthening the prevailing ideology.

The Myth of Propaganda's Connection With
The Means of Mass Communication Only

Another myth associates propaganda only with newspapers, television, radio, and cinema, the means of mass communication. This myth originated in the technological advances which gave propaganda new and very powerful tools, enabling it to reach a virtuosity in the presentation of events and a speed of dissemination previously undreamed of. Events can be transmitted instantaneously from as far away as the moon and edited so as to give an editorial coloration to suit any need.

This capability is proof of the media's power and potential effectiveness in the hands of clever propagandists. This does not mean however that propaganda by personal communication in the home and workplace is obsolete. Discussions, meetings, home study circles, gatherings, parties, and the exchange of letters still fulfill a role in influencing the formulation of opinions although views are divided on the degree of their effectiveness.

The Myth of Propaganda As the Enemy's Ploy

The myth that propaganda is what the enemy resorts to while our side would never stoop to such mean tactics is an accepted but groundless myth. Outstanding in this regard is the example of British photographers who made film diaries during World War I and were insulted when their work was described as political propaganda contributing to the strengthening of morale on the home front. Their photographs were authentic material without editorial direction or dramatic effects. Each picture followed the previous one in chronological order without any attempt to introduce artificiality or an unrealistic optical continuity.

Nevertheless, reality was unwillingly enslaved by the principle of selection. These diaries functioned as propaganda because the war was shown only from one side, and through the camera lens and angle chosen by the photographers. From their point of view, the photographers had indeed shown the war honestly, but it was only a half-truth. The allied side needed to portray a righteous cause, and emphasize the distinction between its method of providing information and the enemy's use of propaganda. The free world has searched for a term that would describe its actions, carrying a positive connotation.

It cannot be said that they have succeeded. The "Information Agency" of the United States which ostensibly deals only with the distribution of information or the Israeli "Center for Information" (in Hebrew the term is *hasbara,* variously translated as information, explanation, justification, retionalization; a term that does not have an equivalent in any other language), are simply semantic substitutes for propaganda. They dress the same lady in a more attractive coat, but if we remove it, we discover that all information is manipulative. This is well described by Jacques Ellul, the French sociologist and philosopher, in his seminal work *Propaganda: The Formation of Men's Attitudes:*

> Information never exists in a vacuum. It is gathered, created, molded, edited, packaged, released, sent out for a specific source to a specific audience in order to achieve a specific end. [8]

If this is the case, is there a way to educate people to correctly assess information? Does the educational system innoculate the student against the malignant effects of propaganda? A surprising answer is provided by Jacques Ellul. He stresses that education is the absolute prerequisite for absorbing propaganda. Education is called the "pre-propaganda phase," the conditioning of the mind with a vast amount of incoherent information already dispersed for ulterior purposes and posing as facts. Along this line, Ellul insists that the individual in a modern technological society needs to be propagandized, in order to be fully integrated. In this way

28

propaganda furnishes him with an explanation for all events. By providing all embracing simple explanations and a doctrinal cause, propaganda exerts a powerful force over the individual. Without it, the news may be unintelligible.

Ellul thus reverses the widespread notion that education is the best prophylactic against propaganda, and concludes by designating intellectuals as the most vulnerable group to modern propaganda. This affinity for propaganda is explained by the fact that intellectuals absorb the largest amount of second-hand unverifiable information; they feel a compelling need to have an opinion on every important question of our time, and thus easily succumb to opinions offered to them by propaganda on all such indigestible pieces of information, and they consider themselves capable of "judging for themselves." They literally need propaganda.

The Definitions of Propaganda

If intellectuals are indeed capable of judging for themselves, what about the ordinary man-in-the-street? Can one define what propaganda is, and what it is not? From a review of the different definitions formulated during the last fifty years by social scientists and experts in the communications field, there is no unanimous agreement in defining propaganda. All the definitions focus on the transfer of information, ideas, or value from one person or group to another. However, the definitions diverge in stressing either the purpose, or the effect of the message, or the techniques used to transmit it.

G. Driencourt has gone the farthest by proposing that "everything is propaganda." [9] Apart from the melodramatic quality of this definition, it does not help us progress towards understanding the concept.

Prof. Clyde Miller, who was the director of the American Propaganda Analysis Institue, emphasized propaganda's intention. He held that it is "the expression of opinion or action of other individuals or groups with reference to predetermined ends." [10] H.L. Childes similarly defined it as "an attempt deliberately to influence the minds of other people." [11] Leo Rosten has also asserted that is is the intention, rather than the effect upon the audience, which is decisive. He continues, however, to point out that what is considered propaganda in one forum may not be considered as such in another. For example, a film about free elections would not be considered propaganda in the United States, but might well be labeled as such in the Soviet Union. [12]

All the definitions we have dealt with up to now have rested on the assumption that propaganda is something planned. Can propaganda

29

nevertheless be unplanned, unconscious, non-voluntary, or subliminal? Leonard Doob, the social psychologist, has dealt with this problem. He analyzes it from a psychological viewpoint, and gives as examples the teacher in the classroom and the judge in the courtroom. The teacher is also an educator even if he is not aware of the role of propaganda in his lecture or lesson. The same is true of the judge when he passes sentence.

I am not sure, however, if these two examples can be considered as pure non-voluntary propaganda. Both the teacher and the judge may be aware of their propaganda roles of passing judgement, sentence, or lecturing a class as an example for others to follow. It seems to me that what Doob calls non-voluntary propaganda is part of a planned complex system of influence and institutional control, but only if neither the teacher nor the judge have any vested interests. This should not be confused with the distinction Doob makes between open propaganda, which reveals the intentions of the propagandist, and camouflaged propaganda which masks intentions.

It is noteworthy that the question of intention in the definiton of the concept of propaganda is considered problematic by Doob. On the other hand he emphasizes the "use of suggestion," and presupposes a certain level of balanced thought and direction. If individuals are controlled by the use of suggestion, then the process may be called propaganda, without considering whether or not the intention of the propagandist was to exercise control. In another work, Doob suggests another definition:

> Propaganda can be called the attempt to affect the personalities, and to control the behavior of individuals towards ends considered unscientific or of doubtful value in a society at a particular time... The dissemination of a viewpoint considered by a group to be "bad," "unjust," "ugly," "unnecessary," is propaganda in terms of that group's standards.[13]

Doob's definition reflects a certain reality in which each group decides which viewpoints to disseminate as propaganda, and also determines the scale of values between positive and negative.

Moreover, Doob's definition calls, in practice, for a conservatism and a rejection of any new idea that does not conform to the established standards of the particular group. In following Doob we are left without any objective definition acceptable to everyone. Nor did he succeed in ignoring the concept of intention which lies at the base of propaganda.

Other researchers have chosen to focus attention on the tools and means of transmission at the propagandist's disposal. Most important of these has been Harold Lasswell, the American pioneer of propaganda research in the United States whose definition of propaganda as an

30

instrument of social control is accepted my many investigators: "The manipulation of public opinion by means of political symbols." [14] It is not the use of bombs or starvation, violence, blockade, or bribery which constitute propaganda, but words, pictures, songs, parodies, and similar methods. Frizer, the author of *Propaganda*, continues this approach in his picturesque metaphor of a donkey. Trying to influence its behavior by whipping is not propaganda. Neither is offering it a carrot. But if the donkey's master shouts at it threateningly or tries to entice it to work harder by sweet words and promises, then the word propaganda is applicable. [15]

A number of researchers have made use of a similarity they see between propaganda and education. In both, knowledge is acquired and both attempt to consolidate or change approaches and opinions. However, a difference can be made on the basis of a consideration of the goals or final results of these two activities. Lester Markel, who analysed propaganda in foreign policy, is one who regards the two as differing only in terms of the objective; education seeks to enlighten while propaganda attempts to persuade. The two may be thought of as two ends of the same stick. [16]

The close relationship between education and propaganda fits the "democratic interpretation" as expressed in British documentary films from the very beginning of the documentary film. It has been well formulated by John Grierson, regarded as "The father of the documentary film," and the coiner of the term itself.

> If we are to persuade, we have to reveal; and we have to reveal in terms of reality... Recognizing the deeper levels of understanding and exposition into which information in a democracy would inevitably reach, it is possible to appreciate that even the once haunted concept of propaganda may have a democratic interpretation, and that its democratic interpretation makes propaganda and education one. [17]

Grierson's interpretation stands in sharp contrast to the totalitarian concept as expressed by Goebbels who boasted in 1939 that "We created the Third Reich with propaganda." The false reality devised by the Nazi propaganda machine in order to rule over millions of Germans was the complete opposite of Grierson's conception that persuasion should be achieved by means of the existing reality. As John Hohenberg has pointed out in the *Professional Journalist,* the temptation is always great to make reality fit expected conclusions, and even journalists who fancy themselves as fair and objective can fall into propagandistic patterns. Did Grierson really imagine himself to be an objective producer of documentary-films, or at least a fair one? Answers to questions like this must take into account the crucial question posed by Mumford about the truth: "Does anyone want to believe this?"[18] In this regard, no one can ignore the fact that as an instrument for both good and evil ends, propaganda has become part of the marketplace of ideas, and that inevitably, in a democratic society there are many competing propagandas, rather than a single one. With all its trappings, it is probably very desirable that propaganda has become vital to our lives in the twentieth century. It behooves us to understand its mechanisms, appeal, power, and potential.

2

FILM AS AN INSTRUMENT
OF PROPAGANDA

The recognition of the almost mystic and hypnotic power of the cinema is today shared by everyone. As early as 1911, V.I. Lenin referred to film as "the most important of the arts," and spoke of the enormous potential of what he called democratic cinematography for advancing the cause of international communism.[1]

Joseph Goebbels realized as well the potential of making the cinema into such a powerful and effective tool that it could be defined as "a weapon." Goebbels even called film "the most encompassing medium in existence for influencing the masses."[2]

On the other hand, the French educator and cinema personality, Jean Benourt-Levy, saw the potential of cinema in influencing the masses in a positive direction," the most powerful medium for nourishing the mind of man among human inventions."[3]

Roger Manwell, however, sees the cinema in a wider framework as "an auxiliary device for the citizens of the world to recognize their problems, the possibilities before them, ... and to understand themselves and others."[4]

While many similarities can be found betwen film and other art forms, in a number of important repects film is unique. Its uniqueness lies primarily in its virtually unrestricted use of time and space. Unlike the stage play, film is capable of providing a continuous, unbroken flow, blurring transitions in time and space while still leaving them absolutely clear. Unlike the novel and the poem, the film communicates not in abstract symbols, but directly through concrete images and sounds. Furthermore, as Ernest Lindren points out, film is capable of treating an almost unlimited variety of subjects.

> It is impossible to conceive of anything which the eye might behold or the ear hear, in actuality or in imagination, which could not be represented in the medium of film. From the poles to the equator, from the Grand Canyon to the minutest flaw in a piece of steel, from the whistling flight of a bullet, to the slow

growth of a flower, from the flicker of thought across an impassive face, to the frenzied ravings of a madman. There is no point in space, no degree of magnitude or speed of movement within the apprehension of man which is not within the reach of the film.[5]

In his analytical study of time, Joseph Boggs discovers some new insights into the range films are capable of spanning:

Film is unlimited not only in its range of subject matter, but also in the scope of its approach to that material. In mood and treatment it can range anywhere between the lyric and the epic, in point of view it can cover the entire spectrum from the purely objective to the intensely subjective, in depth it may focus on the surface realities and the purely sensual, or delve into the intellectual and philosophical. In the dimension of time, film can look backward to the remote past or probe forward into the distant future, it can make a few seconds seem like hours, or compress a century into minutes. Finally, film is capable of evoking the entire spectrum of human sensitivity from the most tender, delicate, fragile, and beautiful feelings to the most brutal, violent, and repulsive.[6]

Another important property of film is the heightened sense of reality and immediacy. The psychologist Doob observes that even though the spectator...

knows that the picture has been produced in a studio and is therefore not a direct reflection of life, nevertheless, sometime during the film or perhaps throughout, he attributes a certain degree of reality to what he is seeing and hearing. Fixation upon the screen reduces the strength of competing responses which might destroy the illusion, and the images he perceives come to represent, for the time being, real people in a real situation.[7]

This is primarily due to the flow of sight and sound together with the uncanny manipulation of time so that everything appears in the present tense. But this immediate sense of reality created by the film does not necessarily mean that the audience will react to the film events as they would to real ones. As Professor Michotte Van den Berck points out:

In real life, an accident or a flight would cause an active reaction; running away, intervention, expostulation. In the cinema there is ordinarily no active bodily response, and the reactions of the audience are largely confined to the expression of emotion.[8]

Siegfried Kracauer emphasizes the feelings aroused when viewing a film. He suggests that we go to the cinema to see a film, and this provides a certain aesthetic distance or removal. People like to be scared to death, or to enjoy a good cry, provided it is in the cinema and not in real life. Although the events on the screen are not happening here and now, film nevertheless creates a powerful impression of being present.[9]

Moreover, the events are happening to other people, not to the viewer. This will affect the film audience more or less strongly according to the type of treatment and to the extent which the spectator identifies himself with one or the other of the characters.

Another significant factor in analyzing the effectiveness of motion pictures as a propaganda tool has to do with the spectator's relation to, and identification with his fellow spectators. Doob notes that the spectator is stimulated by the presence of other people, and by their expressions of approval or disapproval. "He may project his own feelings, or seek to conform to what he perceives to be their reactions."[10] Thus, film comprises a link between collective thoughts and emotions, while as an art form it totally grips the viewer. Here we should add that the individual learns from his fellow viewers, on cue from the film director, how to respond to their behavior.

The uniqueness of the film medium can also be seen in the way in which it can virtually control the attention as well as the environment of the audience by limiting the audience's field of perception to what the camera (director) selects. In the darkened theater the audience's attention is almost hypnotically directed towards the flickering screen, and the sound track is usually more intense than the coughs, conversations, and other distractions. Hence, film can literally capture the audience's attention, fix his viewpoint, and thus prevent him from exercising free thought. The viewer is simply reduced to the level of absorption. Kracauer, in his monumental *Theory of Film,* likens the moviegoer to a hypnotized person "spellbound by the luminous rectangle before his eyes – which resembles the glittering object in the hand of a hypnotist."[11]

It is worth repeating that film viewers in a movie theater are a kind of voluntary captives, and subject to the norms of appropriate behavior which are part of the viewing experience. There is a readiness to believe in the screen images as representing the truth. Most of those viewing a film are not conscious of the fact that they are sitting in absolute darkness for much of the time the film is being screened. This envelopment in total darkness is conducive to the absorption of messages, as Amos Vogel points out in his book, *Film As A Subversive Art:*

During the same infinitesimal period, every image is shown to the audience twice, once as a still photograph; for the film comes to a dead stop in the projector forty-eight times in the course of a single second ... Thus during half the time spent at the movies, the viewer sees no picture at all. Without the viewer's physiological and psychological complicity, the cinema would not exist... Could it be precisely during the period of total darkness – 45 out of every ninety minutes of film we see – that our voracious subconscious, newly nourished by yet another provocative image, "absorbs the work's deeper meaning and sets off chains of associations?"[12]

The degree of susceptibility of the film-viewer also engaged the interest of Brunius. He recognizes the power of the situation of the spectator who "cannot help succumbing to the suggestions that invade the blank of his mind," and in this regard film is an incomparable instrument of propaganda. With his attention thus "held captive" the viewer's judgment and intellect are suspended. He is thus rendered highly vulnerable to the film's emotional impact.

The powerful psychological effect was best understood by Kracauer and articulated by him in his classical study of the theory of film. He claimed that the film's assault on the sensory and visceral processes of the spectator causes him to relinquish a certain amount of control over his thoughts and judgment. The net effect of these attacks is to lower the threshold at which judgement and reason are exercised. To be effective, propaganda must supplement its reasoning power with insinuations and incentives to influence the stomach muscles more than the head.

"Films do precisely this" says Kracauer, ... "provided of course they are not just illustrated sales talk but ... genuine films, with the emphasis on pictorial communication. Since film images lower the spectator's critical faculties, it is always possible to select and arrange them in such a way that they adjust his senses to the idea advertised."[13]

Thus, the influence of the film medium on the "stomach muscles" i.e. the senses, is threefold. First, the physical reality, which the film brings to the screen, leads the viewer to act exactly as he would if the situation and the figures involved in it were real. The cinema is capable of bringing the viewer to a physical as well as a psychological involvement. It can cause him to shed tears, to feel a lump in his throat, to burst into hysterical laughter to the point of causing stomach pain, and even to the point of fainting.

Walt Disney's short film *America the Beautiful,* shown at the Bell Telephone Company's exhibition hall in Disneyland, is an excellent example of the cinema's ability to totally influence the spectator's senses

36

and to weaken his conscious awareness.

The film is shot from above an automobile by nine cameras which exactly cover a circle of 360 degrees. The film is shown by nine projectors on nine screens set in a circle. Each screen therefore shows a segment of 40 degrees of the total picture. The viewer is located in the center of the hall, and can view any side. Wherever he looks he sees the scene which he would see if he were located on top of the car where the cameras are. If for example the sea is located to the right of the car and a chain of mountains on the left, this is exactly what the viewer sees inside the hall at the time of screening.

Second, during the course of viewing, the spectator loses his sense of reality completely. When the car on which the cameras were placed travels at high speed down the slope of famous Lombard Street in San Francisco, known for its sharp winding bends, the viewer loses his balance just as he would if he were on top of the car in reality. The planners of the exhibition hall were well aware of this effect and built a special bannister which the spectator can grab hold of so as not to "fall off" the car.

This proves that the viewer, sitting in his seat which is held fast to the ground in a movie theater, can in effect experience constant motion, from an aesthetic viewpoint. His eye becomes a camera changing directions and distances, and even the space before him is continually moving.

Motion is the foundation of the cinematic art and technique. There is a well-known biological fact that motion which we are aware of causes an internal bodily reaction and stimulates the organic senses to activity. All these in combination with the ability of the film to reach unrealistic dimensions of time and space, create an organic tension, excitement, the result of which is an unconscious sense of liberation from the rational control we normally exercise over making decisions.

In this way, the use of concrete filmatic means, called visual rhetoric, can influence our thought processes. In the 20th century a cinematic language has been created. It is basically a visual and universal language unhindered by the verbal control of a particular language, or the ability to read and write, (when sound films were introduced, this detracted somewhat from the universality of the cinema).

And so the camera has become a central focus in demonstrating the ability of the cinema's visual rhetoric, and with the accompaniment of lighting, it can create without sound a controlled impression of the photographed object on the audience. For example, the filming of an object from a low angle creates an impression of force and strength, and enlarges the dimensions of the filmed object. In contrast, the filming of an object from a high angle creates the opposite effect. Philosophical motifs as well, such as man's powerlessness before the forces of nature, or his loneliness in the universe, can also be constructed beforehand by the proper use of the camera and lighting as part of the visual rhetoric.

Because of its visual expression, film can play upon the emotions of the viewing audience and not only on its intellect. The cinema can create agreement to general ideas such as ideology, the enemy, the leader, without the use of words. From this it follows that the cinema makes less demands on the viewer. Its messages are more easily understood than those of the written or spoken word, and thus its propagandistic appeal can be made at a lower, (even primitive) level, and even subconsciously.

In addition, one must not forget the technical possibility embodied in the film medium, notably the ability to repeat the same phenomenon exactly before millions of viewers, innumerable times, today, tomorrow and even ten years from now.[13]

3

ART AND PROPAGANDA
IN NAZI GERMANY

Art as a Subversive Instrument

In totalitarian states, art plays a critical role in the propaganda apparatus of the regime. Hellmut Lehman-Haupt, in his research on the role of art in totalitarian society, noted that the modern dictator takes art very seriously. It is not a matter of decoration and embellishment.

> He always sees it as a vital part of the very nerve center of the social organism ... that is why he must control it absolutely, must mould it into a completely subservient instrument. He uses art to integrate every single individual into the fabric of the state, and with it he builds the triumphant symbols of his conquest.[1]

Although the rate of the Nazi dictatorship's development varied according to different circumstances, its final goal was always absolute control. Art was one of the most effective means in achieving this control. In a speech at the final session of the International Film Conference on April 25, 1935, at the Kroll Opera in Berlin, Joseph Goebbels said that:

> art must bridge the gap between politics and emotions, and that even the greatest artists are the sons and daughters of the nation who derive their material from the soil of the homeland.[2]

The institutionalization or implementation of the Nazi regime's concept of art and "artistic freedom" was primarily the responsibility of the Ministry of Propaganda and Enlightenment, headed by Goebbels, and other agencies closely connected to it, such as the Reich Chamber of Culture *(Reichs-Kulturkammer),* founded in September, 1933. The Reich Chamber was given the grandiose task of encouraging "all forms of artistic creation or creativity which appear in public;" it was one of the principal instruments of cutural control.[3]

In practice this agency followed artistic criteria which catered to the lowest common denominator of German popular taste. Popular taste in art was exploited as an essential part of a complete world view in Nazi Germany. Emphasis was placed on qualities which served the goal known as creation of an "organic" folk and its "healthy instincts." Among these qualities were the advantages of a pre-industrial society and the family. The farmer was made into the symbol of "the new man," and art served a "purer Germanism."

"What is this Germanism in German art?" asked Kurt Karl Aberlein, literary critic and historian of German art, and answered:

> German art is the fatherland, and longing for home, the same home which the German loves so, the room, the mirror in which his being is reflected ...whoever is familiar with the image of the German room, knows what is meant. The soul is turned into a room, and into German dress ... Today the principal goal of the architect is to create a room for family life in which the spirit of the family resides, and from which it casts its influence.[4]

This definition of art was conducive to the masses who, according to Goebbels, do not like "problematic art" but prefer simple understandable pictures which are not distorted by any kind of "expressionism." Only in this way will art find its close contact with the masses who hate artistic "degenerate" experiments. According to the official line such abstractions were the results of a "sick mind." When this line became well publicized, art criticism was eliminated in "its previous form" and the concept of "art critic" was replaced in practice by that of "art reporter."[5]

By destroying every shred of spontaneity in art, and making of it a consumer product for a mass audience, art too was integrated into the centralized hierarchy and turned into a tool for ideological solidarity and control.

In his address before the annual Congress of the Reich Chamber of Culture on the 26th of November, 1937, Goebbels explained the abolition of art criticism.

> The responsibility for the phenomenon of degeneration in art is in large measure the fault of art criticism. For the most part art criticism has created tendentious issues and trends. It has not judged artistic development in terms of healthy folk instincts but only in terms of the emptiness of intellectual abstractions. The people have never shared in it, but rather turned away in horror from an artistic tendency which could not be brought into harmony with its healthy sensibilities, and which could only be regarded as the abortive product of a snobbish decadence. The abolition of art criticism and the introduction of art observation has, for almost a year now, been criticised as "barbaric and impractical" by large segments of world opinion, but in the meanwhile it has exerted its influence into every corner of our country. Now the public itself functions as critic and by means of

its participation, or non-participation, expresses a clear judgement upon its poets, artists, composers, and actors.[6]

By eliminating the influence of the autonomous and independent art critic, whose aesthetic and general cultural background had its roots in the Western European Liberal tradition, the Nazi leadership attempted to acquire *carte blanche* in forcing every artistic expression to serve its own end: complete and total integration of the individual in the "New Order." In this way, art served as a tool, even a weapon, in the service of the Third Reich.

Both Hitler and his minister of propaganda, Goebbels, were quite articulate about the aim and fuction of propaganda. Hitler, writing in *Mein Kampf*, discussed the "ideal audience" or target for propaganda.

To whom should propaganda be addressed?....
To the scientifically trained, or the less educated masses? All propaganda must be popular and its intellectual level must be adjusted to the most limited intelligence of those to whom it is addressed.[7]

Hitler continued in the same vein on the subjective character of the people whom he described as:

...so feminine in their nature and attitude that their thoughts are motivated less by sober consideration than by feeling or sentiment. This sentiment, however, is not complicated, but very simple and complete. There are not many gradations and abilities to distinguish. There is rather positive or negative, love or hate, right or wrong, truth or falsehood, but never half measures which might have given cause for doubt.[8]

Hitler also viewed the masses unflatteringly as slow and lazy with faulty memories. They always "need a certain time before they are even ready to notice a thing, and they will use their memories only after the thousandth-fold repetition of the most simple ideas."[9]

From these observations, Hitler arrived at the fundamental basis of Nazi propaganda. When dealing with the masses as a target audience one must never approach them with negotiations and discussions, but rather instill in them anger, aggression, and self-confidence. "Propaganda should confine itself to a few points which must be used as slogans until everyone knows exactly what each word stands for."[10] This unsophisticated concept of propaganda served as the cornerstone for the imposing edifice of Nazi organization, and guided the mechanism of the regime's propaganda machine. In spite of the fact that there was nothing new in this concept, the propaganda machine created was awesome in its power and virtuosity.

Goebbel's concept of propaganda supplemented Hitler's. Goebbels, however, emphasized that propaganda must take its target audience into account and speak in different tongues to convince the intellectuals as well as the masses. Both agreed on strengthening the feelings of deprivation and humiliation to increase the desire for Germany's recovery.

In realizing the practical implementation of his concept of propaganda, Goebbels spoke to the intellectuals of Nietzsche's German "blond beast," while in the beer cellars the Nazis sung in the intoxicating language of *Deutschland uber alles* (Germany above all), and in the streets, their refrain was the terrifying battle hymn of the Horst Wessel Song, "When Jewish blood spirts from the knife, all will be so much better."[11]

Thus, the sphere of the "masses" extended deep into the middle and upper classes as well as a strata of intelligentsia. However, propaganda efforts were largely concentrated on the man-in-the-street. In Goebbel's opinion, in order to succeed in propaganda, one must not lose oneself in...

the ivory tower of scientific inquiry. The nature of propaganda lies essentially in its simplicity and repetition. Only the man who is able to reduce problems to the simplest of terms who has the courage to repeat them indefinitely in this simplified form despite the objections of the intellectuals, will in the long run, achieve fundamental success in influencing public opinion.[12]

Thus, from the propagandistic tactical view, Germany's problems were reduced to the war against the Jew, the one enemy who is the source of all evil. The painting of the enemy as the devil, an inhuman demon on the one hand, and a recognizable enemy on the other, only increased the fear of him, and by this means Hitler forged his control over the masses.

The tactics were delineated to prevent fighting a war on too many fronts. Rather, efforts were made to narrow Germany's enemies to one, and ascribe to him every possible defect. Everything which did not match Germany's policies was presented as a result of the machinations of influential Jews so that even the war against Russia was portrayed as a war against world Jewry.

In internal policy, difficulties in destroying German institutions such as the Reichstag were overcome by representing parliamentary democracy as a Jewish institution. This tendency prevented any rational debate. Issues which were uncomfortable for the regime could always be ascribed to a Jewish connection and thus simply resolved.

In order to make the proposed solution more palatable, expressions were coined referring to the Jews which became rooted in public consciousness so that no solution except the Nazi one was possible.

Expressions such as "reptiles and parasites," "cancerous growth," "vision of decay," "microbes and insects," "Bacillus Judaicus," "cockroaches and rats," as well as specific German terms such as *"untermensch"* (sub-human), "unmensch" (non-human), *satansmensch* (devil-man), *"Gegenmensch"* (opposition-man), and *"Anti-mensch"* (anti-man), to stir up feelings of disgust and the need to exterminate such vermin by use of gas. Against this Nazi vision of distorted "political biology" stood the inhibitions of education, religion, and humanitarian feelings. The Nazi methods of propaganda were designed to encourage the ordinary German to cut himself off from any link to such inhibitions from the past.

Goebbels understood that for his concept of propaganda to succeed, he would have to create a situation of total propaganda. This meant that propaganda had to address itself to every audience, to be found everywhere, at any time, and to reach the individual by all existing means. He succeeded in achieving just this in practice by means of anti-Semitic propaganda.

Wherever the German turned, he met his most "dangerous enemy," the Jew. In the press he encountered prominently featured articles against the Jews, including defamatory pictures, sadistic and pornographic caricatures in the style of *Der Stürmer*. When he turned on his radio, he was assailed by the curses and insults of the Nazis against the Jews. While he walked in the street he encountered posters and slogans against the Jews at every square, on every wall and billboard. Even graffiti greeted the German at the entrance to his dwelling: "Wake Up Germany, Judah Must Rot!" "In Pushing Back the Jew, I fight for the Acts of the Creator."

The streets buzzed with trampling marchers, screaming at the top of their lungs the National-Socialist battle cry: Germany Awake, Judah Rot in the Grave," or "The Jews are our misfortune" alongside the slogan: "One People, One Nation, One Leader."

Hitler spoke of this in a conversation with Rauschning:

> In the street, at the factory, in the bakery, in the underground train station, wherever ten or twelve people gather they will react as a mass, and forget all logic.[13]

Wherever there is no debate or attempt to persuade by the force of argument except by decree, without the right to appeal, and by continuous repetition, the absurd eventually becomes the unopposed "truth."

The Mass Meeting and *Triumph of the Will*

The history of the Nazi period falls nicely into two parts. The first, from 1933 to 1939, has been well explained and documented by George Sadoul.[14] The second phase from 1939 to 1945 began only when

> ...Hitler's position at home and abroad was sufficiently consolidated for his war machine to be set in motion... [then] did the Nazi film enter its second phase. The concentration and exploitation had now been carried out completely and prepared for psychologically inside and outside Germany.[15]

Under the Nazis, the cinema reached new heights of brutality, opposed to all the rules of film aesthetics. The film, *The Eternal Jew* became a standard for the constant repetition of slogans combined with the demonstration of force and acts of violence and terror. In this way the Nazis created the feeling of an irrepressible force which could not be defeated, leaving opponents with the feeling of, "if you can't beat them, join them."

In addition to this irrepressible force, Goebbels also understood the principle of constant motion. In this connection, Bismarck's famous remark is recalled, "Enthusiasm cannot be contained like sardines in a can." Goebbels followed the same concept by constantly fanning the "burning, warming, and illuminating flame," feeding propaganda with more propaganda in an endless spiral.

The totality of Nazi propaganda was not concerned only with tactics and techniques. It integrated several streams from the fields of philosophy, science, literature, and art to a melting pot of one ideology, namely race. At its center stood the declaration of the superiority of the German individual, the German nationality, and the German state, raised to the level of a powerful kingdom of the Aryan master race.

This concept of racial identity became the yardstick for measuring and evaluating Judaism, Christianity, "Germanism," nationalism and culture; in short, everything. This faith in the triumphant future of the Aryan race became the most precious possession of the individual German. The ambition to realize this victory through struggle became the national ethos uniting individuals.

In the light of this, the activities of the well-planned and calculated propaganda machine had to appear as the activities of spontaneous enthusiasm which called forth a sense of irresistible power. In the Nazi mass meetings, the flame of enthusiasm was fanned not only by what was said there, but by the very participation in mass suggestion. Hitler wrote in *Mein Kampf:*

44

> The individual...when he marches for the first time from his small workshop or from the large plant in which he feels quite small, and arrives at a mass demonstration surrounded by thousands of people possessing the same faith...he surrenders himself to the magical influence of what we call mass suggestion.[16]

An impressive film document presenting the heights to which Nazi propaganda reached in mass meetings where thousands of people were enthralled in total abandonement and ecstasy, is Lenny Riefenstahl's *Triumph of the Will.* The film documents the meeting of the Nazi Party in Nuremberg in September, 1934. It shows how close bodily contact led to a common sense of excitement breaking down all the natural barriers of individual behavior. From the psychological point of view, the situation created an atmosphere conducive to hysteria.

Nazi propaganda succeeded in eliminating the sense of time during this mass meeting with Hitler. Only thus can we understand the impression of Wolfgang Bruge, writer and critic, who wrote in *When I Hear This Voice:*

> During the last few years I have had the same deep experience whenever I heard this voice ... I always felt that it was directed to me personally. This voice spoke to me, an anonymous person among millions, in order to set me on the right track, to lighten my way so that I would be a German. This voice found its mysterious way inside me. It pulled out the latches behind which my last shred of faith was imprisoned. It broke through the doors and burned away all doubts, suppressed the cowardly dog, and aroused the hero to action.[17]

Lucy Davidowicz has asked:" Was this the physical quality of the hypnotic voice itself, or perhaps the charisma in the message of the superiority of race and the rule of blood?"[18]

In a certain sense, it was the charisma of Hitler. How do we determine this? By the number of people who followed him without relating to the ideological content of his words or political arguments. They followed him because he was the incarnation of their hidden dreams, expressing their most passionate ambitions, speaking with the voice of the masses, knowing how to find a tone which can penetrate one's heart. It was Heine who prophesied to the French eighty years before Hitler, warning against the danger of the charismatic appeal of a leader who is nothing less than the devil which appears in German national poetry.

Shlomo Aharonson spoke of this devil theme in an interview in an Israeli newspaper:

In this poetry the devil resides on a mountaintop of demons, in the image of a black monster, while naked witches dance around him in mad ecstasy. Heine could not have imagined that the mountains and swamps of the North would engender a devil in the shape of a man...around whom a whole nation would ride, bewitched, and driven mad against the background of Wagner's music.[19]

A partial answer to the questions of charisma and the quality of the physical setting can be found in the composition and planning of the mass meetings. Each physical element was meticulously planned in accordance with the Nazi ideology, with the *Führer* in the center whom the masses continually salute. The architecture in the stadium was grandiose. The speakers' stages enhanced the authority of the speakers who were illuminated by sunlight during the day and by torches at night. The stadium was turned into a forest of party flags, a sea of jackboots, and polished and shining uniforms. The individual was made to feel he was nothing compared to the power of the man who orchestrated this entire grandiose spectacle.

How did Nazi propaganda nevertheless succeed in addressing itself to the individual, the intelligentsia, the many university professors, to a majority of members of the liberal professions, the civil service, as well as the army, and the masses?

Germany's defeat in the First World War, the difficulties of the economy, the terrible inflation which followed in the wake of the war, civil strife, sectarian party divisions, and a loss of orientation, all contributed to the success of the Nazis. Everything was ripe for change, and this provided a fertile ground for propaganda. The strategy of Nazi propaganda was to integrate racial doctrines with German nationalism and socialist views. What made the National-Socialist movement a mass one? Was it its special social composition? The planners of the Nazi propaganda strategy understood that it was impossible to demand love of the fatherland from people who felt themselves humiliated and exploited. They also knew that the masses were envious of the bourgeoisie and desired to imitate it. They therefore chose to blend nationalism with social benefits in a way that was impossible to disentangle them. In this manner a traditional German and Christian outlook was interwoven with socialist views.

Social anger was not directed along the path of Marxist Socialism, but rather via channels of nationalism...the national ethos which could provide a feeling of partnership with the upper classes, attracted those of the disintegrating lower classes, and provided a message of redemption and a framework of solidarity.[20]

From the standpoint of the strategy of propaganda, the Nazis became a solidifed movement possessing an identity based on a clear world outlook, and not on the faceless masses motivated by bitterness and foggy and conflicting feelings of frustration. In this the Nazi ideology of "One Nation, One People, One Leader" focused on *Der Jude* (The Jew) rather than *Die Juden* (The Jews) as the enemy. In all their dealings with the enemy (the Jew), the Nazis refused to distinguish among individuals.

Not only this: Nazi propagandists were familiar with the masses. The huge beer halls served as a backdrop to the desires and frivolities of the masses where complicated doctrines were not easily digested. Nazi propaganda presented an entire demagoguery promising superiority which is not dependent on competence and talent, but only on origin. In this way a miserable bar-fly was no longer an unemployed drunkard, but a superior man whose duty it was to defend his superiority. This was not only a simple doctrine, easily accepted and promulgated, but in reality made no demands or imposed obligations. It was limited in practice to one thing: blind faith in the Nazi messiah, and hatred for the Jew.

The Nazi propagandists understood the difficulty of a mass movement in transition between an old doctrine, which had sustained beliefs for hundreds of years, and the acceptance of a new one. Therefore, not everything from the old order was abolished, but rather dressed up in new clothes.

> In concepts, well-known associations familiar to all who had been raised in Christianity were utilized. The unity of the father, son and holy ghost became the Nazi concept of Father of the Nation, The Racial Son, and the Spirit of the People. The image of the Jew as a symbol of the devil in Christian tradition made it easy to turn him into the devil himself, the essence of the symbol. From this point on the necessary conclusion was but obvious: the duty to destroy him. When the *Führer* became the substitute of the redeemer, the Jew became the symbol of the anti-Christ, a target of unlimited hatred. The new language of images matched the old concepts.[21]

From the standpoint of both strategy and tactics, Nazi propaganda succeeded in isolating the Jew within a closed circle, subject to irrational hatred and bestial aggression. There was no possibility to break out of the circle under any condition because such a "break-out" would "endanger" all those who stood outside the circle. All those outside the circle exercised constant vigilance to guard against such attempts at infiltrating their ranks.

The fate of one side was sealed. The more the Jew was humiliated and oppressed, beaten, and looted, the more sublime his attacker. The more the Jew is murdered, the more superior and "racial," his killer. Only in this way can we understand the "pride" of mass murderers who boasted of their lack of any human sentiment in relentlessly carrying out their "duty."[22]

Film Propaganda – Art or Politics?

Both Hitler and Goebbels recognized film as an especially persuasive art form. Hitler was a particularly avid movie fan, and Goebbels often described the many evenings the two of them watched films after a tiring day of work.

David Hull relates that Goebbels was obsessed by films:

> There probably has never been another individual in the history of any modern government who devoted so much of his time to the motion picture in every possible capacity. It is startling to realize that every film made in the Third Reich had to be assessed by Goebbels for public showing, including features, shorts, newsreels, and documentaries.[23]

In one of his first speeches, Goebbels declared that the German film has a mission to conquer the world as a pioneer going before the Nazi armies. He demanded from the studios to produce films which showed clear tendencies of sharp ethnic lines *"Mit scharfen volkischen konturen"* describing people and society as they actually are.

The presentation of these "clear tendencies" left little doubt in the minds of German film producers that the world of the swastika and the myth of the Aryan race would be engraved on the standard of the film industry. The Soviets had paved the way. During the 1930s the Soviet film *Potemkin,* the great production of the Soviet film genius, Sergei Eisenstein, was shown in Germany and greatly impressed film fans including Goebbels.

Immediately upon the Nazi take over, members of the German film industry hastened to prove their loyalty to their new masters. They were invited by Goebbels himself to the building of the Ministry of Propaganda. There, they were shown four films: *Niebelungen,* directed by Fritz Lang, *The Rebel,* by Louis Tranker, *Anna Karenina,* starring Greta Garbo, and of course the most famous of the films on the Russian Revolution, Eisenstein's *The Battleship Potemkin.* The Nazi film industry eventually developed in a different direction than that of the Soviet

Emile Lohkap as the hero in the film *Hans Westmar* (1933)

The Nazi Boys' Meeting in *Hitler Jungequex* (1933)

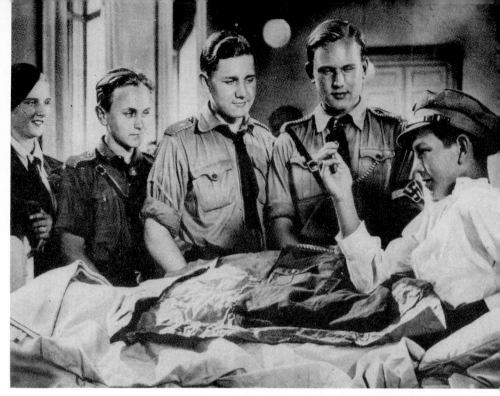

The Nazi Boys Visit Heini in the film *Hitler Jungequex*

S.A. Man Brand

Ferdinand Marian and Emile Jannings in the film *Ohm Kruger*

Emile Jannings as Ohm Kruger in the Sanitarium in Switzerland

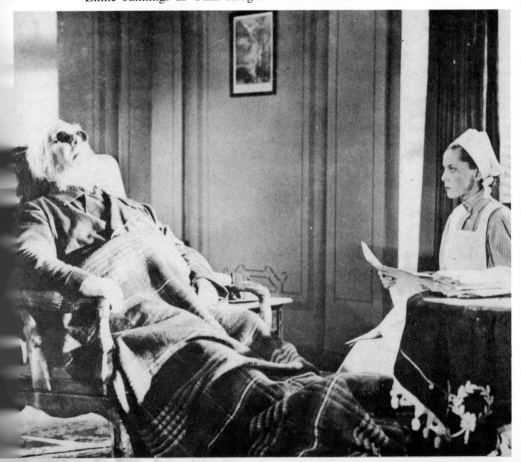

Herbert Hebner as the Jew Impelmayer and Inge V.D. Stratan as his wife
in the film *Robert and Bertram*.

rtram

8/40 b

Herbert Hebner as the Jew Impelmayer in *Robert and Bertram*

Rudi Goden as Robert and Kurt Seypart as Bertram in the film *Robert and Bertram*

Ferdinand Marian in the film *Linen From Ireland* (1939)

Eric Ponto as Rothschild and Hand Steibner as his secretary Bronstein in the film *The Rothschilds* (1940)

The bitter news arrives in the midst of prayer. From the film *The Rothschilds*

Union, but in 1933 film played a similar role in both countries.

A short time after Hitler's seizure of power, he expressed the desire to exploit the cinema as "an instrument of propaganda" but in a way so that:

> Every viewer will be completely aware...that he is about to see a political film. I am disgusted when I find propaganda hiding behind art. It must be either art or politics.[24]

In practice, however, this principle of separation of art and propaganda without any camouflage does not exist. This view also stood in opposition to that of Goebbels' who wanted entertainment films, comedies or musicals, and rejected the idea of including pure propaganda. Goebbels understoood that camouflaged and subconscious propaganda is more effective, and this principle was realized in many of the films made with his support. Therefore, he did not wish to make use of theatrical films to praise the Nazi movement, except in an indirect way, by use of cliches in the dialogue, or evaluations of supposedly "objective" situations which nevertheless leave but one conclusion. This principle explains, among other things, Gobbels' opposition to films such as Riefenstahl's *Triumph of the Will.*

By indirect propaganda, Goebbels meant that actors of "Nordic origin" should never appear in a film as evil characters, traitors, or even disorderly. Such characters must be of other ethnic origins: British, or Jewish, such as was done in some of the sample films to be reviewed shortly.

Goebbels was concerned that viewing the men of the S.A. marching on the screen (as appears in *Triumph of the Will*) would cause the lowering of the constant tension in which he wanted to hold the audience. Nazi propaganda tactics sought to rule in the streets by means of fostering tension and violence. It was less effective to allow the viewer to give vent to his emotions comfortably in a cinema and fulfill his desires and dreams by viewing the screen. Goebbels claimed that "only when they are marching in the street does the S.A. serve ideology." This does not mean that Goebbels opposed the direct medium of newsreels and documentaries. By means of these types of films the Nazis presented the "truth" quickly, selectively, with the first and only means of information. It was a "visual truth," based on the widespread misconception held by the public that a picture cannot lie.

Nazi propaganda strove to suppress rational thought, which it scornfully labeled " the prostitute of the Jews." By emotional means they strove to eliminate the control of rational thought, and replace it with the voice of "Pure Aryan Blood ... the organ by which we think."

This goal was achieved successfully by the cinema among other means.

In a psychologcial study published in Germany in 1936, P. Glaesser determined that the cinema is "the art form which grips the viewer most completely." It does not stimulate thought, but leads the audience in a subconscious way and by consistently holding fast to a desired viewpoint.

> Germany must make use of the cinema to develop the total irrational saturation of the growing spirit taking control of the people while it educates not by means of thought but by environment and viewpoint.[25]

According to Richard Griffith, this policy was the root of Goebbels' decision not to allow a discussion of Nazi principles by the Germans themselves since it could only raise doubts.[26] How did Goebbels implement his Nazi film policy? A survey of films produced during the course of the Nazi period (1933-45) reveals that apart from the first years of the regime, many entertainment films were produced in which the propaganda element was either absent or was drastically limited. The Frenchman, Louis Marcorel, investigator of Nazi films, noted that between 200 and 300 entertainment or escape films were so free of propaganda that they could be frequently shown on West-German screens after the war.[27] The proportion of films containing direct political content was then relatively small. In a catalogue of forbidden films from 1951, published by the Allied High Commission after viewing 700 "suspected" adventure films, only 141 provoked opposition from a political standpoint.[28]

The adventure films of a political nature were mostly produced by a direct order of the Reich Ministry of Propaganda and were completely financed by this body.

These films account for less than 10% (96 out of 1,097) of the fiction films produced in the period 1933-45. In face of the quite apparent emphasis on the pure escapist nature of these films as a principle aspect of Nazi film policy, one must ask how these films could serve the objectives of the state? The answer is that these apparently non-political films also served the Nazis. No less a figure than Goebbels remarked that:

> The moment one becomes aware of propaganda, it loses its effectiveness. However, when propaganda as a tendency, or approach, remains in the background, it becomes effective from every aspect.[29]

Under the disguise of an historical drama rich in costumes, recalling German's imperial past, Bismarck and Frederick the Great, these films approve of the norms of behavior emphasized by fascist ideology such as obedience, discipline, humility, and leadership qualities.

58

In the disguise of sentimental romances and feature films they praised heroism, elitism, and the national German qualities. In these respects one can distinguish essential elements of Nazi ideology even in entertainment films.

INCIDENTAL ANTI-SEMITISM IN THE NAZI CINEMA

A selection of representative films from the Nazi period camouflaged anti-Semitic themes. These are discussed as an introduction to the later films containing blatant anti-Semitic propaganda, and embody the principle of "casual" or "incidental propaganda."

S.A. MAN BRAND (1933)

The first, *S.A. Man Brand,* was released on June 14, 1933. It was made at a Bavaria studio under the direction of Franz Seitz, with a cast of virtually unknown actors. The film belongs to a genre known as "heroic" cinema or "the films of ideological struggle," which simultaneously portray the cult of the personality in the Nazi cinema.

It tells the story of a young Nazi who leaves home because his father is a communist. The anti-Semitic message is inserted in one of the early scenes, where Brand is found working in a factory owned by Neuberg, who represents the stereotype of the "capitalist Jew." Neuberg, apparently for no reason, decides to fire Brand, but, lacking the courage to tell his employee the bad news, he calls in his assistant, a brutal and unkempt man with negative characteristics which Nazi propaganda portrayed as typically Jewish, and orders him to deliver the cruel message.[30] In response to the assistant's question about the reason he is to give, Neuberg curtly replies, "Find any reason." Upon hearing the bad news, Brand straightens his back, and says defiantly to the assistant: "You will have to get used to this (brown) color, you and your kind!"

The central feature of the film was the attempt to awaken anti-communist sentiments in the upcoming elections, and to convey, as if incidentally, an anti-Semitic message as well.

HITLERJUNGE QUEX (1933)

Of this group of "heroic films," *Hitlerjunge Quex,* also called *A film of the Spirit of Sacrifice of German Youth,* was the most successful, and is generally considered a masterful piece of propaganda. It was produced while it was still necessary to build a national socialist spirit on the ashes of the Weimar Republic.

As Goebbels had noted, nothing could remain in a vacuum. The old had to be replaced by the new. Subtle and sophisticated methods of persuasion are used in this film to generate the desired enthusiasm for the new order. This is done carefully by molding the new spirit with traditional ideas, both religious and secular. The film was directed by Hans Steinhoff, who became one of the chief Nazi directors, and was produced by Karl Ritter, a personal friend of Hitler. Ritter became, during the course of time, the chief expert on propaganda films for the *Hitlerjugend* organization.[31]

The central character is the pre-adolescent youth, Heini, later named Quex (quicksilver). His family life is one of poverty and turmoil. He is torn between a communist father, and a mother who is always depressed. Of course Heini cannot live in such a world, and as the film progresses he moves steadily toward Nazism, depicted in the form of the brave disciplined and pure Nazi youth group, in contrast to the loose, slovenly, and immoral communist youth.

In spite of his origins in a broken home, Heini manifests qualities which are quite different from those of his mother and father, and even from those of his communist friends. In the end this leads to Heini's death at the hands of the communists whom he has decided to forsake forever. One day they discover him distributing Nazi election fliers in Berlin and stab him to death leaving him lying in the dark, deserted street. Heini is found in the morning by a Nazi group. His last words are "Our flag billows before...," the first line of the Hitler Youth Song played throughout the film, and which becomes the musical symbol of good against bad, justice against evil. The film skillfully glorifies Nazism, and it depicts the destruction of existing institutions, utilizing the energies thus released for the good of the party.

As direct propaganda, the film purposefully adopts a black and white attitude, especially in the comparison of Nazi youths to communist ones. Neither is there a lack of cliches and slogans, but despite these drawbacks the film indirectly glorifies the Nazis.

The film basically describes the collapse of existing institutions, while paving the way for the establishment of a new institution – the Nazi Party. Within the framework of the regime's penetration into all spheres of life, the film seeks to drive a wedge into the life of the non-Nazi family while pointing out its degeneration. In addition, the film portrays the early and unhealthy sexual relations of much of German youth and its infantile character.

This is not achieved by the use of slogans and preaching, but by persuasion stemming from a simple and highly understandable and emotional portrayal of conflicts which are the result of errors and morbid ways.

The central theme of the film is the disintegrating old family structure. The emotional family ties find a replacement in the ties of the new Nazi "family." Thus, family loyalty is exchanged for party loyalty. The viewer is led to the painful but only decision that, as a result of identification with Heini, one must instill law and order to avoid disintegration and anarchy that would harm him.

This presentation of a scale of values, in which the viewer apparently "chooses" sides, is repeated in the Nazi propaganda films. In love stories, for example, a scale of values is consistently presented linking love and politics. At the apex of this hierarchy, political loyalty is also a form of love. The love represented by *Hitlerjunge Quex* becomes something more sublime, such as love for Hitler, and love of the fatherland is measured by the willingness to die for it.

There are those who see in the flim's last scene hints of reincarnation when Heini's body disappears and is replaced by the flag. After the flag disappears, its place is taken by a triumphant marching band of Nazi youths. They march by and recede from the viewer, and by means of superimposition (the imposition of one picture on top of another) burly adult Nazi marchers stride forth towards the viewer. The viewer is left with the indelible impression that the marchers' power promises a better future. At this moment Heini's soul leaves its body to march with the flag and the comrades to victory.

This form of turning people into symbols is characteristic of both individuals and groups in the Nazi cinema. The masses themselves turn into a disciplined decoration and possess a perfect symmetrical super-human structure. This technique reached its climax in Leni Riefenstahl's *Triumph of the Will*. In the scene of the wreath laying, the Nazi crowds appear to be lifeless geometric figures. This perfection enchanted the Germans, while in this perfection, the individual lost his individuality.

The propaganda impact of *Hitlerjunge Quex* stems from an exploitation of the emotional conflicts that were common to German youth in that period. For example, Heini's amibivalent attitude towards his parents, who are depicted as good and evil, has been so diverted that by the end of the film the positive parental attitudes have been projected onto Nazism, while the negative ones are focussed on the enemy, the communists. Bateson noted that the "complete reorientation of the attitudes and stereotypes that were available in pre-Nazi Germany leads logically and necessarily to the destruction of the old family unit."[32]

It is indicative of the film's psychologcial tactics that the communists are portrayed at first with some sensitivity, and the gradual transition into caricature is so subtle that it is almost imperceptible. With elaborately disarming tactics, Stoppel, the leader of the commune, is introduced as a sympathetic, authoritative symbol of security in Heini's impoverished existence, only to be gradually revealed as a seductively destructive and evil force.

The anti-Semitic component of the film is woven into the film as subtly as is the political message. This is to be found in the scene in which a sloppily-dressed boy, smoking cigarettes and singing bawdy songs written by a Jewish composer, is contrasted unfavorably with the healthy, good-looking members of the Hitler Youth Group. For those in the audience who missed the point, it was broadly stressed in the film reviews that appeared in the daily press.

Evidently, though communism was seen as the most dangerous of opponents, the individual communist could be seen as a potential party member; but not so the Jews, who had no place in either world. Thus, at the end of the film, the communist girl tells the Jewish boy that although Heini crossed the lines and joined the Nazis, she prefers the Nazi Heini to him.

Two more people with Jewish characteristics appear in *Hitlerjunge Quex*. One is the assistant to the communist leader, an underworld type, and the other is the man who pays almost nothing for old furniture. Again the reviews reminded the audience of the fact that these characters were Jewish.

HANS WESTMAR (1933)

The oustanding fiasco of the "hero films" was *Hans Westmar*, directed by Franz Wenzler in 1933, that purported to be a biography of the early Nazi martyr, Horst Wessel, who, according to the Nazis, was killed by the communists. Horst Wessel, in fact, was little better than a pimp who lived on the income of the prostitute, Erna Jaenicke. He was shot in a brawl with another man, (Ali Hoehler, Erna's former pimp and also a Nazi). Goebbels visited Wessel in the hospital and made a great deal of publicity out of his case, planning to make him into a Nazi saint. Wessel's major contribution to the Nazi cause was the compositon of the words for the first verse of the so-called Horst Wessel Song, the party anthem.

The film was previewed on October 3 and was suddenly banned on October 9, the day of its scheduled premiere. *The New York Times* comment attempted to explain the Nazi reservations which probably led to the cancellation decision:

The reason underlying the decision may be summed up in one sentence: the film does justice neither to Horst Wessel whose heroic figure it belittles through inadequate representation, nor the National Socialist movement, on which the state now rests. The film thus jeopardizes vital state interests and Germany's reputation.[33]

Despite the extremely theatrical acting, the film is a good example of the Nazi propaganda film at that time. The influence of the Russian cinema is quite apparent especially in the crowd scenes and the funeral which are shot like a newsreel. Again, the main opponent is communism, but in the film three kinds of communists are juxtaposed. There is the party boss who exploits misery and transmits the Moscow line. There is the small-time official, with Jewish characteristics, who incites a mass rally against the Brownshirts, and warns the "Nazi hooligans" that the streets belong to the communists. When a fight breaks out in the meeting hall, he crawls under the speaker's table; and of course, he and a woman colleague, who also looks Jewish, are held directly responsible for the murder of the hero, Hans Westmar.

Ross, the communist idealist, tells Westmar that only a proletarian can understand the proletariat. In the film, Hans Westmar believes the party's future lies in the masses, so he gives up his studies and becomes a manual laborer.

Not only is Hans not portrayed as a pimp, he is represented as a man of high moral standing who abominates the moral decline of the Weimar Republic, and who is above any erotic desires. He rejects courting an American girl in order to devote his entire time, and the energy stored in his body, to the Nazi movement. He quickly becomes the leader able to triumph over his enemy.

One should not conclude from this that the Nazi films lacked any eroticism, or that the creators of these films were unaware of erotic impulses. In the cinema, however, they repressed these impulses on the one hand, and on the other, they channeled the erotic energy to the party's symbols, such as the marchers, the polished boots, the spotless uniforms, the love of uniforms, the mystical power of the Nazi group, the image of the *Führer,* and the charismatic concept of the leader.

Here too, as in *Hitlerjunge Quex,* the individual communist is a potential member for the Nazi party, but not the Jew. This is expressed in the last scene of the film in which a torchlight parade of the S.A. is held just prior to the seizure of power by the Nazis. During the march Ross' fist opens and extends into the Nazi salute.

While the anti-Semitic component in the above-mentioned films of 1933 was small, it was nevertheless significant. At that time, the Nazis did not feel that it was necessary to portray Bolshevism in films as a Jewish idea.

According to Dr. Fürstenau, Director of the German Institute for Film Art, it was not necessary to establish an automatic connection between Jews and Marxism in films, since all other media did it.[36] Such Nazi terminology as "Jewish Bolshevism" was common, irrespective of the support among Jews for the conservative parties, and the fact that many of them were patriotic Germans.

Thus, an important principle of propaganda was realized: to make a thorough presentation of the image of the enemy (the Jew) in terms well known to the intended audience.

UM DAS MUNSHENRECHT (1934)

In the film, *Um Das Munshenrecht,* which relates the brief "reign of terror" of the communist republic established in 1919 in Bavaria, there is a clear anti-Semitic dimension. In it, the Jews are held responsible for all acts of terror that occurred during that period, by inciting the workers, exploiting their naiveté and the resulting shortages.

In one scene a citizen is seen speaking to revolutionary workers who have been incited by the Jews. The workers are urged to continue performing communist acts of terrorism.

Citizen: You were indeed once all soldiers!
Worker A: Yes, but they deceived us when they called us.
Worker B: We object to this. We are not second-class human beings.
Jew: What does a worker know of human rights?
Citizen: B: I spoke to comrades-in-arms, not with the Jews!

The fact is that approximately 100,000 Jews were mobilized for war in 1914 in the name of Germany, and 12,000 of them fell in battle. This, the film does not mention.

TOGGER (1937)

Incidental anti-Semitism also appears in a scene of the film *Togger,* produced in 1937. The scene deals with a Berlin press conference held in 1932. A Jewish journalist appears as a provocative element, and a debate ensues between him and the other journalists until one from the Nazi Party puts him in his place.

Jewish Journalist: It has to do with a planned robbery of international capital against our popular economy, and I thank my colleague from *Ziebenstadt* for his actions.

Nazi Journalist: We too would like to know where our government stands in this war!

Jewish Journalist: Whom does it interest?

Nazi Journalist: Perhaps not you, but it certainly interests us.

Jewish Journalist: I don't think it's honorable to shout in this house.

Nazi Journalist: We don't need to speak of honor with you. Who are you to speak of honor? We will worry about honor.

The scene ends stormily.

PETTERSON AND BENDEL (1938)

It is noteworthy that until 1938 there was no German cinematic production which was completely devoted to the anti-Semitic theme. However, the need for such films was felt, and therefore use was twice made of the Swedish film *Petterson and Bendel,* in order to fill this gap.

The film is about a young unemployed Swede, Petterson, who meets the Jew Bendel after the latter has been expelled from Sweden, and then returns in disguise. Together they start a business where the Jew Bendel uses Petterson as a cover, and becomes rich until Petterson discovers that the Jew has used illegal means and is fleeing with both the money and his fiancée. At the very last moment justice triumphs, of course, and Petterson arrives at the ship and takes back his fiancée and the money from Bendel who was about to flee to distant lands.

The banal film did not achieve any measure of success and at its premiere performance, held in Berlin in 1936, whistles of disapproval were heard in the cinema. The Nazi press claimed, of course, that this had been a Jewish provocation. However, quite quickly the film disappeared from cinema screens, and it appears that not only its quality but also the German subtitles were not looked on favorably by the viewers.

In 1938, right after the "Night of Broken.Glass," *(Kristallnacht)* the movie was presented again with a totally new synchronized sound track in German. The film was intended as a justification for the events of the *Kristallnacht.* Critics wrote: "This film offers an important answer to a question which has been decided by the German Führer and 'the people.' " This time there was no protest, as it would have been too dangerous even in a dark cinema. Goebbels liked the German version of Petterson and Bendel, and *Robert and Bertram,* his own first anti-Semitic film, showed patterns similar to those of the Swedish film.

Robert and Bertram, and perhaps the anti-Semitic film, *Linen From Ireland,* signalled a departure from the previous policy of incidental anti-Semitism in the Nazi cinema. After the production of these films, the Nazis no longer dealt with hints, but engaged in open, direct, and vulgar anti-Semitic propaganda in their films in accord with their ideology.

HEIMAKER (1941)

The film *Heimaker* deals with the *Volksdeutscher* (ethnic German minority) in Poland in the Spring of 1939. One may definitely regard it as anti-Polish, but the propaganda of incidental anti-Semitism is woven into the film.

In the relevant scene we are in the Jewish marketplace in Poland where an ethnic German teacher and her female companion are shopping. They speak with a Jewish merchant whose language is a grotesque mixture of German and Yiddish. He resembles the anti-Semitic stereotyped image of the Jew.

Jew: I love to do business with the Germans. Why? Because they are honest. The German people are a great nation, a proud people and the *Führer* Hitler is a brilliant man. It is a shame that he doesn't want to regard us correctly.

Teacher: (in a sarcastic laugh) I shall write to him.

Jew: Why are you laughing at an unfortunate Jew. All I want is to do business with you.

(The teacher passes by him and continues on her way)

Jew: (curses behind her back) *Yimach shmam vizikram* (Hebrew for "May their name and memory be blotted out.")

OHM KRUGER (1941)

One of the most famous, if not the most famous, of the Nazi propaganda films was *Ohm Kruger,* directed by Hans Steinhoff, which premiered on April 4, 1941. The film is essentially anti-British, but does not refrain from anti-Semitic allusions.

The film traces the life of the Boer leader, Ohm (Uncle in Dutch) Kruger, (played by Emil Jannings), by means of flashbacks as he lies dying in a Swiss hospital. In the gallery of figures appearing in the film, we find the Englishmen Cecil Rhodes, the sinister financier, eager for the gold beneath the peaceful farmlands of the Boers, and the cynical and cunning Joseph Chamberlain. These two are contrasted to Kruger, the simple, modest elder statesman.

In the end, the old, blind, fugitive Kruger tells his Swiss nurse that one day a great nation will arise to avenge the Boers for their treatment by Britain, the enemy of civilization. Britain's viciousness and depravity are conveyed by showing scenes of British concentration camps in which the prisoners are subjected to inhuman forms of torture. It is quite amazing that in so doing, the British are made to resemble the Germans. This characteristic of unconsciously projecting one's self-image on to others was also apparent in Steinhoff's depiction of the communist youth in the earlier *Hitlerjunge Quex,* and reflected one of the basic weaknesses in much of Nazi propaganda, at least to outside observers, if not to German audiences.

Where are the anti-Semitic allusions in this basically anti-British film? In the beginning of the film when Kruger is shown dying in the sanatorium, there is a scene in which some correspondents are trying to get in to interview the old man. The nurse and doctors refuse to let them in because of his grave condition. All the journalists understand this and ·relent in order to let the old Boer leader die peacefully, except for a fat and slovenly journalist who represents the liberal newspaper, *Berliner Tageblatt.* In the event that the German public missed the pointedly Jewish characteristics, film reviews in the popular press explained that the Jew, Theodor Wolf, had been the editor of the *Berliner Tageblatt.*

The Jewish journalist is portrayed as crude and offensive as in the scene where he bursts into the midst of the journalists

Jewish Journalist: Here, *Berliner Tageblatt* – 135,000 readers. I have to have an exclusive report by tomorrow on how Ohm Kruger lives in exile, what he thinks of the peace agreement with the English, and what he has to say about it.

Gatekeeper: (pleadingly) Really, for the last time, the reputation of our institution forbids us to allow our guests to be bothered.

Journalist: (aggressively) Don't give me that crap!

When the gatekeeper refuses to allow him in, the Jew tries to bribe the director of the sanatorium. He takes out 100 francs from his pocket and offers the money to the director.

Journalist: Let me up to see the president. One hand washes the other.

Director: (takes the money) Ahh, a hundred francs. Thank you very much. (puts the money in his pocket)

Journalist: (with pleasure) Ahh, I knew it.

Director: I will donate this money to the Red Cross.

Journalist: Don't do something stupid.

Director: But you won't get to see the president.

In spite of everything, the Jewish journalist manages, with a heavy camera strapped to his back, to break into the room of the sick president. The nurse and doctor present are astounded, but the journalist does not consider anything.

Journalist: Here, *Berliner Tageblatt,* pardon me, I won't stay long. It's a great honor for me, Mr. President. Permit me to ask you a few questions: What's your opinion of the political situation?

(silence reigns) Well, perhaps I can open the curtains a bit (runs to the curtains).

Nurse: (interferes) That is impossible. The president is suffering from an eye disease.

Journalist: So a flash instead! (takes a photograph with a flash). Thank you Mr. President. The picture will be a sensation.

KARL PETERS (1941)

Another film worthy of mention from the same period is *Karl Peters,* directed by Herbert Selpin, which was first shown on March 21, 1941. Like so many of the uniformed hero figures of the Nazi cinema, Karl Peters clashes with his superiors in his obedience to the call of a higher duty.

The film is full of incidental anti-Semitic messages. It is Berlin, 1882, and Peters learns that his rival in the Foreign Ministry is a Jew in charge of colonial affairs although he is opposed to Germany's colonial policy. In light of this, Peters requests an audience with Chancellor Bismarck. The dialogue needs no further commentary.

Peters: With your permission, I shall leave, because I don't want to bother you further. I shall find my own way to reach Bismarck.

Clerk: Your attempt to meet with Bismarck is doomed to failure. There is only one way to reach him: through me. Besides, I can just imagine what Bismarck will think of your ideas.

Peters: I'm not so sure.

Clerk: That's what you think.

Peters: Von Bismarck and I speak the same language. The two of us were baptised in the waters of the Elbe. And where were you baptised? Better not talk about that.

Clerk: I refuse to continue this conversation.

In the next dialogue, the hints are even clearer. Karl Peters speaks with his friend, a German, who supports his colonial plans.

Peters: We shall never be able to reach Bismarck. This "Kayser" with the letter "Y" will see to that (reference to the Jewish official whose name resembles the Kaiser). He has kidnapped the office dealing with colonial affairs. But the subject is too sensitive and he is afraid.

Four years later Peters is about to be nominated as Commissioner for Colonial Affairs and things are reversed. The Jewish clerk will now be subject to Peters' authority. Here, too the dialogue speaks for itself.

Clerk: (in submission) I am open to any suggestion, Herr Reichskommisar.

Peters: I already told you four years ago that we spoke two completely different languages. But perhaps you will understand me today when I explain to you in detail that I don't want our colonies to be under your influence ... Have you understood me this time?

Clerk: Of course, Herr Reichskommisar. You have a very clear manner of speech.

Peters: Don't forget that I can be even clearer, much clearer.

Peters is later accused of ordering the execution of two Blacks without a trial. Thus, "by his irresponsible action he has damaged the reputation of the German people in the eyes of the whole civilized world."

On the surface there is nothing here to do with Jews or anti-Semitism, but "by chance," two of Peters' accusers are a senior government official and a Social Democratic member of parliament, who are both Jews. The whole scene tries to prove that Jews are behind the fight against men like Peters. When the Jews ask Peters how he can talk of peace when he has hanged people, adding that they themselves would never have countenanced this, Peters replies:

True enough, YOU would never have done it . And YOU wouldn't have won German East Africa either. If I hadn't hung those two Africans on the spit as a deterrent, the rebellion you were plotting would have broken out there and hundreds of decent German farmers would have been massacred. Should I have first put in a request to Berlin? Or maybe I should have asked you or the permission of the *Vorwärts?* (Social-democratic and later communist newspaper.)

WIEN 1910 (1942)

This film affords another example of incidental anti-Semitism. The object of the relevant scene is to demonstrate that Jewish journalism is sensationalist, revelling in scandal, wicked, sick, and blood-thirsty, always searching for the dirtiest affairs.

A Jewish journalist speaks in a flattering and nasal tone with the editor of the newspaper, who is also Jewish, and holds out the promise of a scoop for him.

Journalist: I have a sensation for you. You will kiss my hands for it... (I have a story about) a mental case who fondled a girl for four hours and sixteen minutes ... I have found material on the leader of the Austrian Christian Social Party to show his involvement with a young girl. The leader of the party is known as a sick man, and the angle of the husband betraying his wife will certainly be well received by you and our Vienna readers.

REMBRANDT (1942)

The popular biographical film about the great Dutch painter, directed by Karl Ritter, has very little to do with Jews, but it achieved a certain credibility, and its artistry effectively enhances one brief anti-Semitic scene. In the scene, three obviously Jewish money lenders, though not explicitly identified as such, cheat Rembrandt's landlady by buying one of the master's paintings at a ridiculously low price. Soon after the landlady dies, apparently having found out that she had been swindled. The money lenders try to sell the painting at a high price to a British art dealer, but when he hears of the death of Rembrandt's landlady, he cancels the deal. To this, the money lenders callously respond. "Let's go, we have nothing to do here anymore."

From the examples outlined above it appears that the heroic films of historical and biographical dramas which comprised the cult of the personality of the Nazi cinema, were not directly aimed against the Jews, and dealt with anti-Semitism only indirectly. However, the German film critic Dr. Fürstenau claims that these allusions were much more effective than the blatantly anti-Semitic Nazi propaganda films of 1940.

4

IDEOLOGY AND PROPAGANDA

"A propagandist is a man who canalizes an
already existing stream. In a land where there is
no water, he digs in vain."[1] (Aldous Huxley)

Huxley's general assumption regarding the effectiveness of propaganda
is also correct about Nazi propaganda. The operations of the Nazi
anti-Semitic propaganda machine did not involve any originality,
according to Peter Pulzer who claims that in practice the Nazis'
anti-Semitic argumentation was already found in the works of Deuring,
Lagarde, Chamberlain and their ideological colleagues[2]. Hitler had the
satanic will to put into practice a program which had been promulgated
before the beginnings of National-Socialism.

If this indeed is the case, then a number of questions occur regarding
Hitler. Was this satanic program the vengeful act of a private individual
who sought to punish the Jews for failing to have bought his paintings?
Did Hitler's relationship with Jews create his ideological mold and in this
way lead to the doctrinal base of National-Socialism?

Was Hitler the god who descended from on high to the masses in
Nuremberg, as staged so demonically by Riefenstahl in the opening of her
film *Triumph of the Will,* or was Hitler an orator who knew how to
instinctively exploit the deepest emotions of the Germans, and channel
powerful streams of anger and unbridled bigotry?

So great was the hatred that even at the very end when dreams of the
Thousand Year Reich lay shattered in smithereens against a background
of horror surpassing the visions of Dante's hell and Wagner's apocalyptic
last day of judgement, at a time when Berlin stood rent asunder and
utterly helpless before the Red Army, and Hitler had already made
preparations for suicide, he left the following final bequest to the German
people:

> Above all, I charge the leaders of the nation and those under
> them *(Die Fuehrung der Nation und Die Gefolgschaft)* to
> scrupulous observance of the laws of race and to merciless
> opposition to the universal poisoner of all peoples *(Weltvergifter
> aller Völker),* international Jewry.[3]

Some psychoanalysts have suggested that Hitler's hatred of the Jews
was a projection of his self-hate. There is an extensive body of literature

71

which seeks to explain, either in psychoanalytic or socio-historical terms, the reasons for Hitler's obsessive preoccupation with the Jewish question and its final solution. But it is not within the bounds of the present study to deal with this issue. The harsh fact about the Holocaust is hatred for the Jews, and their persecution was not a means to achieve a limited objective:

> It was not caused by the exigencies of war, nor was it a political maneuver to cope with internal unrest and domestic conflict. These people were killed as the result of one of Hitler's ideas: the idea of a superior race, and the need to exterminate what he considered to be vermin that were attacking it. The horror of Hitler was this: he meant what he said, he lived by his ideals, he practiced what he preached.[5]

What is of particular relevance in Huxley's approach is the fact that anti-Semitism was already deeply rooted in the European Christian tradition. As Hitler noted to Bishop Berning in 1933 shortly before he seized power:

> I was attacked because of my reaction to the Jewish question. Nevertheless, the Catholic Church considered the Jews as pests for 1,500 years. The church expelled the Jews into ghettos, etc. At that time the people understood what the Jews were. I am repeating the same action which was pursued for 1,500 years and perhaps by this action I am doing the greatest service ever for Christianity.[6]

How did Hitler find such a receptive audience to canalize his insane ideas in the German people? How was one of the greatest and most developed nations swept along in the current of a madman? This same nation that had given the world Goethe, Schiller, and Beethoven could be made to believe in "good blood" and "bad blood," social Darwinism and a racist Jesus?

In tracing the roots of German anti-Semtism, we must first turn to the towering figure of Martin Luther. Luther not only dominated the period of the German Reformation but cast a lengthy shadow across centuries.

The period of the Reformation sought religious liberation but ended in brutal political enslavement and, according to Thomas Mann, it bequeathed patterns of political tradition to the German people in subsequent generations. These patterns embraced blind obedience, submission, and self-denial in the face of authority. Luther was originally the hero of the simple people, but in the Peasants Revolt (1525-1529) he supported with all his strength the brutal suppression of the people by the feudal princes and secular authority.

Mann, in his well known essay "Germany and the Germans" wrote that the heritage of Luther was an inability to appreciate the right of the individual to exercise political freedom. For Luther, the concept of freedom was tied to the concepts of grace and free acceptance of Christian faith.[7]

It is worthwhile to note that in his novel *Doctor Faustus,* Thomas Mann took up the challenge of the rise of Nazism in Germany, and regarded Luther as one of those who sowed the seeds preparing the way for Hitler's seizure of power.

Popular German historiography tends to neglect his theological achievements, and remembers him as the national hero who broke the universality of the Roman Catholic Church, established the modern German language, and demanded that the Jews be expelled from the country.

In spite of this, it would be a calumny to speak of Luther as "Hitler's spiritual ancestor." Indeed this relation has been asserted in a book entitled just that, written during World War II. In his analysis of Hitler, Robert Waite wrote:

> A spiritual universe separates the Christian leader from the racist demagogue. Luther would have been appalled by the Third Reich; with magnificent moral courage, he would have denounced Hitler as an Antichrist incarnate; he would have been among the first executed by the Gestapo. Yet having said that, we must also say that the great religious reformer did unwittingly help pave the way for Hitler.[8]

It is interesting that Luther, like Muhammed at the beginnings of Islam, believed that the Jews would accept his doctrine, renounce their religion, and repent for their sins in the past. At the beginning of his career as a reformer, Luther did not hesitate to rail against the church and accuse its leaders of being pig-headed by treating the Jews as dogs instead of human beings.

> They did nothing for them, only cursed them and desired their property. I request and plead that everyone treat the Jews with tenderness, and show them our doctrine. In this way we may hope that they will come to us.[9]

When the reality became clear that the Jews would not follow him, the great reformer changed his tune and became infuriated, attacking the Jews with the most unrestrained, crude verbal assaults.

Waite cites the following example of Luther's anti-Semitism. It was selected from the pamphlet entitled "Concerning the Jews and Their Lies," (1543).

> While Germans toil by the sweat of their brow, Jews stuff themselves, guzzle, and sit around the stove.... fart and roast pears [a proverbial expression for laziness], ...they fleece us out of our money and goods. Know, Christian, that next to the devil, thou hast no enemy more cruel, more venemous and violent than a true Jew.[10]

Luther outlined a program to get rid of them:

> First, set fire to their synagogues or schools...Second, I advise that their houses also be razed and destroyed...Third, I advise that all their prayer books and Talmudic writings, in which such adultery, lies, cursing, and blasphemy are taught, be taken from them...Fourth, I advise that their Rabbis be forbidden to teach henceforth on pain of loss of life and limb...Fifth, I advise that safe conduct on highways be abolished completely for Jews...Sixth, I advise that...all cash and treasure of silver and gold be taken from them. Seventh, so much the better, and if this be not enough, let them be driven like mad dogs out of the land.[11]

This program was set forth in 1543. "Centuries later," writes the noted psychoanalyst, Erik Erikson:

> ...there appeared in Germany another young man who radically underbid Martin [Luther] in his choice of temporary nothingness, a young man who likewise reemerged from his moratorium as a leader of the German nation, matching Luther little in constructiveness, and outdoing him totally in systematic political destructiveness. This man, of course, was Adolf Hitler."[11]

Hitler himself, in an early conversation with Dietrich Eckart, in 1924, asserted that the violently anti-Semitic Luther, was the genuine Luther.[12] Hitler's tribute to Luther may be seen in the fact that Hitler launched his first major attack against the Jews, in which Jewish schools and synagogues were set afire and vandalized known as "The Night of Broken Glass" *(Kristallnacht)* on the night between the 9th and 10th of November, 1938, that is, on Luther's birthday.

One of the immediate consequences of the Reformation was the aggravation of the situation of the Jews in regions that remained Catholic. Another result was the introduction of ghettos on a large scale beginning in the sixteenth century. As the eighteenth century Catholic publicist, G.

B. Roberts, remarked: " A Jewish ghetto is a better proof of the truth of the religion of Jesus Christ than a whole school of theologians."[13]

Nevertheless, the central feature of the national-socialist doctrine is found in the ideas generated by German Romantic philosophers and historians at the beginning of the nineteenth century. This century came to be called The Century of Emancipation by many Jews, whereas anti-Semites regarding the entry of the Jews into European social life as a decisive event in world history referred to it as The Jewish Century.

Among them was Johann Gottlieb Fichte (1762-1814), the so-called Father of German Nationalism, who in his famous "Address to the German People" (1807) proclaimed the Germans to be unique, the primal people (Urvolk), and praised them as "archetypal people" compared with the Latins (especially the French and the Jews) who were "second rate" and "stale." Only Germans, asserted Fichte, possess the possibility of regeneration. Under them, a new era in history would blossom. The state would be led by a small elite, free of any moral restraints of a private nature. This concept of the state gave rise to the idea that the individual was unimportant as compared to the nation which, if need be, could demand the sacrifice of the individual.

Germany's special mission, and the preeminence of the nation, were thus given a pseudo-historical underpinning. They combined it with the idea that the national community was fundamentally different from an administrative union in the sense of the classical "social compact." Instead, the nation was regarded as if it were a natural, primary "organism."

Fichte has also been called the "Father of modern anti-Semitism." In 1793 he argued against Jewish emancipation, characterizing the Jewish community as a state within a state that would undermine the German nation. He also described the Jews as masters of the economy by means of the stock exchange. He wrote: "In a country where I preserve my rights before the Almighty, any Jew who so desires, plunders me without punishment."[15]

Fichte was succeeded by George Wilhelm Friedrich Hegel, (1770-1831), the most influential political theorist of the nineteenth century. "For decades, none but Hegel's disciples occupied chairs of philosophy and political economy in all the universities in Prussia."[16]

In Hegel and Fichte the Nazis found a rational justification for their exalted notion of the state, and the subordinate role of the individual. In reaction to the Enlightenment, Hegelianism held that the individual's freedom could only be realized within the state.

Hegel's emphasis on the Gemeinschaft shows his indebtedness to the political Romantics. Apart from the state, "the people" have no moral meaning, and no political form. The people are a shapeless mass who do not know what they want until welded into the "community of the state."

Hitler was inspired above all by Helgel's theory of *Volk*, whose agents would carry out "the will of the world spirit." As in the case of Luther's influence, Waite has warned against a direct causal relation between Hegel and Nazi notions of supremacy:

> Like every other responsible German, Hegel would have been appalled by Hitler's brutal dictatorship. But his endorsement of the concept of a World Historic Leader, the World Spirit Incarnate, and the World Soul, helped create a tradition of political hero worship in Germany that was not uncongenial to Hitler's concept of the *Führer*.[17]

Another important source for the National-Socialists was the philosopher Friedrich Nietzsche. His most celebrated works, *The Will to Power*, and *Thus Spake Zarathustra*, were appropriated and grossly distorted by the Nazis. In 1914, when Hitler's generation went to war, they took Nietzsche's *Thus Spake Zarathustra* with them, along with Luther's translation of the New Testament.

Although in spirit and intent Nietzsche was a world apart from Hitler, his slogans eventually became the ideological tools of aggressive nationalism, and proclaimed the coming of the master race and superman. Only thus could a Nazi theoretician from Berlin University, Alfred Beumler, proclaim that "When we call Heil Hitler to German youth, we are blessing Friedrich Nietzsche."[18]

How was this ideological connection between the Nazis and Nietzsche established? In contemplating a new order of society, Nietzsche wrote:

> Great Politics intends to make physiology the mistress of all other questions. She will create a power strong enough to breed a more complete and higher form of humanity with merciless hardness against the degenerate and parasitic in life – against that which corrupts, poisons, defames, and destroys .. and which sees in the annihilation of life the mark of a higher form of the soul.[19]

Even Nietzsche's defenders might find this thought appalling. Predictably, the Nazi philosopher Alfred Rosenberg quoted this very passage to demonstrate his thesis that the Nazis and Nietzsche were "spiritual brothers."[20]

In his masterly synthesis of the history of the Nazi dictatorship, Karl Dietrich Bracher writes that , based on such theories about the political power of the state and the nation, race theoreticians and social hygienists were able to connect this with their demand for official breeding of "superior" beings and extermination of the "inferior." From this it was only a step to the total submission of the individual to the state, the nation, and the race principle.[21]

Nietzsche's defenders rightly emphasized that he would have been adamantly opposed to Nazi ideology. He despised the anti-Semitism and racism of his own time and had high praise for Jews and only one major criticism: they had produced Christianity.

In a letter to his sister, who married a racist, Nietzsche notes:

> You have committed one of the greatest stupidities – for yourself and for me. Your association with one of the anti-Semitic leaders expresses an unfamiliarity with my whole way of life and fills me again and again with anger or sadness. It is a matter of honor with me to be absolutely clear and unequivocal in relation to anti-Semitism, namely to oppose it ... the fact that the name of Zarathustra is used in every anti-Semitic publication, has made me ill many times.[22]

Nevertheless, Nietzsche was joined in his contempt for "nineteenth-century morality" by Heinrich von Treitschke, a polished stylist and investigator of German history who was considered by many as the spokesman for The New Germany.

Treitschke envisaged the state as the true embodiment of mind and spirit, as an all-embracing, self-determined entity, unbound by rules of behavior and morality. The state was in its totality, the "divine will as it exists on earth." The people, the subjects, are little more than slaves in the nation. "It does not matter what you think," he exclaims, "so long as you obey."

Even before anti-Semitism was systematically exploited as a political weapon, it was Treitschke, among others, who encouraged German conservative nationalists to identify the Jews with the twin dangers of liberalism and internationalism. "What stake could the Jews possibly have in the future of the German state?" Treitschke asked. "Were they not everywhere revolutionaries or atheists?"

In a series of articles in the *Prussian Jahrbuch* in the autumn of 1879, Treitschke called attention to the growing problem of Jewish solidarity and the emergence of a separate German-Jewish caste. He warned his countrymen that Germany must be transformed into a Lutheran *Kulturstaat,* and cleansed of all cosmopolitan influences. Moreover, he argued that an international "network of Jews was using liberalism to fasten a stranglehold on German life." After all, what were big business and dynamic capitalism, if not Jewish creations?

In this context, Craig tells of Treitschke's attitude toward Heine and his poetry. For him, the Jewish poet who changed his religion cannot be part of the new German nationalism. In spite of the enormous popularity of Heine's poems...

> It is impossible to conceal the fact that he is the only one who has not written drinking songs. With him, heaven is full of nut cakes, purses full of gold, and street prostitutes. That is because the Oriental is incapable of celebrating in the German tradition.[23]

In Treitschke's theory of "Germanomania," the Jews comprise the antithesis, and his attitude towards them can be summarized in one of his popular lectures:

> In plain words, the Jew has always been an element of national decompostion ... Whenever [the German] finds his life sullied by the filth of Judaism, he must turn from it and learn to speak the truth boldly against it.[24]

The writings of Treitschke were very influential among young German intellectuals. And it is in Treitschke's writings that one first finds the slogan which was later to become the rallying cry of the Third Reich: "The Jews are our misfortune."

As is known, early anti-Semitism focussed on the murderers of Jesus the Christ, the blood-thirsty leeches who suck Christian blood and worship Satan. Nevertheless, to the extent that they repented, they could obtain forgiveness and thus a loophole was left for the physical survival of the Jew. Others in fact demanded the survival of the Jew – as a homeless wanderer, humbled and persecuted, as proof of the truth of Christianity.

The Nazis went even further, and created the "Antitype Jew" who embodied total negativeness and as such has no right to exist.

Constant confrontation and obsession with the Jews was the hallmark of anti-Semitism. Its ideologues received no rest from the survival of the Jews and their failure to assimilate into other peoples.

In the 1880s, new, professional anti-Semites arose who were considered "modern." They held a fundamentally different view than the traditionalists. It is in their pamphlets and lectures that the basic fundamentals of Nazism appear. Among them was Karl Eugen Dühring (1833-1921), who objected to the term "semites," and demanded the use of the exclusive term "Jews". He called for the destruction of the "foreign" and parasitic" Jews by means of violence and terror. Paul De Lagarde, who has been called the prophet of German nationalism, also called for the destruction of the Jews as harmful pests and, if this was not practical, their exile to Palestine or Madagascar. Wilhelm Marr is considered the originator of the term "anti-Semitism" which was borrowed from the teachings of anthropology.

For these modern anti-Semites it was not simply a matter of the Jews not being Germans, due to their religion but also because of their "unique Jewish essence" which by its very nature is a foreign element in German society, an element bearing contagious diseases and destroying the vital forces in German society, and constituting a threat of degeneration and death.

Hannah Arendt notes that:

> the explanation of this conflict is based on the qualities of the "Jewish race," a concept borrowed from the anthropological and linguistic terminology to which social significance was attributed in the second half of the 19th century. Its application to the Jewish question in its most sinister aspect owed much of its success to social phenomena and convictions which virtually constituted a consent by public opinion.[25].

Thus, the Jewish question became a social question, and as such, it served as a platform for political spokesmen for whom there was no moral barrier to their opportunism. The way to power was dependent on winning the hearts of the masses, and flattering the prejudices of the voters by openly or subtlely channeling hatred and envy of the Jew through ostensibly rational arguments. This technique appeared to be an excellent means of winning votes.

The Jews themselves tended to believe that the hatred towards them stemmed from their religious stubborness, and the Christian prejudice against them as Christ-killers. They hoped that with the spread of enlightenment they would be recognized as equals. They believed that the principle of legal equality without religious differences, which spread with European scientific philosophy, would also apply to them.

In their desire to resemble their surroundings, they changed their traditional dress, and abandoned many Jewish customs. They spoke fluent German and became involved in modern society. This, however, not only did not win them favor among the Germans, but increased the hostility of the latter, and became a new theme of anti-Semitic propaganda which emphasized that the modern Jew resembles the traditional one, and is more dangerous because he hides his "Jewish characteristics."

The start signal was thus given for a campaign of slander and anti-Semitic literature that strove to frustrate the assimilation of the modern Jew. This literature emphasized that there is no possibility to change the defiled character of the Jews, this "foreign," "Asiatic," and "dangerous" people. As one leading anti-Semite put it so graphically, "Instead of washing their minds, it is better to cut off their heads and replace them with heads without one Jewish idea."[26]

Even authors not considered blatant anti-Semites, such as William Raab, Gustav Freitag, and Felix de Haan, could not avoid using stereotyped descriptions. The Christians of their works always appear as loyal and honorable as opposed to the Jews who are described as egotists, cowards, materialists, and unscrupulous.

While these authors exerted influence in the salons of the intellectuals, the German masses were fed a diet of gutter tracts which appeared each week at popular newspaper stands on street corners. In these, readers were instructed to see in the Jew a money lender at high interest rates, the "poisoner of wells," "child killer," and international criminal. For a large part of the German public there was no need to emphasize the differences between traditional and modern Jews. The emancipation did not reach them, and scientific development and enlightenment had not touched them.

A large part of the German masses passed directly from the Middle Ages to the 19th century without any fundamental change in their value system or the heritage of hatred brought with them from the past, especially regarding the image of the Jew in popular consciousness. The Jew of the present was the same one they had known from the past, The Eternal Jew.

However, there were Germans who, in this same period when racial anti-Semitism began, accepted progressive thought and scientific rationalism that accompanied the spread of enlightenment. The discovery of the New World, and the many different cultural patterns existing there, led to an innovative attempt to explain these phenomena in a rational way in place of the supernatural Christian doctrinal explanations. By and large, this period was nevertheless one of disappointment in the belief that man could liberate himself from past traditions and build a new world on a completely rational basis. In the wake of this disappointment, a reaction set in, leading to a desire to return to a glorious past of romantic nationalism.

Thus the historical philosophy of Jean Jacques Rousseau was interpreted in this way. It was no longer conceived as the inspiration of the rights of the simple natural man as described in *Discourse on the Origin and Foundation of Inequality Among Men,* better known as *The Second Discourse.*

As Lucy Davidowicz noted:

The glorification of the natural man, the simple life, uncontaminated by the artificialities of civilization and the fetters of organized society, was a romantic Rousseauist idea. The romanticization of the peasant as a natural man turned him into a receptacle of certain mystical qualities in his relationship to the land. The Voltairist conception turned these universal qualities into specifically Germanic ones. The peasant, by virtue of his descent from Germanic-Teutonic stock and by virtue of the mysterious qualities of Germanness in the very soil he worked, became the embodiment not merely of natural man, but of Germanic man. The antagonist of Germanic man became the Jew, the embodiment of urban man, the man of civilization. A money economy, for example, as the product of the disintegrating civilization, was associated with Jews, who were buyers, sellers, and lenders. Where rootedness was an essential element of *Volk*, the Wandering Jew became the symbol of the flesh and blood Jews, condemned to eternal homelessness for having rejected the Messiah, whose fathers or forefathers had lived outside Germany, in other lands.[27]

Thus, along with the appearance of new lofty social ideas, the image of the Jew developed in an opposite direction, and the foundations of traditional anti-Semitism did not disappear, but instead were emphasized all the more. The internal solidarity of the Jews was especially stressed as the key to understanding their power. The various social, religious, economic, theological, and racial arguments presented the Jews in an unfavorable light as a powerful group ready to struggle in a battle for survival with its enemies. Instead of bringing about the greater acceptance of the Jews into world society, the struggle against them passed from the religious sphere to the racial one. The roots of such an approach could be found in the works of Lessing and Herder who conceived of history as the rational process in which human development proceeded through a series of stages until the final completion or fulfillment of human nature.

In this multi-staged process the Jewish character also reached its final stage of being "a parasitic plant growing upon almost all the European nations and sucking their marrow" in contrast to the German *Volk* which developed in a different way.

The "German national spirit," and the German myths are, according to these theories, to be found in the concept of the *Volk*. Friedrich Ludwig Jahn in his book *German Volkdom*, declared that:

> a state without *Volk* is nothing, a soulless artifice; a *Volk* without a state is nothing, a bodiless, airy phantom, like the Gypsies and the Jews. Only state and *Volk* together can form the

Reich, and such a Reich cannot be preserved without *Volkdom*.[28]

According to George Mosse, *Volk* is one of those perplexing German terms which connotes far more than its specific meaning. It is a much more comprehensive term than "people." Since the birth of German Romaticism at the end of the eighteenth century, German thinkers regarded the term *Volk* as the union of a group of people possessing a transcendental essence. This essence might be called nature or cosmos or myth but in each instance it was fused with man's innermost nature and represented the source of his creativity, depth of feeling, individuality, and his unity with other members of the *Volk*.[29]

The Jews were regarded as the very antithesis of a *Volk*, lacking a state and therefore any substantiality. As a so-called "desert people," they were viewed as shallow, barren, and "arid" people, devoid of all profundity and any creativity. Thus they stood in marked contrast with the Germans "who live in the dark mist-shrouded forests and are deep, mysterious and profound." Because they are so constantly shrouded in darkness, they strive towards the sun and are truly *Lichtmenschen*.

One of the basic inspirations of German National Socialism was the musical genius, Richard Wagner. Wagner strove to create national symbols in which the romatic invocation of a barbaric-heroic past played a decisive role. It was a myth-making nationalism built on Nordic-religious foundations which was to furnish justification for Germany's pretensions to supremacy. One of the recurrent themes in Wagner's writing is anti-Semitism. His most influential statement on the subject was a long article entitled *Das Judentum in der Musik* (Judaism in Music), which originally appeared in a musical periodical in September 1850, under the pseudonym of K. Freigedank (Freethought).

In his writings, in which he also coined the saying, "The Jew is the satanic incarnation of humanity's degeneration," we do not find opposition to the Jews on political, religious, or economic grounds. Wagner believed that his contribution was to prove once and for all that "Jewish blood" is incapable of producing anything of creative value in thought, art, literature, or music, and that emancipation from the yoke of Judaism is an essential necessity.

He declared:

> I consider the Jewish race the sworn enemy of man and all that is noble in him. That we Germans in particular will be ruined by them is beyond dispute.[30]

Peter Gay observed that such a view:

...could not be so suavely exorcised. It was something more than the telling of a few offensive jokes, or certain social snobbery; it was a philosophy from which it was easy to derive a deadly program, a philosophy not casually held and marginal, but passionately believed and central to Wagner's notion about the world.[31]

In his articles, Wagner stressed the necessity of a "grand solution," and looked forward to the time when "there would no longer be any more Jews." He also called for " a war of liberation against this enemy of the human race." His support for such a development is expressed concisely in this segment which was frequently quoted by Nazi authors: "But bethink ye that one thing can redeem you from the curse that burdens you: The redemption of Ahasuerus: destruction."[32]

It was not in his political writings however, but in his operas that Wagner developed his idea of a German religion extirpated of Judaism in which Teutonic and Christian elements would merge.

Wagner's immense power to arouse emotions lay in his capacity to present in his muscial dramas what most people found necessary to repress: impermissible erotic fantasies. His *Niebelungen Ring* operas, which were inspired by the great German epic myth *Niebelungenlied*, gave Germany, especially in the Third Reich, much of its primitive mythology.

As the poet Max Mell, a contemporary of Wagner, wrote in his modern version of the *Song of the Neibelungen:*

> Today only little has remained of the Greek gods that humanism wanted to implant so deeply into our culture...But Siegfried and Kremhild[33] were always in the people's soul.[34]

Not without reason did Hitler compare Wagner's contribution to German nationalism to that of Luther and Frederick the Great, and declare that whoever wished to understand National Socialism should first become familiar with Wagner.

In the course of his life, Wagner came into contact with two men who influenced his philosophy. One of them, the Count Joseph Arthur de Gobineau, was a French diplomat whom he met in Rome in 1876. The other was an Englishman, Houston Stewart Chamberlain, who became Wagner's son-in-law. To the Nazis, the racial doctrines and the doubtful theories of these two, which occasionally even contradict each other, became accepted as the gospel.

The other crucial components of the Nazi ideology were contributed by Dietrich Eckart and Alfred Rosenberg. They lent a historical weight and dimension to the racial theories of Chamberlain. Gobineau was another protagonist of racial purity. His four volume work, *Essay on the Inequality of the Human Race,* was published in Paris between 1853 and 1855. According to his cultural-anthropological theory, the Aryans compose the highest ethnic group among the whites. The Semites, according to Gobineau, occupy a much lower place. While modern racism, according to Gobineau, is directed against all Semites, it in fact concentrated on the Jews.

According to Gobineau, the Aryans are composed of many groups and nations, among which are the Slavs, the Celts, the Latins, and the Germans, but the Germans alone have an exclusive monopoly on cultural creativeness. Wherever the Germans went they brought about improvements. In contrast, the Jew, with his inferior culture and civilization, brings nothing but disintegration and destruction. Therefore, he must be prevented from contaminating the finer and purer German race.

Intermarriage between Jews and Germans would therefore endanger the source of German superiority, the purity of blood, since racial characteristics cannot be erased. Houston Stewart Chamberlain, like Gobineau, found the key to history, even to all of civilization, in race. However, in contrast to Gobineau's "Aryanism," Chamberlain sees German superiority in their Nordic and Teutonic sources. In his *Foundation of the Nineteenth Century,* published in 1908 by the Munich publisher Bruchmann, he describes the Aryan peoples as "very mixed in blood," and agrees that "the more we study the writings of the experts, the less certain we become."[35] Chamberlain views the "German race" as the savior of civilization and the most superior on earth. The end justifies the scientific theory, and accordingly it is possible to understand how, in another segment, Chamberlain describes Gobineau's hypothetical Aryan as a being

> of whom we know nothing at all, whom we construct out of the remotest, most incomprehensible sagas, and patch together from linguistic indications, which are extremely difficult to interpret, a being who everyone can, like a fairy, endow with all the gifts that he pleases.[36]

It was the tall, golden-haired, long-headed Teuton, Chamberlain contends, who created all that is worthy in modern civilization. According to this assumption the man from Nazareth was also of Aryan descent, although his religion and upbringing were Jewish. In this way a loophole is created for the clever "Germanization" of Jesus by presenting a negative Christianity (influenced by Judaism) versus the positive (Aryan) image of Jesus.

84

The longest chapter in *Foundations* is devoted to the Jews. Chamberlain claimed that the Jews' racial origins are a mixture of the Semites and the desert Bedouins with the round-headed Hittites who had a "Jewish nose," and afterwards with the Amorites who were Aryans, tall, blond and handsome, but who came too late to improve the "corrupt Hebrew strain." History is conceived as the struggle between the Teutonic and Semitic races. The former is creative and constructive, the latter harmful and destructive, and therefore condemned to annihilation.

Thus did the Englishman Chamberlain hitch pseudo-science to the wagon of racism. In the name of some kind of mystic intuition he made selective use of facts that fit his theory without any need for control or reliance on scientific methods. Hundreds of thousands of copies of this book, lacking any scientific foundation, were distributed and influenced a large part of the German intelligentsia. No less a personage than the Kaiser himself suggested that it be included in the curriculum of officers' schools. Thus, anti-Semitism gradually became an essential ingredient of the ruling class.

Another source of the national-socialist doctrine was the conflicting economic theories of capitalism and socialism. Jewish economic activity has been so closely interwoven with the history of capitalism that many historians had forgotten that, while Jews helped to shape the history of capitalism, so did capitalism contribute in determining the fate of the Jews. It was a matter of reciprocal influences within a system of conditions and possibilities, and it was therefore an error to overemphasize only one side of the equation.

For example, in his book, *The Jews and Modern Capitalism,* the German economic historian, Werner Sombart, identified the spirit of Judaism with the spirit of capitalism. Judaism, he claimed, was characterized "by the close relationship between religion and business, the arithmetical concept of sin, (punishment is meted out in direct proportion to fit the severity of the sin), and above all, the rationalization of life."[37]

In addition, Sombart suggested that the "racial instinct" of the Jew was akin to that of the nomads, and expressed itself in a hostile and opportunistic attitude towards Christians. Sombart claimed that the Jewish character had been formed in the desert. The Jews were wanderers, and so they wander in the world carrying capitalism with them. Thus, an eternal conflict exists between the European farmer, working on his land deriving sustenance from it, and the wandering Jew.

Such an identification between the Jews and capitalism had been made in 1844, (seventy years before Sombart), by the young Karl Marx in his essay, *On the Jewish Question.* A few segments from this work suffice to show the general tendency:

> Money is the zealous one God of Israel, beside which no other god may stand.[38]

> The God of the Jew has become secularized, and is now a worldly god. The bill of exchange is the Jew's real god.[39]

> What was the essential foundation of the Jewish religion? Practical needs, egotism."[40]

> What is the Jew's foundation in our world? Material necessity, private advantage. What is the object of the Jew's worship in this world? Usury. What is his worldly god? Money.[41]

Although one of the declared goals of the socialists was to liberate all people from the oppression of the past, including the Jews, their attitude towards them as a group was hostile. They emphasized the Jewish role in the development of European capitalism which they naturally regarded as a negative social development that must be fought with all their strength. The anti-capitalist struggle thus created a clear anti-Jewish tendency because, from the socialist point of view, the Jews comprised an antagonistic group that would have to be eliminated for the good of socialism.

Marx wrote in the same vein: "Emancipation from usury and money, which comprise real practical Judaism, would constitute the emancipation of our time."[42]

The various components of the national socialist doctrine that have been described above, were all given popular expression, usually in the form of stereotypes. These stereotypes provided the creators of anti-Semitic films with a reservoir of images which the viewing audience could identify easily, watch on the cinema screen, and believe that "pictures do not lie."

In the light of these images, Huxley's characterization of propaganda closely fits the Nazi anti-Semitic type. Waters filled with hatred towards the Jews flowed through open channels that had existed for generations. There was no need to invent new ideas. Anti-Semitic ideology was there already waiting.

> In this atmosphere, the idea of race was twisted into the myth of the race at the end of the 19th century. From the status of racial inferiority according to a scientific biological concept, the Jew was made into demonic incarnation of all that is evil, corrupt and destructive.[43]

When Hitler began his propaganda he did not have to plow barren ground. He found channels in the hearts of the German people along which the waters of hatred could be funneled, together with the mythology of "northern blood" and the symbols of blood and war.

Thus the Nazi ideology was constructed, layer upon layer, each ideological element adding to the pseudo-scientific structure. In the light of this, Rosenberg did not feel any need to prove Chamberlain's racist theory. He simply accepted it as a scientific axiom and added his own *Myths of the Twentieth Century* to Chamberlain's *Foundations of the Nineteenth Century*. This mythology speaks of the sin of the blood committed by those peoples who did not defend blood purity but engaged in racial mixing, and as a result of which they disappeared from the world. Chamberlain did not claim that racial mixture is a sin, only that it leads to cultural impoverishment. Rosenberg went further in portraying racial mixture as a "crime" against the race and the blood of the superior group. Hitler blended this ideology with Darwinism, free choice as it exists in nature.

It was the historian Theodore Momsen, as early as the late 1870s, who warned against Treistchke and his writings, and urged a war against anti-Semitism through the use of reason:

> This is a terrible epidemic, like cholera. It is impossible to explain or to cure it. There is nothing to do except wait patiently until the poison will destroy itself and lose its venom.[44]

In the meantime, however, the poison had destroyed close to half the Jewish people.

5

PROPAGANDA AND STEREOTYPE
IN THE ANTI-SEMITIC FILM

The International Encyclopedia of the Social Sciences cites the source of the term "stereotype" in the technology of printing. After preparation of the order of the letters, a metal cast plate is made: the stereotype is in essence a block of print that can be used over and over again without change.[1]

When propaganda engages in stereotypes we are dealing with what Webster's dictionary defines as " a standard mental picture common to members of one group that represents a simplified opinion, emotional approach or uncritical judgement."

In other words, we are dealing with a closed and solidified structure that opposes any change and rejects any additional knowledge liable to injure the thought structure or interpret it in any other way. Social psychologists claim that for every stereotype there are several basic elements which are the reason for the rejection of knowledge liable to injure the formation of the structure.

The first ingredient is the grain of truth which does exist in the stereotype. For example the portrayal of the Jew as a talented financial dealer is undoubtedly based on the historical experience of the Middle Ages when Jews were forbidden to acquire land or engage in other professions. They were restricted to money matters while lending money at interest was forbidden to Christians.

Since this activity was forbidden to Christians, it added another calumny upon the Jew to further humiliate him. The problem arises when the same facts are viewed differently. In the case under discussion the Jews had no choice, and the Christians disregarded this fact. The attempt to find a grain of truth in the view of only one group is an accepted principle of propaganda.

A second element of the stereotype is the unjustified generalization where, on the basis of the evaluation of a single individual or small group only, judgments are made upon the entire group, and this ingredient, no matter how fragmentary or distorted, is used to create either general sympathy or to arouse hatred. This is done by the presentation of information in a simplified, unsophisticated, and one-dimensional way that is not subject to change, i.e. in the form of a stereotype.

Through the use of such propagandistic elements the Jews were portrayed to the masses of Christians by the Church during the Middle Ages:

> Alongside the statue of the triumphant glorious Church stands the blind and depressed Synagogue. The image of the Jew in his special form of dress is connected with the image of the devil. Occasionally the Jew is pictured with a tail and horns like a demon. Sometimes he is illustrated together with a pig. The Jew rides the pig facing backwards, or is shown nursing from it. His magical powers stem from the dark forces of evil and this explains his treacherous acts: Judas Iscariot who betrayed Jesus is, according to Christian Medieval tradition, the embodiment of the Jewish character.[2]

The central stereotype of the Jew was his very personification of evil. This was generally portrayed visually in the form of caricatures. One of the most important characteristics of the caricature is its power to concentrate a complicated and complex idea into a single picture possessing one significance. When the single picture is joined with a mythologcial imagination already existing in the viewer's mind, the power of the caricature is increased. When all of these are focussed on the negative character of the image, the caricature becomes a weapon.

In the second half of the fifteenth century, caricatures of Jews appeared in Germany. This was an indirect way of eliminating the enemy by distorting his likeness. Jews were portrayed with long noses and twisted bodies. The idea behind this caricature was to portray the Jew as a comic and grotesque image. Under the Nazis, this image was further extended and made more sinister. The image of the Jew became a dangerous, evil, avaricious, and lustful one.

In the hands of the Nazis, the political caricature became a weapon.

> Because of its destructive power, it is capable of turning the image, symbol or concept it is describing into a sacrifice to the reader's aggression. The political, national, social and personal significances are unified with the emotional burden of the reader, thus creating the special influence exerted by the political caricature.[3]

This destructive power was not ignored by the Nazi propagandists. They contrasted the proportional and handsome features (in their opinion) of the Nordic man in with the distorted and exaggerated

89

characteristics of the Jews as represented in the sadistic and pornographic style of *Der Stürmer.*

> Racially it was decreed, and popularly believed, that all Jews bore the same marks of distinction; they were ugly, bearded, and wore caftans. If they diverged from the mean, it was to disguise their conspiracy to dominate Germany and the world.[4]

The vicious stereotype of the Jew was often projected to the public by the authorities. In an official police poster which appeared in Hamburg in 1912, the "distinctive characteristics" of a certain criminal were described as "a fat Jew with a Jewish nose and the missing link between man and ape."[5]

Later Nazi propaganda referred to the Jew as:

> a sub-human, a creature of nature which apparently is equal in the biological sense of having hands, feet and a kind of brain, eyes and a mouth. But to tell the truth he is a terrible creation, essentially different, a travesty in comparison to man, with a human-like face, whereas in his soul and spirit he is less than any animal.[6]

What, then, is the Jewish stereotype? It appears that, because of this personification of all things negative, it is easier to describe the stereotype in terms of what it lacks. In the light of this concept, an S.S. who was educated under the Nazi system could address a member of the Warsaw Jewish Council at the end of 1939 as follows: "You are not a human being, you are not a dog, you are a Jew."[7]

The Arch Enemy

The Jew appears in the Nazi film not only as a demonic figure, but also as the incarnation of modernity – a symbol of all those forces in the modern world which the German anti-Semites themselves feared and hated.

The Jew was blamed for capitalism, liberalism, democracy, socialism, and the urban way of life. Even Christianity was, for them, a Jewish creation which had helped to destroy the ancient Germanic world. The Jew was the anti-*Volk*, the Antichrist, the embodiment of the enemy. As such, he was the agent for all acts against the state and the German people.

As such, a modern Jew was even more dangerous than the traditional one, and therefore, for the sake of Germany, there were only two possiblities: "Either victory of the Aryan, or annihiliation of the Aryan and victory of the Jew."[8]

Regarding the latter possiblity, Hitler wrote in *Mein Kampf:*

> If the Jew conquers the nations of this world, his crown will become the funeral wreath of humanity, and once again this planet, empty of mankind, will move through the ether as it did millions of years ago.[9]

"What are the Jewish aims?" Hitler asked rhetorically in a speech made in 1923. "To spread their invisible state as a supreme tyranny over all states in the whole world."[10]

Nazi Propaganda Minister Joseph Goebbels, in his Nuremberg speech of September 10, 1936, declared that the Jews aim at destroying the civilized nations of Europe and at founding a Jewish international world regime that would subject all nations to their power.[11]

There are those who claim that the representation of the Jew as the arch enemy helped the integration of the bourgeoisie in the Nazi movement, allowing them to proudly take part in what Hitler called in 1933 "the greatest German racial revolution in history."

Racial Defiler

The concern with "blood poisoning" and "racial pollution," or more directly with interracial sex, occupied a central position in Hitler's thoughts. In *Mein Kampf,* he wrote:

> For hours the black haired Jewish youth lurks in wait for the unsuspecting girl whom he defiles with his blood, thus stealing her from her people. With every means he tries to destroy the racial foundations of the people he has set out to subjugate. Just as he himself systematically ruins women and girls, he does not shrink back from pulling down the blood barriers for others even on a larger scale.[12]

Elsewhere, he wrote of the "nightmare vision of the seduction of hundreds of thousands of girls by repulsive crooked-legged Jew bastards."

Most of Hitler's biographers have come to feel that the key to Hitler's racial bias lies hidden in these notorious passages. In *Mein Kampf* he referred to the Jews repeatedly as "the seducers of our people," and equated *Rassenschande,* racial shame, with venereal disease, both leading to blood poisoning.

The countless stories about affairs of rich Jews with Aryan servant girls cannot be attributed merely to the sexual frustrations of the writers, but to the creation, as well as acceptance of, the image of the Jew as a racial defiler by the general public. Here, after all, was an image which could strike terror in the heart of every German who loved his wife and daughter. Also, the Germanic revival had idealized female virginity and the Aryan woman's primary role as a wife and mother: the receptacle of the seed of the race, a role which the Nazis idealized and worshipped.

One of the most widely distributed novels, *Die Sünde Wider das Blut (Sins against the Blood),* by Arthur Dinter, told of the violation of a German woman's racial purity by a rich Jew, and even though she left him and married an Aryan, her blood has been "defiled" and her offspring continue to look "Semitic" and resemble Jewish stereotypes. The novel attempts to show the harmful effects of racial intercourse, and communicates the horror of racial defilement by portraying a completely inhuman image.

In the light of this, it is interesting to note that even after the Nuremberg racial legislation, a German woman could still marry a Japanese man, whose racial characteristics were pronounced, without defiling her "German blood and honor." The strictest punishments were proscribed, however, for her relations with a Jew who may have had a more Aryan appearance than the average German.

The reason was that when the blood is "defiled" there is no return or remedy. The tragedy lasts for generations, and it becomes hereditary. This is made clear in the novel where the "Jewish method" is to seduce untouched, innocent, blond virgins. The object of this Jewish lust is the corruption of the Aryans.

At the end of the novel, the Aryan husband is tried for murder of the man whose Jewish blood had defiled his wife. Of course the jury understands his patriotic motives and the murderer is absolved of any guilt.

An attempt to portray the differences between "Aryan blood" and "Jewish blood" was made by Max Bauer, writer, poet and publisher,one of the initiators of the anti-intellectual movement called The Rembrandt Movement. For example, Bauer says:

> Skin color in the East is brown and Jewish blood is oriental so that it is also dark, black. This darkness is simply an expression of the dark characteristics of the Jew. The Jew is sombre, asocial, "petrified," ugly. He is completely negative and defective, and an indication of Jewry's black soul.[13]

The same claims are made in reverse for "Aryan blood" which is red and also royal blue with white and silver representing purity and prestige. A mixture of two such different bloods and interracial marriage is therefore against the laws of nature, and the result is the creation of monsters.

But not only the Aryan women violated by Jews are the victims. A man lying with a Jewish woman is also contaminated. Therefore, in the list of crimes which an S.S. man is liable to commit, sexual relations with a Jewess was considered the most serious.

> Such a transgression committed by an S.S. man was considered more serious than the sin of having intercourse with a woman of any other inferior race, with a negress for example, although the Negro race was considered to be similar to the apes by Nazi theology; somewhere on the border between human beings and beasts. Therefore, the death penalty was proscribed for an S.S. man for sexual relations with Jewish women, whereas he would be punished for intercourse with a Negro woman (in France) by imprisonment and expulsion from the order.[14]

The Negro was looked upon with revulsion by the Nazis, but the Jew was considered to be "a son of the devil." Therefore, an S.S. man who had sexual relations with a Jewish woman was punishable by death, and "contaminated" without reprieve. The precise nature of the Jew's sexual contamination was not defined. The Nazi attitude was one of revulsion that was spiritual as well as physical. This was the case even where there was no chance of pregnancy. The revulsion extended to all physical contact, and as a result there were even police officers and hangmen who wore gloves in order to deal with Jews, and in Vilna the commander of the S.S. ordered that the cups used by Jews for drinking be destroyed.

In Poland there were ghettos where the Nazis forbade the use of the Reich's paper money out of fear that the touch of Jewish hands might pollute the image of the *Führer* and transmit a contagious contamination. Extreme ideological hairsplitting was even the subject of debate by Nazi jurists concerning whether pollution also resulted from the contact of a Jew and a German prostitute, and what was the degree of intimacy required with a Jew in order for a German to be contaminated.

While playing on social and individual prejudices of many Germans, the anti-Semitic stereotype did not omit the link between Jews and money, and thus Jewish lust for Aryan women was always connected with lust for money. The resulting image pictured a fat Jewish banker caressing a blond woman on his knee, or lying in wait to ravish the native blond Aryan maiden.

This image was propagandized by Hitler, theorized by Rosenberg and Darr, and depicted graphically in cartoons, drawings, and public posters by Julius Streicher, Hitler's specialist in inflammatory journalism.

The following appeared in *Der Stürmer* in August 1935:

93

The Jew has in his veins a large element of Negro blood; his frizzy hair, his wolf lips, the color of his eyeballs prove this as effectually as the insatiable sexual greed which hesitates at no crime and finds its supremest triumph in the brutal defilement of women of another race. This bestial lust obsesses even a barely mature Jew-boy.[15]

The fear of racial contamination and degeneration connected with mixed marriages was accompanied by the natural fear of senility which accompanies old age. This comparison increased the fear of contamination from a drop of semen carrying with it "Jewish venereal disease" or the slightest physical touch bringing with it a fatal result for which there could be no remedy.

Strange and Foreign

The hate/fear of the Jews was also connected to a general xenophobia especially after the First World War, when Germany served as a transit for emigrating Jews. At this time these foreign Jews became a stereotype of all foreigners. The Jewish migrants stood out in their "foreignness" and were used as easy tools to incite feelings of a "foreign take-over in Germany."

At times, there was a differentiation between native Jews, and those who "invaded" the country from the East. Many of the leaders of the German-Jewish community actually preferred to lay the onus of hatred on some eighty thousand East European Jews who had entered Germany between 1917 and 1920 as refugees from Ukranian nationalism. "The Jews of Eastern Europe are our misfortune" was a frequent German Jewish exclamation, but they hoped it was a passing phase, until the *Ostjuden* (East European Jews) became acculturated.

The tendency to present the problem as one of education, a conception held by many Jews and non-Jews originally, was a case of mere wishful thinking. Even the outspoken friends of the Jews, eager to stress the basic unity of mankind, tried to make Jewish origins more exotic than they actually were. This did not prevent the masses from regarding them as aliens, "strange peoples of Asia," or " the Oriental horde camped on the Brandenburg sands." Thus, to call the Jew an Oriental was more often intended as an insult than a source of pride. Stereotypes of this sort converted the Jewish question into " an ethical question,"[16] a phrase used by Adolf Stocker in the Prussian Diet. It was not simply a matter of race, nationality or religion, but a whole way of life that was endangered by "alien values." In the words of Goethe, this was a foreign people living at Germany's borders and infiltrating the so called higher cultures of the

94

Western nations.[17]

The theme of the Jew as an alien, and the contrast of his roots with German ones, was taken up by other German writers as well. In the *National Socialist Times,* Eberhard Wolfgang Moller, winner of the national book award of 1934-35, portrayed Eastern Jews as "the Jews" without any further qualifications. Tudel Weller in his preface to *Rabauken,* uses the term "half Asia" to describe the Jewish milieu in general, and Alfred Rosenberg's periodical *Die Judenfrage (The Jewish Question)* put it succinctly: "Eastern Jewry was the reservoir of modern Jewry, the root of its strength."[18] Such strength, according to German writings, was rooted in surroundings of dirt and filth, of milling crowds who talk in an unpleasant language.

It is true that many of the Eastern immigrants were palpably different from the old German Jewish settlers, in speech, gestures, habits, probably even in values. However, to force all Jewish immigrants from the East – Russians, Ukrainians, Lithuanians and Galicians – into a single mold and thus to fashion a convenient stereotype seemed to be obvious propaganda too. In spite of all the efforts of enlightened groups both among Jews and non-Jews, the terms *Ostjuden* and "pimp" were popularly accepted almost as synanomous terms.

According to Peter Gay,

> After the World War , the Eastern Jews ... lived in distinct quarters of the city. But they were also set apart by their trades, their appearance, their speech. Thousands of Berlin Jews, well educated, impeccably German in their accent and their convictions, thought themselves superior to these invaders from the East, and conducted an intermittent civil war with their fellow Jews.[19]

In that "civil war," the term used for the Eastern Jews by the native Berliner Jews was "foreigners." The "natives" especially looked down contemptuously upon the new arrivals who spoken a broken German or Yiddish dialects.

> Berlin German Jews made fun of their brothers from beyond the border not merely because they wanted to demonstrate that they were Germans, but precisely because they were Germans .... Thus, while the German Jew found *Ostjuden* embarrassing to him for fear that he might be identified with them, he found them so also because they were to him, really embarrassing.[20]

With the rise of racial anti-Semitism, the distinction between German Jews and *Ostjuden* began to dissolve, and the attempt to separate one's fate from that of the Eastern Jews proved to be a desperate miscalculation. There seems to be a general law concerning the acceptance of an alien. His treatment depends on the degree to which he is judged an asset or a liability for the realization of the values of the in-group, and the degree of visibility of his differences and their importance to the in-group. Propaganda, of course, could provide the clues whereby the enemy can be identified, especially in cases where he tries to lower his visibility.[21]

Nazi propaganda emphasized the German Jews' "tribal" character, "a people without a homeland," the very incarnation of foreignness. Nevertheless it was found that the visibility of the Jew was not a perfect guide for his identity. Hence, the requirement to wear yellow arm bands.

Many anti-Semitic writers pointed to statistics on the amazing migration of Jews to the capital city, thus linking the themes of strangeness, nomadism, and urbanism. The legends of The Wandering Jew and The Eternal Jew were thus revived and gained new currency. The non-Jewish nomad, however, retained a certain positive image. He is foreign but has a positive attitude towards work, a bit of an idealist even though appearing strange to the Aryan peoples. Nevertheless, he is not totally different from them in character; but not so the Jewish nomad. His foreignness is totally different and stems from a negative attitude towards work. The wandering nature has been the result of constant expulsions by the host peoples who were exploited by the Jew. The dispersion and nomadic nature of the Jew is thus a sign of his worthlessness since it is a response by a parasite seeking a new fertile soil to nourish his race.

The Nazis succeeded in their propaganda to effectively isolate the Jews through emphasis on the latter's mysteriousness and strangeness. This was the first necessary step in breaking the social and economic ties between them and German society.

Another aspect of the "foreign" and "alien" character of Jews is the exotic and exclusive practices Jews engaged in, particularly those relating to dietary laws. One of the most provocative of these practices, from the point of view of the host countries, was that of *shechita* (ritual slaughtering) in which the animal's blood is completely drained in accordance with strict ritual practices by an especially trained religious functionary – the *shochet*. It is based on the commandment found in Leviticus 17:11-13.

> The life of the flesh is in the blood. Therefore, I said unto the children of Israel, no soul of you shall eat blood, neither shall any stranger that sojourneth among you...

Anti-*shechita* agitation long predated the Nazis in Germany and was a staple of anti-Semitic propaganda which depicted it as a brutal and inhumane practice.

During the 1920s there was an anti-*shechita* campaign in the state parliaments and under its influence Bavaria enacted an anti-*shechita* law in 1930. On April 21, 1933, a law was promulgated banning *shechita* in all of Germany.

The Nazis made full capital of the public row over *shechita* to whip up popular resentment against the Jews. The complete draining of the blood after the *shechita* was cited as evidence of cruelty of the Jews to animals as well as a Jewish blood rite. This contributed to a deeper entrenchment of the blood libel.

The French historian and investigator of anti-Semitism, Poliakov, in seeking to identify the psychological basis of the strong popular reaction to this practice, wrote:

> The Jews' fearful and respectful attitude towards blood (and towards human life in general) may have contributed its share. If they made so much of blood, if they attributed so much value to it, then they desired it, just as they desired money.[22]

The fact that such practices as these took place behind the walls of the ghetto further enhanced their mysterious, occult, strange, and outlandish character.

The Ghetto Jew

The Ghetto Jews with their medieval style of dress were the favorite visual objects of Nazi anti-Semitic propaganda in the cinema. For Germans, the existence of the mass of East European Jewry within ghettos could be taken to typify Judaism and Jews. The barren stones of the ghetto streets were said to epitomize the soul of Jewry. Moreover, behind the ghetto walls, with its dark streets and mysterious caftanned inhabitants, conspiracies were plotted, the object of which was to take power and to destroy all non-Jews.

In addition, the ghetto has also come to represent the physical embodiment of the urban nature of Jews. It symbolized emptiness, in contrast to the spirituality and solidity of the German peasant or the German petite bourgeois.[23]

The Arch Conspirator

In invoking the Jewish World Plot, the Nazis had only to turn to the infamous *Protocols of the Elders of Zion,* a document purporting to be the plan for the establishment of a Jewish world state.[24]

The source of the *Protocols* was an obscure French journalist, Maurice Joly. It was orginally a satirical dialogue in hell between Machiavelli and Montesquieu about the seats of power and how to gain them. No mention was made of Jews. Joly's work was ignored for several decades until a German, Herman Godsche, used it as a source for a novel. Godsche, writing under the pseudonym, Sir John Radcliffe, introduced the scene in which the Rabbis met in a mysterious cemetery of the ghetto of Prague, where they plotted to take over the world. The plot is so secret that it is even hidden from ordinary Jews.

In many editions of the *Protocols,* an appendix appeared at the end of the text dealing with a symbolic snake. The snake's body represents the Jewish People whose characteristic traits are guile and lies. The snake winds around the world beginning from Zion (Jerusalem). It bores through the hearts of the nations while its tail remains in Zion. Its head coils around Europe seeking to return to Zion, symbolizing complete Jewish control of the world. This will be achieved after the destruction of Europe by means of economic crises, spiritual disintegration, and the corruption of values. This is aided by Jewish prostitutes who hide their Jewishness and entrap the leaders of Europe in their web.

For the Nazis, Godsche's fictional account served as documentary proof of the world conspiracy of Jewry, and in the 1930s Johan van Leers reprinted the chapters dealing with the Jewish conspiracy as support and justification for an increased anti-Semitism. Therefore, for their purpose, the *Protocols* had to be authentic. The fact that the Berne Court in Switzerland in 1934 found it a "plagiarism of Joly's ridiculous nonsense," and referred to it as "gutter literature" was used by Hitler as proof of Jewish influence over the court, and the "genuineness" of the *Protocols.*

The conspiracy legend adroitly played upon the economic fears of the peasants by raising the specter of Jewish domination. Anti-Semitic propaganda claimed that a Jewish conspiracy was in control over every facet of life except, typically enough, labor, which the Jews shied away as from a plague, and that the Jews were in fact the kings of the present epoch.

Agent of Change

The image of the Jew as a symbol of urban culture and as an agent of change had its roots in social and economic causes, but its political importance increased when Nazi agitators compared the sneaky, dishonest, selfish, overclever, ambitious Jew to the ideal life of the farmer who lives off his soil. The Jew was the symbol of change, dislocation, and revolution, everything that the rural folk abhorred and fought against.

Their concentration in towns and cities had a considerable influence on the Jewish way of life and on its relation with the non-Jewish environment. This concentration strengthened anti-Semitic trends. In spite of Jewish concentration within the new ghettos, a large non-Jewish public came in close contact with them. This was principally an economic tie but included social aspects. These connections were inimical for Nazi propaganda which presented an image of the Jew that clashed with everyday reality. Thus the Nazis were interested in totally isolating the Jew to prevent a comparison of contrasting images.

In Europe, the falling away from rural occupations continued among Jews, as did the transition to a typically urban economy. As such, the Jew appeared in Nazi propaganda as yielding to the materialistic urban values engendered in the city. He was seen as one whose life is dominated by high finance and shady politics. He is the big city Jew who comes down from the city to trick the German peasant.

The "Fat Cat" Image

The image of the Jew as one who is primarily concerned with money runs the gamut of money-lending, pawnbrowkers, merchants, bankers, financiers, and the "fat cat" capitalist. The image of the Jew as money lender is historically rooted in feudal society, where the Jews were considered as landless. Being social outcasts, they had no legal, social or economic status, but were juridically classified as *Servi Camarae,* or *Kammerknecht* – The King's Servants. Their opportunities for earning a livelihood were painfully limited. They could not belong to Christian trade or merchant guilds, nor could they own a house or land, and were strictly enjoined from engaging in farming.

The occupations which remained open to them by law were limited to the despised or marginal trades, such as junk dealing, street hawking, the buying of old clothes and bones, and lastly, and most hazardously, money lending and money changing, and pawnbroking, all three usually being united in one establishment.

Until the Third Lateran Council of 1179 passed a decree against it, money lending had been a highly profitable activity of the Church itself. But after the passage of the decree, lending at interest or "usury" as it was called, was prohibited for all Christians.

The Church action failed to consider the realities and historic developments taking place at that time. The primitive system of barter was making way for the more efficient money economy. At that time a new middle class was emerging in the cities and towns together with the rapid growth of manufacturing and commerce. All those enterprises urgently needed liquid capital. For this, the money lender – the banker of feudal society, was indispensable. No less necessary than the large loans were the innumerable petty loans extended to small people in distress who pawned their household and personal possessions for small advances of money. But the Church had forbidden Christians to engage in money lending.

At this critical juncture the Jews entered the scene. They were already considered accursed since they had rejected Jesus the Messiah, and so, because they were damned anyway, the sin of usury could hardly increase their total wickedness.

Actually, at no time did Jewish moneylenders constitute more than a small group, and then only secondary in importance to the Christians, even during the period when the Church ban was formally in force. Nevertheless, the myth of the Jewish moneylender who trafficked with the devil, and who, "in his ancient hatred for Our Lord the Messiah Jesus, conspires to rob and destroy honest Christians," became entrenched over the centuries.

It was about a hundred years later in 1349 that the Black Plague struck Europe. The Jews were accused in all lands of having caused it by poisoning the water supplies. In Strasbourg 2,000 Jews were burned on St. Valentine's Day. The Council of Strasbourg declared that it was not just the charge of poisoning that sealed their fate.

> The money was indeed the thing that killed the Jews. If they had been poor, and if the feudal lords had not been in debt to them, they would not have been burned.[25]

The image of the sharp-dealing, merciless, gloating Jew, demanding his pound of flesh is embodied, indeed immortalized, in Shakespeare's Shylock, the merchant of Venice. The theme of the pound of flesh that appears in Nazi films was a very old one, perhaps dating back to the harsh Roman laws codified in the Twelve Tables. The lender had been presented in various forms as a pitiless creditor who was either a resentful slave or the obvious reincarnation of the devil. Then around 1378, the Florentine author, Sir Giovanni Fiorentino, in a tale from Le Pecorone (Day 4, Story 1), decided to transform the character into a Jew.

A similar tale in the *Gesta Romanorum,* the most widely read collection of popular stories in Europe, tells not about a Jew, but about an avaricious Christian money-lender from whom a lovesick knight had borrowed a thousand florins. The two had signed an agreement which included the pound of flesh formula. When the knight defaulted on the agreement, the moneylender dragged him into court. The verdict of the judges was almost identical with what was pronounced in *The Merchant of*

Venice. The merchant should have the power to cut the knight's flesh, but there was no provision for the shedding of blood.

Shakespeare, without doubt, must also have been familiar with the popular "Ballad of the Jew Gernutus," or the "Jew of Venice," in Percy's famous collection, *Reliques of Ancient Poetry,* which shows the cruelty of Gernutus, a Jew, who demands a pound of flesh from a merchant who could not repay a loan of a hundred crowns on time. In presenting Shylock as a verminous creature, a composite of several classic anti-Semitic stereotypes was used, and in spite of the individual humanity of Shylock, Shakesapeare did not abolish the negative stereotype of the merchant of Venice.

From the Christ-killer and Wandering Jew images, Shakespeare derived the compulsive vengefulness and capacity for gloating; traits which supposedly were intrinsic to the Jewish character. He also endowed his Shylock with the treachery made odious to Christians by the example of the notorious Judas Iscariot. These images were part of the cultural heritage of the period which was steeped in deep-rooted Christian motifs. In the early part of the seventeenth century, the dramatic works of Shakespeare and Marlowe appeared often on German stages. Today, the word Shylock has become a figurative term for avaricious and ruthless dealing. Worse, it is often synanomous with Jew.

We have seen that the Shylock image and the bizarre pound of flesh device with which it is associated in people's minds have their roots in medieval English history, social conditions and culture. Their genesis and development furnish a striking illustration of how anti-Semitic myths have been invented and propagated. In the Nazi era, the Shylock slander of Shakespeare was projected in a number of disguised forms, chief of which was the International Jewish Banker whose tentacles reached out everywhere.

By the middle of the eighteenth century, Jewish financiers and bankers had come to be influential forces in Central Europe. Even before the French Revolution, Frankfurt had become the center of international banking and enjoyed much of its pre-eminence because of Jewish enterprise. Indeed, the growth of international Jewish banking has long been one of the most intriguing phenomena of modern European history. A small, but immensely imaginative group of Jewish investment bankers (in no way typical of the great mass of Jews living in Western Europe), had an impact on European high finance far out of proportion to their numbers. They virtually affected the economic policies of the Western state system. The legends that grew up around their names had profound consequences for the destiny of all European Jews. The group that was hurt most by the rise of investment capitalism was the lower middle class who risked their small savings and had been permanently ruined.

Hannah Arendt explains that "they were becoming aware that if they did not succeed in climbing upward into the bourgeoisie, they might sink down into the proletariat."[26] At first they hoped the state might shield them against emergencies but soon...

> they had to accept the help of bankers. To the small shopkeeper the banker appeared to be the same kind of exploiter as the owner of a big industrial enterprise was to the worker. But while the European workers, from their own experience and a Marxist education in economics, knew that the capitalists filled the double function of exploiting them and giving them the opportunity to produce ... bankers looked like the exploiters not of working power and productive capacity, but of misfortune and misery.[27]

Many of these bankers were Jews. These Jewish financiers, many of them direct descendents of the *Hofjuden* who had financed governments since the eighteenth century, were endowed with long experience in dealing with portable funds. Most of them had capital which had been accumulated over several generations, and thus the entire propaganda against banking capital became anti-Semitic.

Arendt points out that "the social resentment of the lower middle classes against the Jews turned into a highly explosive political element because these bitterly hated Jews were thought to be well on their way to political power."[28]

The foremost Jewish bankers, like the Oppenheimers, Seligmans, and Rothschilds, were the most influential financial power in Germany, not to speak of the Speyer Bank, which was the vital link between Germany and the American market. In 1800 it was many times more powerful than the emergent House of Rothschild. The rise of the "Frankfurt Tradition," however, was best illustrated in the career of the Rothschilds, who, like many of the other Jewish banking houses, came from the Frankfurt *Judengasse*. It was in this light that, when Nazi propaganda raised the slogan of the defense of the ordinary man from the exploiting capitalist, Rothschild became a symbol of capitalism and King of the Jews in Nazi film.

Although the stock exchange speculator and the corpulent banker had become widely accepted and disseminated through popular literature as exploiters of the people from a material point of view, their supposed immoral sexual behavior added the element of moral exploitation as well. According to Mosse:

It fused the image of Jewish hunger for money with his lust for Aryan women. The resulting image widely used a fat Jewish banker caressing a blond woman on his knee. The same agent who milked Germans of their wealth also depleted their racial strength; that was the Volkish anti-Semitic theme. This was the image which became accepted by many Germans.[29]

The connection between the Jew and high finance found a responsive echo among academic circles, and was not limited to the masses. Many of the anti-Semitic propagandists relied on the work of the economic historian Werner Sombardt's *The Jews and Capitalism* (1910), which served as a basis for the view that the Jew brings capitalism with him wherever he goes.

Thus, the belief that everything Jewish high finance did was in the service of a world-wide conspiracy against either national interest or against the Aryans, had great propaganda value, and epitomized the stereotype of the Jew far more than had the traditional European prejudice. The picture of capitalism and liberalism as an expression of the spirit of an exploiting and oppressive Jewry was explained by Hitler himself:

> The Jew suddenly becomes liberal and begins to praise the need for progress for the human race. He gradually turns into a pioneer of a new era. But he destroys more and more of the economy essential to our people by indirect means. By means of shares, he pushes himself into the stream of national production and turns it into money to be traded and used as an object of speculation. He thus prevents firms from becoming stable. As a result, a process of alienation between classes begins. However, the influence on the economic sector increases quickly by means of the stock market. The Jew becomes the owner or the supervisor of the national work force.[30]

This belief in the power of "Jewish big money" embodied the stereotype of the Jew more than the traditional one. It was no accident that the Nazi charges were not levelled simply against the Jew, but rather "the modern international Jew."

The Bolshevik

In the nineteenth century, conservative aristocrats seeking to preserve the political status quo had found it convenient to brand liberalism as Jewish. In the twentieth century, agrarian and industrial monopolies sought with equal desperation to find a political technique for preserving the economic status quo. They found it by stigmatizing Marxism together with international banking as a Jewish phenomenon.

This political technique was applied with notable success in Germany. After the First World War, the Jewish world conspiracy came to be linked with the communist conspiracy. The theory was that the Jews pretended to be communists for the sake of their conspiracy to take over the world. This was very clearly asserted by Goebbels in a speech which was also reprinted as a pamphlet, *Bolshevism in Theory and Practice*. Goebbels asserted that:

> It [Bolshevism] is nothing but a pathological and criminal kind of madness, devised by the Jews who aim at destroying the civilized nations of Europe and founding a Jewish international world regime that would subject all nations to their power ... Jewish Bolshevism is a past master in the manipulation of lies. Decent and truthful people are so stunned by this method that they are incapable of offering inner resistance.[31]

There is no doubt that most Jews in Russia were opposed to Bolshevism and to the bolshevik scheme for a totalitarian government. Every one of the eight Jewish members of the first Saint Petersburg Soviet, the group which overthrew the Kerensky regime, voted against the bolshevik plan of action. The kind of ruthless proletarian dictatorship established by Lenin violated the deepest instinct of nearly every Russian Jew, socialist or non-socialist. Side by side with the threat of the death penalty for anti-Semitism, Lenin sought to destroy the Jewish national entity in the Soviet Union

There were, however, individual Jews who played a role in the bolshevik uprising quite out of proportion to the number of Jews in the Russian population or even in the Bolshevik Party. Jacob Sverdlov was the first president of the Central Executive Committee; Grigori Zinoviev became president of the Third International. Maxim Litvinov became Soviet Commissar for Foreign Affairs; Karl Radek was Soviet Press Commissar. D. Riaganov was chairman of the Marx-Engels Institute and the leading Marxist historian; Jakob Yoffe, Lev Kameniev, Lazar Kaganovich all became leading figures in the Soviet regime; the last two receiving appointments as commissars and members of the highest body, the Politburo.

Perhaps the most influential Jewish Bolshevik of all was Leon Trotsky. His neatly trimmed goatee and his jackboots were a caricature so frequently portrayed in the European press that for non-Russians they virtually became trademarks of the revolution. After the Bolshevik revolution, Trotsky was appointed Commissar for Foreign Affairs and

Defense. It was Trotsky, a Jew, who organized the Red Army and, as Commander in Chief, personally led the military campaign against the counter-revolutionary forces. In 1929 Trotsky was outmaneuvered by Stalin, and exiled.

In no other period in modern time did Europe produce so influential a minority of powerful Jews. The appearance of Jewish names upon the rosters of socialist and communist parties provided the reactionaries of the twentieth century with a most effective propaganda weapon. In their view international Jewry stood behind the bolshevik regime.

It is important to note that Nazi propaganda did not fight against Bolshevism as an ideology as much as aganist the actual Bolshevik, portrayed as a Jew. To this end, the cinema was an ideal medium.

In his book *Racism in Hitler's View*,[32] Tzvi Bacharach writes that Hitler believed that Nordic-German elements comprised the elite strata of the Russian population before the First World War. These elements suffered a hemorrhage *(Ausblutung)* during the war and were eliminated not by the "Slavic racial instinct" *(Slawische Rasseninstinkt)*, but by the new Soviet leadership which was primarily Jewish. Soviet Russia was thus weakened and subjugated by Jewry's destructive plans.

It was therefore "fortunate" that Germany's pressing need for expansion *(Lebensraum)* would inevitably involve a final showdown with the Jewish racial enemy. This added justification was a convenient one for Hitler who stated:

> We must regard Russian Bolshevism in the twentieth century as an attempt by the Jew to gain world control....The struggle against Jewish world Bolshevisation demands a clear stand towards Soviet Russia. It is impossible to expell the devil with a fly-swatter...[33]

In this chapter I have indicated the principal stereotypes which appeared in the Nazi cinema. Their appearance on the screen as flesh and blood, eating, drinking, raping and carousing, strengthened the negative image of the Jew which had been rooted in the minds of many Germans for generations.

PART 2
THE NAZI ANTI-SEMITIC FILM

1

PRELIMINARY ANTI-SEMITIC FILMS

ROBERT AND BERTRAM – 1939

Frankly anti-Semitic themes had previously been used only for party films until 1939 when they appeared before the general public in the form of a seemingly inoffensive light comedy called *Robert and Bertram*.

The use of stereotypes is characteristic of many propaganda films. The process of transforming the image of the Jew from comical and grotesque to dangerous and sinister began with this film. It was produced as a simple light comedy, but its roots can be found in the vulgar and quite popular comedies in which distorted and ridiculous Jewish types were portrayed during the 18th and 19th centuries.

The production of the film at, Terra studios, started on December 29, 1935, with Ludwig Manfred Lommel and Kurt Vespermann in title roles. This contrived comedy had its premiere in Hamburg on July 27,1939. It was the cinematic version of a play by Gustav Radler which had been shown in German theaters since 1865, but in the stage version no attempt had been made to portray the typical Jew.

The director selected for the project was Hans Heinz Zerlett, a prolific specialist in both musicals and action pictures. Zerlett was highly regarded by Goebbels as an actor's director. However, most of his work until then was non-political.

The story takes place in 1839. Two carefree vagabonds, who have just escaped from jail, manage to get along without money for a while, but soon have to find a source of income.

One day they meet up with the daughter of a local inkeeper who tearfully tells them that she is being forced to marry the Jew Biedermeir. He is a friend of another Jew, Impelmayer, who owns a mortgage on her father's inn. When the two friends hear the story, they decide to steal Impelmayer's money. They pose as dishwashers and offer their sevices to Impelmayer on the occasion of his engagement party.

During a costume ball Bertram entertains the guests with a song while Robert tries to steal jewelry, and at the same time courts the grotesque and fat Frau Impelmayer.

Impelmayer is drugged by mistake, and the two friends succeed in robbing him and his guest of their jewels and money. They flee and send the loot to the blond-braided blue-eyed daughter of the innkeeper, enabling her to pay off the mortgage, and to marry the man of her choice – a loyal soldier in the army of a local prince.

Although the film is shown as filmed theatre (with a curtain in the beginning), several scenes, especially the anti-Semitic ones, show a high of grotesque exaggeration. These scenes are meant to be a parody of the Jewish lack of taste, culture, and education; the supposed nouveau-riche behavior of the Jews. Nevertheless, Impelmayer and his wife are portrayed not only as noveau-riches, but in an extremely derogatory way. As Robert puts it: "They are blown up like peacocks and waddle like ducks." The Jews have flat feet and speak a terrible German. They use exaggerated gestures, and their manner of dress and hairstyle allow them to be identified easily.

Here is one of the typical dialogue passages of the film which reveals its tendency and style. Robert, who has introduced himself as the Count of Monte Cristo, converses with the master of the house.

Robert: Your house appears to be a real temple of art!

Impelmayer: (gesticulating with his hands and speaking in broken German) What do you mean a temple? Are you by chance also a......? (understood as Jew)

Robert: (referring to his title) No, that's hardly possible.

Impelmayer: Why not? For example I know an archbishop called Cohn and a Lord Rothschild.

Robert: No....

Impelmayer: What do you mean by no? Word of honor!

The rich Jew Impelmayer says to Bertram : "I have a secret ... I am an Israelite." "I also have a secret," answers Bertram, "I have a belly." Since Bertram is very fat, the idea is clear. The assimilated Jew, no matter how hard he tries to penetrate German society, cannot hide his origin just as a fat man cannot hide his paunch. This motif is repeated many times in Semitic films.

German critics appreciated the "true" image presented by the film, and praised the actors who had taken upon themselves the unpleasant role of playing the parts of Jews.

Although the Jewish types appear comical and grotesque, they are also dangerous. They involve simple naive German farmers in financial problems which leave them helpless. Although the two vagabonds engage in theft, they are sympathetically portrayed, for the simple reason that they are so anti-bourgeois. Bertram in fact describes himself as a "fugitive bourgeois," who "prefers to be a tramp than city trash." Still, several critics wrote that the Jew had not been presented in his true light, i.e. as

110

the dangerous element he really is, and Hitler himself criticized the bad image of the two Germans, shown as tricksters. At the end, Robert and Bertram are rewarded for their good deed and allowed to go to heaven where they can continue their pranks upon chubby-faced Biedermeir angels for all eternity.

As a precautionary measure (the time was 1939), a second ending to the film was shot. Here we see Robert and Bertram serving under the blond husband-warrior of the maiden they helped, and march joyously with a group of soldiers under his command. This version was shown in 1942 at the time when the ordinary German citizen was beginning to show signs of war weariness.

It was a primitive type of satire which did not meet Goebbels' plans for hard-hitting and provocative anti-Semitic films. Nevertheless, *Robert and Bertram* may be regarded as a precursor to those pictures which aimed at the justification of the murder of the Jews.

LEINEN AUS IRLAND – 1939
(LINEN FROM IRELAND)

Another film which may be included in this group is *Leinen aus Irland*. In this film, however, the image of the "dangerous Jew" appears for the first time. It was produced in Austria after the *Anschluss,* and was supposed to be proof of ideological coordination of Austria and the Reich. This movie was based on an anti-Semitic theater play, written by Stefan von Kamera, which in itself was not anti-Semitic, but was exploited for propaganda purposes.

The film's premiere was in Berlin in October 1939, and dealt with the problem of Jewish assimilation. The director, Herbert Helwig, was eager to prove that the Austrian film industry adhered to the propaganda line laid down by Goebbels, and thus made it a German product.

The film is about a Jewish boy, Kohn, from Krotoschin, who manages to become the general manager of the Libussa Agency in Prague. He is not content with his position and wants more. With his unbridled ambition he plans to become the linen king of the world, and one of the ways he thinks he can achieve this is by marrying the boss's daughter.

In his greed he plans to take advantage of the free import of Irish linen, regardless of whether hundreds of thousands of Bohemian workers lose their jobs, but in the end he fails.

The film portrays Kohn (later Kuhn) as a human being without instincts and, through his uncle Sigi, we are reminded where the Jews who have adapted themselves to modern society come from: "the dark holes of the ghetto."

111

The film tries to explain Kohn's failure as a result of his moral corruption, as well as to give proof that the healthy instincts of the Germans cannot be fooled.

German critics praised the film as a new genre, "political entertainment." Nevertheless, the film was not very well received by the public.

Together with *Robert and Bertram,* this film prepared the ground for films such as *The Eternal Jew* and *Jew Süss* that made a significant contribution to creating the psychologcial climate in which the Holocaust took place, a theme we shall expand upon in the following chapters.

2

THE ETERNAL JEW: THE *MEIN KAMPF* OF THE ANTI-SEMITIC NAZI CINEMA

The Documentary Film as Propaganda

From the outset, cinema has displayed a dualistic nature, encompassing both realism and fantasy, following the example of Lumiere to record actuality, and Melies in the invention of new cinematic techniques to create fantasy images.[1] This quality has been reflected in the ongoing controversy regarding the basic nature of the documentary film. The controversy can be reduced to the question: "Should documentary films be defined as objective or subjective?" That is, does a documentary present fact or fiction, truth or mere opinion; an impartial report or a personal editorial; untouched reality, or an individual interpretation of reality?

Siegfried Kracauer has based his elaborate theory of film on the medium's capacity for recording and revealing physical reality. According to Kracauer, film and science stand in the same relation to their subject matter. "Like science," he writes, "film breaks down material phenomena into tiny particles, thereby sensitizing us to the tremendous energies accumulated in the microscopic configurations of matter."[2]

While conceding the fact that films "cling to the surface of things," that they do not penetrate matters of spirit and intellect, Kracauer argues that "film forces us to explore the blind spots of the mind;" areas of perception that habit and prejudice cause us to overlook, things that we "know by heart," but not with the eye.

Film forces us to notice these things, and perhaps see them in new ways, in new relations. Film is a celluloid memory, preserving events, customs and fashion from our past, retaining a level of objectivity that is often beyond the capacity of the participant activated by strong emotions.

In this context, John Grierson, in the 1920s, defined the documentary film as "the creative treatment of actuality," even going so far as to call it a "propaganda film" based on his democratically oriented interpretation of propaganda as outlined in the first chapter.

In the late 1930s, the leading American prewar documentarist, Pare Lorentz, continued the debate by offering his own definition of documentary as "...factual film which is dramatic."[3] Lorentz soon discovered that what he regarded as fact, others viewed as lies or, at best, a subjective value judgement supporting partisan political programs.

While the semantics of these definitions are not completely satisfactory, they should put any student of film on guard concerning the problems involved in using documentaries as visual historical records. Just as people must learn a foreign language in order to utilize essential written documents, they must be familiar with focus, camera placement, framing, lens selection, lighting, film emulsion, editing techniques and other factors, combined to determine the form, content, and meaning of a given segment of film.

We will now analyze the *Mein Kampf* of the Nazi anti-Semitic Cinema, *The Eternal Jew,* which Hull called "the hate picture of all time," and one of the greatest examples of the way in which the film medium can be used as a propaganda tool, with a far greater effect than the printed or spoken word alone.[4]

Although the question of subjectivity and objectivity is not relevant at all to this film, which openly calls for genocide, its classification as a documentary film has to do mainly with disposition and style. Disposition refers to the arrangements of the elements of presentation to achieve maximal effect, and distinguishes the documentary film format from the feature film. The feature is inevitably both narrative and collaborative; a product of teams rather than individuals. The documentary film may be both or neither. That is why the documentary can allow its content or message the time and structure most naturally required.

Other aspects of form are also left open. That is why the documentary is able to adapt to many different dispositions that will be acceptable to the audience, and what might distract and detract from the narrative in a feature, may be legitimate in a documentary.

What about style? Style is the personal expression that gives the presentation impact and movement. Style may also be defined as the way the filmmaker uses the "productional rhetoric" of film. From this it follows that any investigation of the style practiced in a documentary film must be extremely careful to prevent a rapid descent into banalities. In other words, the belief that today's critics have a complete understanding of how film affects the audience is only an illusion. In reality, very few conventions have been identified and described.

One must examine the principal techniques and tools used to get and maintain audience attention, create variety, convey information and emphasize meaning. In addition, one must examine how the general principles of propaganda are applied in synthesizing verbal with visual communication means, since film does not rely solely on spoken rhetoric, but also employs its own resources in sound and vision.

The Eternal Jew

In the film, *The Eternal Jew*, the images are extremely diverse in origin and situation, from newsreel clips of the Jewish ghettos in Poland, to evidently staged sequences (as in the portraits of Jews with and without the stereotyped markings of Jewishness), maps, diagrams and animated statistics, paintings and sculptures, and excerpts from a Hollywood feature film, *The House of Rothschild*.

It is the particular way in which these images are ordered and structured, that determines the meaning and impact of the film. The scenes do not follow a logical thematic structure or continuity, and thus the film's impact is adversely affected. However, this is not a unique approach of the cinema. The scenes of *The Eternal Jew* are purposely constructed so as to provoke emotions, and create an atmosphere and mood, an experiential happening to evoke a direct identification rather than to persuade as a result of information or relevant considerations. The verbal part of *The Eternal Jew* takes the form of a commentary and statement that serve, on the one hand, to unify and verbally mark out an order for the images, and on the other, to provide the possibility of a direct address to an audience. It will be seen that although the images have their own figures of repetition and symmetry, they are not constrained by the need to motivate and be motivated by the narrative.

The verbal part of the film is presented in the form of description and commentary. The description assists to unite and denote verbally the order of the scenes and the accompanying pictures. The simplistic, poster-like description does not leave the viewer time to wonder about the essence of what he sees, and it reduces the burden placed upon the viewer from a propagandistic point of view. The viewer is not forced to interpret or think for himself and reach conclusions.

The Nazis saw in the legendary figure of the Eternal Jew an arch enemy of the Eternal Germany.[5] In the promotional material that was published, it was emphasized that the story or legend of the Eternal Jew antedated National Socialism, i.e. that this figure was not a creation or figment of the Nazi imagination, but was a symbol of the anathema in which the Jew was held by the world throughout history.

The story of Ahasuerus, the Jewish shoemaker who did not let Jesus rest in the shade, and was condemned by Jesus to wander until his second coming for having rebuffed him on the way to the crucifixion, is a

115

characteristically anti-Semitic legend. It was known in various versions already in the first centuries A.D., but its final and popular form took shape in the period of the Reformation, and brought with it a wave of hatred towards the Jews.[6]

In 1602, a book of legends was printed in German which accentuated the anti-Jewish implications of the tale.[7] It is told that in 1532, the Bishop of Schleswig, while attending church in Hamburg, saw a tall man with long hair, dressed in threadbare garments, standing barefoot in the chapel reserved for the priests and the choir. Each time the name of Jesus was mentioned, the man reportedly bowed his head, beat his breast and sighed profoundly. He was supposed to be Ahasuerus.[8] According to the film's promotional material, the adjective "eternal" signified the unchangeable racial characteristics of the Jews.

While the Aryan has inherited eternal life from his ancestors, the Jew, in contrast, had been branded with the eternal motive of his race to destroy all other races in order to rule over the entire world.[9]

This was the theme of the film, *The Eternal Jew,* which was first shown in Berlin on November 28, 1940. The idea of making a documentary film on this subject was that of Eberhard Taubert. It was Fritz Hippler, however, the head of the Reich's Film Chamber, who produced the film. *The Eternal Jew* contains footage which was shot in Poland right after the invasion of 1939, in the newly established ghettos of Lodz, Warsaw, Crackow, and Lublin. It was described in the German press as a *Kulturfilm,* an educational documentary on "the problems of world Jewry."

Hippler, who saw in the film his life's work, found it necessary to personally promote the film with a full page report of how it was made, which appeared in the the weekly film journal *Der Film* on November 30, 1940. It was intended to counter possible objections of the public. To anyone who said: "Again a movie about the Jewish problem,"[10] Hippler pointed out that "the Jewish problem would not stop being acute until the last Jew had departed from all the non-Jewish nations of the world."[11]

Despite the risk of objection from a public uninterested in documentaries, Hippler believed that the Germans would be very interested in seeing the new picture because two other anti-Semitic fims, *The Rothschilds* and *Jud Süss* had brought "unbelievable box-office results."[12] He went on to point out the superiority of this film project. There was something new about it because the two other entertainment films mentioned above, which showed the behavior and the way of life of the Jews,

...have, despite the greatest art and inner truth, missed out on telling the full truth. To aim for an immediate effect, you have to show reality, and you have to make a documentary. This is the case with the film, *The Eternal Jew*. Here Jews are not being portrayed, rather they show themselves as they really are. Not one picture is posed, and no Jew is forced to do anything special, or act against his will.[13]

To strengthen his assertion, Hippler said that the camera team caught the atmosphere in the Polish cities before the German administration started to make changes. After the overwhelming German victory over Poland, the Jews were "anxious to appear friendly and obliging." Thus Hippler assumed that easy-going Germans would consider any documentary scene to be a true reflection of reality. Hippler went on to say:

If one lets the pictures sink in, it has to be admitted that even the most hateful cartoons and performances remain far behind what reality is in fact. Everybody who saw these pictures said the same: A symphony of disgust and horror.[14]

Hippler explained:

We picked out some very particular types of ghetto Jews, and portrayed them as they were, running around in the ghetto with full beards, caps, and caftans. We then shaved them and sheared their hair, put them into European suits and filmed them again. The ghetto Jew was not recognizable even if the second picture was not attractive either.[15]

Analytical Abstract

The film begins with a statement in the credit titles that

The civilized Jews we know in Germany only give us an incomplete picture of their racial character. This film shows genuine shots of Polish ghettos. It shows us the Jews as they really are before they concealed themselves behind the mask of the civilized European.

The thesis of the film is clear and it is stated right at the start. The "Oriental barbarian" has disguised himself as a cultured person, and interfered with European civilization. The documentary film will reveal the true Jew.

As indicated, the film does not follow any direct line of logical progression, but the effect is a cumulative one, especially for those viewers who can bear it to the end. Images and various stereotyped illustrations of the Jew are piled one on top of each other and culminate at the end of the film with the barbaric attitude of the Jew towards animals by means of a description of Jewish ritual slaughter.

The place is Poland. The narrator, Hippler, speaks of the familiar Jews of Germany who appear civilized, as opposed to those from Poland whom we see in the film. The purpose of the comparison is clear. Both represent the same low form of the human race. With affected noblesse oblige the commentator tells of the Polish defeat, and indirectly praises the German victory.[16] He describes the feelings of defeat manifested by the Poles while the Jews sat "safely in calm ghettos" and returned to their haggling as soon as hostilities ceased.

There is a shot of the Warsaw ghetto, compiled from newsreel footage. During this extremely long shot, the camera slowly moves in for closeups. of Jewish types. Some of the men have enormous beards and twisted, misshapen faces. Their appearance is generally comic, grotesque, and not at all frightening.

Here the narrator uses direct commentary. The viewer's impression of the Jew as a comic figure misses the mark. Therefore the commentator directs the conclusions of the viewer and analyzes the photographs . A sophisticated interpretation will reveal that the Jews are the source of a plague which threatens the health of the Aryan peoples.

To strengthen the conclusion the camera pans the streets of the ghetto and the strange black-clad figures. As we have noted earlier, much of Nazi ideology focused on the German family, home, and room. In comparison, the Jewish family lives in a place lacking honor. The message of the scene is that the Jewish family has no honor. There is a closeup of vermin on the wall, a crawling black mass. An objective view of such a scene might be that we are watching a very poor neighborhood, but such a conclusion is not desirable, and once again the commentator offers his direct interpretation. These Jews are not poor, he tells us. They made huge profits from their business dealings over the years and could well afford to live in clean and pleasant homes, but they prefer filth. In such disgusting surroundings they offer their prayers.

We see a band of old men, dressed in black, with thick beards who move the upper parts of their bodies to and fro. Whoever is not familiar with the prayer ritual must regard it as strange. The camera closes in on the men at prayer and exaggerates their motions even more. "The movement of the upper part of the body is the required manner of reading the Jewish scriptures," explains the commentator, thus generalizing about all Jews wherever they may be.

Again we go outside into the streets where we find ourselves among

118

people who are all involved in some outlandish arguments. "They hardly ever make anything for themselves," claims the commentator, "so they do not work, and if they work, they do so only under pressure."

Several Jews are shown at work removing rubble. One of them moves slowly, holding a brick in each hand and then dumps them into a wheelbarrow. He performs this action with obvious distate and returns to his lazy brothers. They are resting passively on their shovels. Then we are back in the streets of the ghetto.

The commentator continues: "Their desire is to trade. Their pride lies in haggling over a price. They have no ideals; divine law teaches them to be selfish, to cheat any non-Jew." Scenes with quarreling women; men buying second-hand clothes, handling, feeling, tugging at the cloth all illustrate the image of the rag-trading Jew.

Inside their walled town, these poeple speak Yiddish. We hear excited Yiddish voices. Everywhere there are scenes of filth and a lack of hygiene. A woman in a stained apron is trying to sell slaughtered chickens that have been set out uncovered in the sunshine. Someone is trying to sell a cake which everyone is handling while another picks his nose, and a shopkeeper stares out apathetically at the street.

And of course, the scene is not complete without children. We see them also haggling in the streets over prices. They are of school age and school is where they should obviously be at this time of day. The commentator explains that "it would be naive to see in their street activity as little merchants a sign of poverty. They are proud to be like grown-ups. The young have no ambitions. They are not idealists, and their religion teaches them to cheat any non-Jew." (Here, to strengthen his assertions, a Torah scroll appears on the screen.)

The viewer is called upon to understand that for the Jew engaging in trade is part of his religion. It is not simply an economic activity, but a holy one. Only in this way can the viewer understand how an entire people is uninterested in creativity and is solely occupied with trade. Here an answer is provided to the claim that the Jews have been limited to trade because other occupations were closed to them. "The opposite is the case," summarizes the commentator, "their passion is trade."

Of course, during the course of viewing, the spectator is making an unconscious comparison with what he has seen on the screen and his own self-image. In such a situation of extremism, the viewer clearly rejects any aspect of similarity between himself and the Jew.

The producers of the film were not content with presentation of the negative stereotype, and reinforced it by presenting an idealized positive self-image of the German. The narrator pauses dramatically before moving on. We now see Germans diligently at work, accompanied by the words: "The Aryan individual finds dignity in every action. He seeks to create something."

From the propaganda point of view, a comparison is utilized by means of the principal of repetition. Once again faces appear in closeup on the screen. They are, however, nothing like the Jewish faces we saw earlier. These faces have "Aryan lines." The closeup shows hands. These are not the hands of merchants, but hands involved in creativity, operating machines, engaging in art, in the work of flailing hammers. We see strong bodies and muscular arms, the figures of Aryans engaged in creative work.

The music in the background has also changed. It is no longer frail and screeching, but harmonic with Wagnerian motifs. These figures are shot from a low angle with the sky as a background. This serves to increase their height on the screen.

There is a feeling of vision, majestic honor, and, above all, of power. This is the power which emanates from the screen to the German viewer; a power which the Jew has no chance of achieving. It is a visual situation enhancing an idealism which is borne aloft to great heights. From here the abysmal descent to the Jew is thereby magnified.

A figure with Jewish characteristics appears on the screen, counting money. From the German ideal of the creation of valuable objects we again move to Jewish ideal of money. The transition is sharp, abrupt, and rapid. In the coming shots we see a Jewish junk dealer and his wares. Another Jew brutally removes geese from their wretched cages while others are selling vegetables from improvised stalls.

"Soon, the more clever Jews become petty shopkeepers while the least scrupulous acquire department stores and banks, and live in opulent villas." By means of still photographs the grand houses of successful merchants are shown. The commentator points out how Jewish merchants have risen to such wealth by unscrupulous means. If nobody stops them, Jews will move into the wealthiest neighborhoods.

Scenes follow of Jews on the move with all their worldly goods packed on their backs. The effect is created of a massive migration of Jews wandering from places of poverty to wealthy states in order to purchase goods, which the Jew is unable to produce himself, and then to sell them at a profit.

> The Jews are a race without farmers and without handworkers, a race of parasites. Whenever a sore shows itself on the body of a people, they settle themselves firmly and feed on the decaying organism. They find their businesses among the diseases of the people, and for this reason they do their utmost to increase and

120

Advertisement Poster for the film *The Eternal Jew*

er ewige Jude

"This Jew Was Created As a Result of a Mixture Between the Asiatic-Oriental and the Negro" from the film *The Eternal Jew*

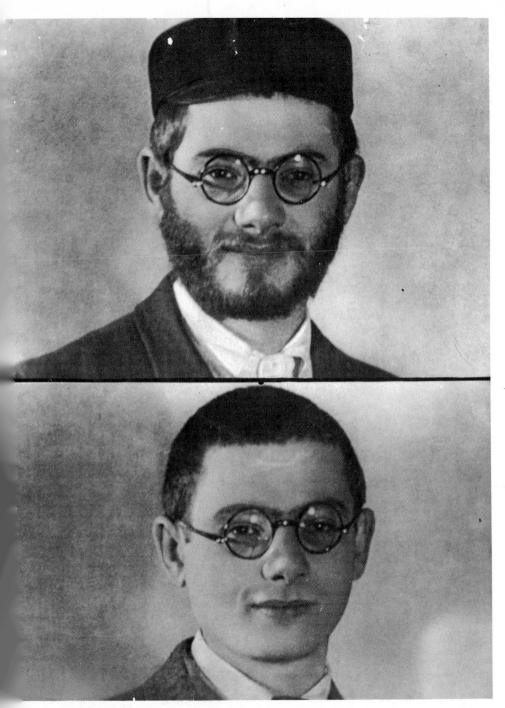

"...e Jew Knows How to Disguise His Jewish Characteristics," in the film
...e *Eternal Jew*

From a Montage of Jewish types, from the film *The Eternal Jew*

Montage of Jews hiding their "Jewish Characteristics," from the film *The Eternal Jew*

Profiles of Jewish Yeshiva Students from the film *The Eternal Jew*

The Jewish Slaughterer and Jewish types in the film *The Etnernal Jew*

perpetuate every form of sickness. This is the case in Poland and how it once was in Germany.

There follows an historical survey of the Dispersion with accompanying maps.[17] With the Wailing Wall as a symbol for Palestine, we see, by means of animated maps, the spread of Jews over the face of Europe.

The Western (Wailing) Wall symbolizes Palestine, but the origin of the Jews is not there, but in Mesopotamia, the land between the rivers. From there their wanderings began to Egypt where they engaged in the trade of grains until they were expelled by Egyptian farmers who had reached the limits of their endurance of Jewish exploitation. They leave Egypt and begin a journey of merciless plunder of a people who possess a higher culture than they do, and live in the land which the Jews regard as promised to them.

The points of Jewish concentration of settlement visually accumulate, and resemble multiplying insects from which a snake emerges to wind around the world – a reminder of the symbolism in the *Protocols*. After dominating Palestine they continue to expand, moving without rest, because "such is their nature." The "mobility neurosis" from which they suffer brings them to Spain, England, France and South Germany. This is illustrated as a dense network over the map. In each new country they make themselves unbearable, and are expelled by the natives. Suddenly the continuity of the animation is interrupted to present figures with "Jewish characteristics." These are repellent faces, the commentator explains, and the Jew is a mixture that developed from mating the Asiatic-Oriental Peoples with the Negroid race. For the viewer, "the pictures speak for themselves," and he is not to wonder why the Jews are an inferior race.

After this short interruption the animation returns and we see the Jewish snake winding itself around the world, sending out threatening tentacles, and creating a spider's web, embracing not only Europe but the entire Western hemisphere.

The spider webs lead the viewer to a montage presented in the form of swarms of insects (white spots created by the animation technique) located in Mesopotamia. The viewer expects a retelling of the story of the Jews' origins, but instead the commentator speaks of the "Asiatic rat." The narrator provides the analogy: "Like the Jew, the brown rat, which has a similar Asiatic origin, has also spread across Europe." In the following sequence, rats come out of gullies and flee in wild haste. They fill up the frame. For the viewer who has still not yet caught on to the analogy, the commentator adds:

In this way they spread disease, plague, leprosy, typhoid, cholera, dysentery, etc. They are cunning, cowardly and cruel and are found mostly in large packs. In the animal world they represent the element of craftiness and underground destruction – no different from the Jews among mankind.

The commentary underlines the parallel. Then the camera returns to the Jewish faces in the crowds of the Lodz ghetto who are moving in the same direction as the rates moved. The comparison between Jews and rats not only creates disgust but turns the Jews into non-humans. The fear of the "Barbarians from the East" seeking to invade Germany and destory its culture was a fixed element of the thinking of many Germans, and it often appears in German literature. In the German cinema we have the well-known example of Friedrich W. Mornau's, *Nosferatu,* who, like the Jew, is from the Orient and carries in his wake rats and disease.

From the preceding, it appears that the propagandistic principal and poster-like style of films served a clear and extremist ideology. The visual-logical principal declares that whoever appears on the screen as "bad," "ugly," "filthy," proves also that his inward character is the same. In the example of *The Eternal Jew,* it is the principle of racism which is the connecting thread unifying the entire film. In this connection the producers of the film were unable to disregard an additional element of propaganda: statistics.

Once again stereotyped close-ups of Jews appear on the screen. The figures chosen for the purpose of this scene are hardly flattering, to put it mildly. With this as background, the commentator brings the audience statistics, illustrating the place occupied by Jews (in terms of very high percentages) as such criminals as drug merchants, bank robbers, international burglers, and pimps. The faces seen on the screen acquire another significance: they are not only disgusting, they are dangerous.

The use of a "dissolve" is a cinematic device which served Nazi propaganda in a perfect way and, in my opinion, the scene in which the Jewish faces lose their Jewish characteristics by means of a dissolve, is the most technically successful one in the film. The producers of the film were anxious that the German viewer might reach the conclusion that owing to his familiarity with the German Jew, the latter might be really different from the East European Jew, especially if compared to the selection of faces presented on the screen. To forestall this possibility, the dissolve scene was planned to reinforce the assertion that the German Jew and the East European Jew belong to the same race, and that the former is even more dangerous because he has learned to camouflague his racial characteristics.

This is accomplished by the presentation of a group of Polish Jews dressed in caftans. They have long earlocks and thick beards. After having been filmed, these Jews were shaved and dressed in the European clothes customarily worn by the Berlin Jews. They were filmed for a second time without even any head covering. They were then presented on the screen in the form of before-and-after. We see the East European Jew and immediately afterward the same Jew appears in European clothing while the commentator emphasizes that only a sharp eye can distinguish the special racial characteristics of the Jew.

The danger is not in the first generation, warns the commentator, but primarily in the second and third generations. There the level of Jewish cleverness reaches its peak and the danger of assimilation and racial defilement increases substantially. This conspiracy begins with the Jew concealing his origin.

At this point, the film turns to a "docu-drama" presenting long excerpts from the Hollywood film, *The House of Rothschild,* featuring George Arliss. This early Rothschild is played as a rich merchant concealing his wealth from the tax collectors by claiming that he is poor and hungry. He is helped in this deception by his wife and children. For the purposes of *The Eternal Jew,* the scene of Rothschild and the tax collector is taken out of context, (Rothschild actually supported Prussia, England, Italy, and Austria against Napoleon). The commentator covers over the original soundtrack, and intervenes at critical points to orient the viewer, providing the terms of reference for its comprehension. In the second fragment, Rothschild is talking to his children, telling them of his plan to set up banks in various European capital cities.

> If money is to be sent to London, no one needs to risk his life. You send a letter to Nathan in London to pay so and so. As a counter account there will be loans from London to Frankfurt. Soon there will be many wars and all the states will come to the Rothschilds. The money will be safest with you.

The dialogue continues, but the sound is dimmed to inaudibility, and the commentary intervenes:

> At this point, it must be noted that transfer of money by check was not an invention of the Jews, nor was it cultivated by them for the good of mankind, but simply to serve them as a means of obtaining international interference over and above the heads of their hosts.

In this sequence Hippler deals with capitalism, Rothschild's dual loyalties, manipulation of politicians, and his war profiteering.

It is interesting that American film critics praised the original Hollywood film, among other things, for its positive treatment of Jews, and even called it a "contribution to humanity."

A return to the documentary style of the film does not, however, abandon the preoccupation with Rothschild who has become a symbol for all of Jewry. The expansion of the Rothschild family over Europe is then traced on an animated map, by way of introducing a sequence on the power of the great Jewish houses in international banking and politics. The Rothschilds sent "hands" into every financial center of the world, until "the world is captured."

How is the world controlled? Through the stock market of course! We move on to the bustling floor of the New York Stock Exchange where influential Jews, financiers and statesmen, are masked to look like Americans. Also fitted into this sequence are Leon Blum, Prime Minister of France, and Hore-Belisha, the British Secretary of War.

The next section deals with German politics of the 1920s, and accuses Walter Rathenau and others of having brought about Germany's humiliation. In still photos we are shown Jewish executives, financiers, and publishers holding their grip on Germany. These Jews, however, do not resemble the ghetto Jews. Indeed it is difficult to tell that they are Jews at all. The narrator is therefore quick to warn us that people without instinct can be fooled by this mimicry, and may actually see them (the Jews) as one of their own kind. This bears great danger, because these assimilated Jews will always remain alien in the organization of their host countries no matter how much they resemble their inhabitants.

This sequence is followed by animated diagrams illustrating the proliferation of Jews in the arts and professions. Fictitious statistics are quoted: for example, "52% of German physicians were Jews whereas for every thousand workers in Berlin only two were Jews." In addition, it is pointed out that while millions of Germans were unemployed, many Jews became millionaires by lending money at high interest.

Demonstrations with red flags give the commentator the opportunity to say that German youth had lost its nobler values and had been corrupted by treacherous ideas such as the class struggle ... all because of the twisted mind of a Jew named Karl Marx. The still picture of Marx is followed on the screen by pictures of Lasalle, and Rosa Luxemburg, whose real name was Emma Goldman, (a fact emphasized by the commentator), and three Jewish political assasins, Levin Nisan (a Russian-born revolutionary figure who acquired influence in the German workers' movement immediately following World War I), David Frankfurter, who killed a leading member of the Swiss Nazi Party, and David Greenspan who assasinated a Nazi diplomat in Paris, an event utilized by the Nazis to

132

perpetrate the Night of the Broken Glass. This sequence was inserted to convince the viewer that the Weimar Republic had been "poisoned by the Jews."

A film critic of Goebbels' newspaper, *Der Angriff,* verified this opinion by saying that:

> poison flowed from numerous channels into the German people to paralyze them until finally they would be totally subdued by the Jewish spider.[18]

With a montage of still photographs and newsreel clips the names of Jewish swindlers appear, in which a long sequence on art and culture is introduced, with the intention of railing against Jews who dare intervene and even express critical opinions regarding beauty and purity in that most holy of holies, the fields of art and culture. We are shown a montage of classical and Renaissance images of human figures: a Greek temple, classical sculptures, Gothic faces, Michelangelo's Sistine Chapel paintings and Boticelli's The Birth of Venus, while a Bach chorale is played on the sound track. This is followed by another montage of the images of human figures from Modern Art, notably by Expressionists such as Picasso, Grosse, Nolde, and others. The effect is the juxtaposition of the "ideal" and "harmonious" with the "disfigured" and "distorted."

After a description of these "sick" images, the narrator concludes that "a wave of vulgarization and degeneration has swept through all fields of German cultural life: the Jew is instinctively interested in everything abnormal and depraved. He is continually looking for ways to disrupt the healthy judgement of the race."

The conclusion is clear: the Jews cannot grasp the Aryan concept of beauty. Instead, they give their nature full rein in tastelesss manifestations such as cubism, expressionism, and jazz. As publishers, they specialized in pornography: pornographic postcards appear on the screen. They have imposed themselves upon science: Einstein, "the relativity Jew" appears on the screen.

A long chain of Jewish "distortion and deviation" continues. The theater is represented by Max Reinhardt, "the Jewish dictator of the stage," followed by Curt Bois in female impersonation acts. The Jews dominate the worlds of music and film. In the field of the cinema Fritz Kortner is introduced, and an excerpt from the film *M* by Lang is shown where the child murderer is played by the Jewish actor, Peter Lorre. The German film industry is portrayed as "the playground for Jewish intellectuals," and "even the Jew Chaplin (the groundless rumor that Chaplin was Jewish was uncritically accepted by the Nazis) was greeted in Berlin by an enthusiastic crowd."

This long montage segment of stills presented a gallery of Jews who were well known to the German viewing public, but it failed to hold its interest.

It is true that an undisguised propaganda film is generally directed to an audience who is expected to share the values which the film portrays. For this audience the open propaganda film provides events which satisfy long-felt needs. In spite of these factors, film producers should never lose sight of the prime function of film, to entertain, and to grasp the attention and emotions of the audience.

In the above-mentioned montage segment this principle was disregarded and the film becomes nothing more than a collection of slides which even the vulgar narration fails to imbue with life. There is no movement of the camera, and the change of slides lacks any rhythm or dynamics. The narration dominates the picture, and whoever closes his eyes and only listens to the narration does not miss anything.

This is an anti-cinematic element and its use here makes the film lose whatever "free audience" it had. It continues to appeal only to a "captive audience," like those found in a military camp, or in the meeting rooms of the Hitler Jugend, etc.

A new theme is introduced when the film speaks of "Christian beliefs," used here as a catch phrase to point out that Christian and Jewish beliefs have nothing in common. Whereas Christianity has a certain moral basis, Judaism is entirely devoid of one. While Bach's music is played in the background, the narration continues to lecture that Christianity has conveyed a deceptive image of the Jews in the form of idealized Biblical figures. In Christian art the Biblical figures have been presented as human ideals. We must correct this impression, declares the narrator, before embarking on a brief presentation of Jewish religious services.

Trading is carried on in the synagogues and not just in the streets. The scenes from the synagogue service are interwoven with close shots of hands (without faces) exchanging goods under the cover of the wooden benches. The praying men rock back and forth almost as if they were in the throes of sexual ecstasy.

With the aid of misleading and falsified quotations from the Bible and Talmud, the narrator defines the rabbis as "masters in the art of deception," and their religious education as "political education designed for future world rulership, the politics of a parasite people" created in secret.

The conclusion is drawn:

This is no religion and no religious service; this is a conspiracy of a cunning, unhealthy, contaminated race against all non-Jews, against the health of the Aryan peoples and against their moral laws.

The film concludes with a sequence about Jewish ritual slaughter *(shechita).* It is introduced as follows:

One of the most instructive customs of the Jewish so-called religion is the slaughter of animals. The following pictures are genuine. They are among the most horrifying that a camera has ever taken. We are showing them in spite of this, without regard for objections on the grounds of taste. Because more important than all objections is the fact that our people should know the truth about Judaism.

On the screen, a cow bleeds to death from a knife wound in the neck. The butcher wipes the blood from the knife with his left hand. Another butcher digs inside the living cow to make the heart pump the blood out more quickly. There is then a shift of scene to the butchers who are laughing at the suffering of the animal. The head is practically severed from the body, but the cow is still moving in a pool of blood.

Press clippings follow, showing the National Socialist campaign against ritual slaughter; idyllic shots of living animals; herds of cows and flocks of sheep are followed by scenes of Jewish ritual slaughter, slashed throats, and leering Jewish butchers.

The climax of the film occurs at this point. Newsreel shots of Hitler before the Reichstag on January 30, 1939, announcing "the extermination of the Jewish race." This is immediately followed by shots of handsome, blond SA troops marching in precision. The narrator says of them that "through their greatness and heroic figures, the ugliness and inhumanities coming from world Jewry which plagues us for an hour, could be alleviated."[19] This is followed by a scene of flags and enormous Nazi banners. The commentator concludes: "Keep our race pure. Racial purity forever."

With regard to this scene, German film reporters remarked that the ending is like seeing light again. "German people and German life surround us once more. We are returning from a long distance which separates us from the Jews."[20]

COMMENTARY

The fact that *The Eternal Jew* takes the form of a documentary is itself significant, since documentaries are presumably objective film accounts of actual events.

The documentary, as opposed to a feature film, establishes a certain distance between the viewer and the subject matter. The use of commentary is one way of creating a feeling of distance. In *The Eternal Jew* it serves a dual purpose: to accentuate the otherness of the Jew and at the same time to promote and consolidate the feeling of sameness and unity of the viewers. This is done by the constant use of the first person. For example:

> We Germans had an opportunity twenty-five years ago to cast a glance into the Polish ghetto. This time, however, our eyes have been made keener by the experiences of the last decades. We no longer see, merely the grotesque and the strange...

The obvious implication is that this social degeneration must be eliminated. The communal sense of identificaiton contained in the word "we" is one of the propagandist's primary goals. Here, the commentary establishes the sense of community. It aggressively draws up frontiers against "the others," and suggests that beyond these frontiers lie dangers and enemies that threaten "our" community. Thus, the spoken commentary does not stand outside, at a distance from the subject, to provide a description. Instead it becomes a personal call which elicits the full quality of emotional involvement.

The commentator's reporting is done with unconcealed bias against the enemy, and the spectator feels that the film commentary is speaking for him even if at times he is also spoken to.

The commentary is structured as a set of arguments. It poses a question and gives the answer or an interpretation. The following narration is heard while the viewer sees Polish Jews:

> Rarely will *you* find Jews engaged in useful work.... *You* can easily see that they aren't used to hard work and don't like it either.

Another way of creating this dual effect is through the presentation of visual images which accentuate their one-dimensional character and strange, alien appearance. Thus, in many scenes Jewish figures are virtually paraded before the audience for examination and scrutiny. Moreover, except for the images of Germans working at productive labor and agriculture and those from the Classical and Renaissance paintings, and agriculture, and those from the Classical and Renaissance paintings, which the viewer could use as a comparison. This absence helps maintain a perpetual distance which is also the effect of the commentary.

Since the film *The Eternal Jew* is long and inevitably episodic, the analysis will focus on the rhetorical treatment of those sequences which, in my opinion, best exemplify the exploitation of the documentary style for political purposes: the ghetto scene, the rats montage, the set of images of Jewish faces, and the dissolve to new faces without Jewish markings.

Selection and half truths are the cornerstones of propagandist documentary. Events can be arranged, even staged, for the documentary camera to film.[21] A more detailed and eye-opening description of the way Nazi documentarists created their newsreel foootage is described by Emmanuel Ringelbaum, the historian of the Warsaw ghetto:

> Jews were herded together and then the Jewish security police were ordered to disperse them. Scenes showing very Jewish-looking men locked together in the ritual baths with young women were manufactured to create the impression that the Jews bathed together in the nude. A restaurant owner was forced to lay his tables to suggest to the audience an abundance of delicacies and champagne; then Jews were indiscriminately rounded up on the street and filmed eating and drinking. Grocery shop windows were filled with rare delicacies before being filmed; a boy was made to steal a loaf of bread and run off with it to his friends, who were supposed to be hiding him and his loot.[22]

Although it describes the work of a film crew in the summer of 1942, the methods of selection, staged events, and elimination were the same as those used in the filming of the ghetto scene in *The Eternal Jew*. This was confirmed by an eyewitness, Bernard Goldstein, who watched the film-makers in Warsaw. Later he wrote:

> The Nazi cameras were carefully aimed when they shot actual scenes as well as when they took posed shots. Dead bodies lying around the streets, the starving human skeletons, the half-naked, lonely, begging children; such pictures they never took.[23]

The falsification of reality was also achieved by what the film did *not* present; i.e. the background or underlying reasons for the Jews living in this way. The "calm ghetto," as it was described in the film, was an area of 10 square kilometers, which used to be the poorest section of town. Before the war this distrcit held 240,000 Jews and 80,000 non-Jews. The non-Jews were forced to move out, and they were replaced by several hundreds of thousands of Jews who were forcibly transported to the ghetto.

According to Leiser:

> Here lies the cynicism of a "document" like *The Eternal Jew*.
> People confined in a world of dirt, like animals, in overcrowded
> cages, and their subsequent degradation presented as though it
> were completely normal, an existence which these victims of the
> Nazi terror had supposedly chosen for themselves, a simple
> demonstration of the theory that Jews are not people like you
> and me.[24]

For these ghetto shots, the cameramen had foraged around the streets
of the Lodz ghetto searching for the worst looking types of the Jewish
poor. Dressed in rags, some of the men had enormous beards and strange
eyes, or twisted faces, an effect emphasized by the use of a wide-angle lens
which tended to enlarge the nose and give the smile a comic or even a
somewhat sinister and leering appearance.

Whether the characters belonged in the German camp or the enemy's
was clearly spelled out by their outward appearance which acted as a
reflection of their moral values. The Jewish faces selected are a good
example of how much the propagandist can achieve simply by a careful
choice of unattractive types for the part.[25]

This is a primitive mechanism that sets in motion conditioned reflexes
rather than arguments. It initiates a distancing process which in *The
Eternal Jew* involves the spectator and the Jew. Once the viewer's distance
has become well established, propaganda can indulge in any maneuvers
without jeopardizing its aim. Thus, the mere fact that the camera is
against somebody, establishes a relationship, an aesthetic commitment.
This is purely formal, but it has psychological implications. On the other
hand, using the same shots in another context might produce a fascinating
ambivalent effect; for example the use of shots from *Triumph of the Will*
where the original intention was to glorify the Nazis; in the American
series *Why We Fight,* where the motive was just the opposite, namely to
justify the war against them.

This is not the case with the images of the Jews in *The Eternal Jew*.
Hippler himself provides an insight into the use of his film techniques.

> In the cinema the spectator must know with greater certainty
> than in the theatre whom to love and whom to hate.

Criticizing the Nazi film, *The Rothschilds,* he goes on to point out:

> If, for instance, I am making an anti-Semitic film, it is obvious
> that I must not make the Jews attractive... but if I put the Jews
> against the English, that is to say unattractive people against
> other unattractive people, the effect will be the same as if I were

to put a cut-out silhouette in black paper, however artistically executed, on an equally black background, exclaiming: "Look how artistic it is!" The most perfectly shaped profile would be doomed in advance to complete ineffectuality.[26]

Faithful to this cinematic principle, and in order to make the Jews look sinister, he uses photographic contrast. The black-garbed Jews against a white background, and by again using a wide-angle lens they appear as a black dot on a light surface. Thus, they are "locked" in the frame, "locked" within the ghetto border.

The rat sequence is an excellent example of how film functions according to an internal logic of its own – in this case, establishing a compelling connection between rats and Jews. With impeccable editing, the premises of the argument are set out.

A map is shown illustrating the density of the Jewish population centers throughout the world. On the map they appear like hordes of insects. Then a few rats are shown emerging from gullies. They tear open a sack of flour and race in wild haste toward the spectator. Their number rapidly increases and soon an army of rats is advancing toward the audience, threatening to break out of the borders of the frame which are the borders of the film in reality, and into the theater. The overall rhythmic correspondance gives the scene a sense (filmic content) of being unstoppable.

Partly because of the number involved within such a small area (the screen), the treatment of the rat scene clearly exemplifies a technique which is used repeatedly throughout the film, namely, the combination of great masses in a small area to create the impression that the subject is a giant. In the case of *The Eternal Jew,* waves of rats move forward, whereas in Riefenstal's *Triumph of the Will,* waves of marchers and flags create an indomitable force that cannot be stopped (Nazism, a force larger than life). Instead of being a threat, however, as in *The Eternal Jew, Triumph of the Will* encourages the audience to identify with it.

The message of *The Eternal Jew,* however, could hardly be stated more clearly: the killing of one or of many Jews is not a crime but a necessity. Jews, the film implies, are not human beings, but pests that have to be exterminated.

Hippler could be sure that the repulsive scenes with the rats would call forth strong feelings of disgust and aversion. He reinforced this psychologcial effect by smothering the viewer with hard-to-verify statistics showing the high percentage of Jews committing all kinds of crimes. These statistics are interwoven with selected photos of Jews whose facial expressions were supposed to create the impression of criminals, reinforcing the point. The sequence consists of a set of images of Jewish faces, in which there is a dissolve from each individual as marked by "Jewish characteristics," such as hairstyle and beards, to the same face shorn of these features. The sequence culminates in shots of Jewish businessmen in German high society accompanied by the following commentary: "Even these 'civilized' Jews remain foreign bodies in the organism of their hosts."

The visuals are clear "proof" of the attempt of the Jews to assimilate with civilized people by camouflaging themselves. In this way the Jew interferes with the healthy judgment of the race. The physiognomy of the revealed faces is intended as proof of the Nazi racial theory. It proves that racial differences cannot be totally erased and remain unrecognized.[27]

Thus, the film did not leave any time for critical thoughts. The overall theme pertained to the "Jewish capabilities to assimilate," as Hippler put it. He also disclosed the reason why this theme played such an important role in the film. He wrote:

> The ordinary citizen will take people he has to deal with as they are. If a Jew has lived in a European city for decades, he will think that he will make a civilized and normal impression. But how different will it be when, at the same time, a picture of the Jew prior to his immigration appears before the spectator's eyes? The juxtaposition of these contrasts was my very special task.[28]

Here again Hippler demonstrates one of the guiding principles underlying *The Eternal Jew,* an emotional approach which is relevant to rhetorical aspects of cinematic communications.

However, despite the skillful editing and camera work in some scenes, *The Eternal Jew* fails both as a film and as propaganda. One reason is that Hippler simply went too far, both artistically and aesthetically. The relentless parade of images and the frequent cross-cuts tended to anaesthetize the viewer, while the harsh voice of the narrator constantly dinned defamatory phrases in his ears. The constant cutting from the shocking to the tranquil sequences was much too obvious and did not succeed in building any kind of tension.

All of this taken together has the effect of disassociating the images from reality. For a film to be a documentary, the viewer needs to interpret it in this specified sense; that a shot must retain its direct relationship to what is actually happening while functioning as an element of cinematic recording of actuality.

The term documentary thus describes not the nature of the material, but the way it engenders our response to it. If we fail to respond in the manner desired by the propagandist, then the significance of the events which are supposedly being portrayed is lost. A sample indication of the film's ultimate failure is the lack of interest shown by the public. The Nazi Security Service reported that the number of spectators diminished rapidly after the first local openings.

The report states that in eight major cities in Germany only the politically active people saw this documentary while the typical moviegoer avoided the film. Also, locally, there was criticism of the repulsiveness of the film as a whole, particluarly the butchering scenes. The film was repeatedly declared to be "very taxing on the nerves."[29]

Growing disinterest was noted by the agents in much of the country and in Austria as well. According to the reports, viewers left the theater during the showing because they found the film repugnant.

Of course, it must be expected that the agents had something to praise about the film, but the note that the public applauded "very enthusiastically as if relieved" when Hitler spoke, need not be interpreted as complete agreement with the persecution of the Jews; for at the peak of the audience's revulsion, Hitler appeared and broke the tension. The applause may very well have been a sign of general relief freeing the viewers from the effects of the butchering scene.

Fritz Hippler was asked: Did the viewer automatically become dizzy with hatred? He admitted that the question was relevant when viewed against the background of Auschwitz. At the time of the filming there was no talk of exterminating the Jews, but Hippler confirmed that the viewer could not view the film without becoming "dizzy with hatred." He continued:

> Immediately followimg the end of the war in Poland, I was given the task of traveling to Poland with a documentary film crew to take pictures that would be preserved in the archives. But Goebbels said that the pictures were too good to be left to rot in the archives and thus a film was made... The film was personally approved by Goebbels, the text was endlessly rewritten and all possible film tricks were used. Thus the most terrible defamatory anti-Semitic Nazi film was created, the most terrible film which can be imagined.[30]

This interview was held in 1983. Hippler claimed that his hands had not shed the blood. Without believing his claims of innocence, there is nevertheless a powerful confirmation in his words of the power of visual rhetoric of the documentary film and its use as a first rate instrument of propaganda.

From Hippler's words and views regarding the documentary-propaganda film, his obvious attempt throughout the film *The Eternal Jew* becomes clear. Figures are presented provoking subconscious and visual associations instead of those based on content and rational contexts. This technique is one of the fundamentals of cinematic propaganda leading the viewer to anti-logical conclusions by means of attitudes, emotions, moods, and imagination. When these elements become powerful they are absorbed in the consciousness as a myth, and attitudes towards them achieve a normative status.

3

JUD ŠUSS
PROPAGANDA THROUGH
ENTERTAINMENT

BACKGROUND

The film *Jud Süss* was first presented before the public at the Venice Film Festival on September 5, 1940. Nineteen days later, on September 24, *Jud Süss* was shown in Berlin. According to Hull this film was

> unquestionably the most notorious film of the Third Reich. It brought disgrace and worse on everyone connected with it, and was in the public limelight when it became the central exhibit in Veit Harlan's postwar trial for crimes against humanity.[1]

Here is a synopsis which was distributed to viewers in Berlin:

"Süss Oppenheimer of Frankfurt, acted by Ferdinand Marian, who has specialized in playing the part of villains, makes a large loan to Duke Karl Alexander of Württemberg (Heinrich George), and in return he is given financial control of the Dutchy with auhority to collect taxes and tolls. Against the advice of the old Rabbi Loew (Werner Krauss), he overextends his power with the help of his near hysterical secretary Levy; abducts the beautiful Dorothea Sturm (Kristina Söderbaum), and brutally rapes her while her husband is tortured by Süss' servants in the cellar. Dorothea manages to escape, and then drowns herself. The whole story is made known, and the Dutchy is on the verge of revolt when the Duke suddenly dies. His protection gone, Süss is brought to trial and condemned to death. As the Jews leave the city, the judge remarks: 'May the citizens of other states never forget this lesson.' "

The execution of Süss Oppenheimer attracted great attention and was the source of inspiration for a profuse biographical literature including novels and short stories.

A short novel titled *Jew Süss,* the work of Wilhelm Hauff, was first published in 1827 and achieved wide popularity. Although it was in favor of segregation between Jews and Gentiles, it nevertheless cast doubt on the justice of the verdict.

In 1925, Leon Feuchtwanger's novel bearing the same title, was published, and pictured the Jew as the eternal scapegoat.

This novel served as the basis for a British film with a pro-Jewish bias, filmed in England and directed in pronounced German style by Lothar Mendes, and starred Conradt Veidt in the title role. This film was more or less faithful to Feuchtwanger's novel.

Goebbels, after screening the British film many times, played with the idea of turning the story into an anti-Jewish film. Before discussing the immediate background to Harlan's Nazi film, it is advisable to sketch the historical background of Josef Süss Oppenheimer and the several fictional treatments of his life.

Little is known of him until he sprang into prominence as fiancial advisor to Duke Karl Alexander of Württemberg. It is definitely known that he was born in Heidelberg. His mother was a beautiful Jewish actress. Ostensibly, his father was Issachar Süsskind, the manager of a troupe of Jewish actors, but rumors circulated that his real father was Freiherr Georg Eberhard von Heydersdorf, Imperial Field-Marshal and Knight of the Teutonic Order.

Süss was a relative of the important banking family, the Oppenheimers, but apparently achieved no success whatever until 1732 when he met Karl Alexander who was then the Imperial Regent in Serbia. Süss was said to have made a prophecy based on the Kabbala, that the prince would inherit the throne of Württemberg, and when this actually occurred, Süss' star rose and he was invited to Stuttgart and quickly became the chief financial power in the country.

The political ambitions of Karl Alexander demanded the creation of a powerful regular army, and in order to finance it, Oppenheimer's unlimited genius for inventing new taxes was exploited. Everyone believed that Karl Alexander intended not only to abolish the constitution of Wüttemberg but to impose the Roman-Cathloic faith upon the Protestant Dutchy. But the Duke died suddenly of a stroke on March 12, 1737. If there were designs of a Catholic *putsch* either at his or someone else's initiative, they collapsed. Süss was arrested and tried by a special commission. He had never served in any official capacity outside of the Duke's household, and it is difficult to claim that Karl Alexander, an experienced and authoritarian ruler, was led by the nose by Süss.

After the accusations against Süss for improper administration of the treasury were proven false, the commission switched to an investigation based on his supposed immoral personal life with the intention of finding an excuse to seal his fate. This approach also failed and finally he was condemned to death against all legal precedent and accepted judicial procedure.

At the same time, those responsible from a legal viewpoint, the Duke's ministers, were left unpunished and managed to retain their illegally acquired gains. After being imprisoned, Süss was brutally tortured and interrogated for close to a year. He was hanged in a barbaric fashion inside an iron cage on September 4, 1738.

Süss was sentenced to death even though Professor Johann Heinrich Harprecht, the most renowned and respected lawyer at that time, argued that a sentence of exile would have been sufficient. Süss vainly asserted his innocence and, after the verdict, cursed his judges. The new Regent, Karl Rudolf, signed the sentence with the following words: "This is indeed a rare occurence when a Jew must pay the bill for Christian scoundrels."[2]

It was nevertheless the image of the criminal and evil Jew which found its way into ostensibly learned and respected publications, as well as into Wilhelm Hauff's short story where Süss is portrayed as an evil spirit in whose shadow a sentimental love affair ends miserably.

Hauff's is the only well-known version before Feuchtwanger's. As long as Süss Oppenheimer was regarded simply as an unmitigated villain, and used as a vehicle for anti-Semitism, the whole story could not acquire a deeper significance.

A more reasoned and objective account of Süss' personality and career was given by Manfred Zimmerman in his *Josepf Süss Oppenheimer, ein Finanzmann des 18 Jahrhunderts,* which was published in 1874. Then in 1929, Selma Stern argued that Süss' financial innovations, many of them subsequently regarded as recognized practices, "restored the finances of Württemberg and put them on an organized footing."[3]

Leon Feuchtwanger was the first writer to master sufficient imaginative insight to make Josef Süss Oppenheimer not only a problematic individual, but a symbolic figure whose spiritual development had philosophical implications.

The first product of this penetrating insight was the drama *Jud Süss,* a work that is of interest only as a prelude to the novel. In 1921-22, Feuchtwanger attempted to write a fictional work about the career of a contemporary Jewish politician, Walther Rathenau, Foreign Minister of the Weimar Republic, who was assassinated by German nationalists on June 23, 1922. Feuchtwanger wrote:

> I was concerned to illustrate the progress of a man from activity to passivity, from action to contemplation, from a European to an Indian view of life. It naturally occurred to me to model this figure on the career of a topical figure, Walther Rathenau. I tried and failed. I moved my material two hundred years back in

time to describe the career of the Jew, Süss Oppenheimer. In this way I came closer to achieving my aim.[4]

The fact that both Süss and Rathenau were victims of anti-Semitism might not seem an adequate basis for a parallel between Württemberg in the 1730s and Germany in the 1920s, but

> Feuchtwanger, seizing the evidences of spirituality and idealism in Zimmerman's biography of Süss, set out to refashion him, not only in the image of Rathenau, but also as the epitome of the spiritual dilemma of the Jewish race.[5]

Such an attempt at parallelism provides an example of that endemic anti-Semitism which, as Pinson says, "always comes to the surface in Germany in periods of political and social crisis." [6]

Rathenau also felt anti-Semitism just below the surface and, in spite of his contributions to Germany in World War I, he wrote:

> Neither of the groups concerned [the soldiers and industrialists] could forgive me, a private citizen and a Jew, for serving my country at my own initiative, and I am not certain that this attitude will change during my lifetime.[7]

In the light of this attitude towards Rathenau as a Jew, it is no wonder that when he was nominated as Foreign Minister in February 1922, the reaction of radical nationalists was extremely emotional and expressed itself in slogans like "Now we are in for it." A right wing newspaper wrote: "His nomination is an absolute provocation against the German people, without precedent."[8]

Not long afterwards, the slogan "Shoot Rathenau, the dirty goddam Jew," became the banner slogan of anti-Semitism in the immediate post-war period.

In an atmosphere in which such sentiments were unchecked, there could be little hope for democracy. The murder of Rathenau while he rode in an open car along *Königstrasse* in Berlin was by no means the only evidence of savage anti-Semitism in postwar Germany.

Apart from the issue of anti-Semitism, the general political situation in Württemberg under Karl Alexander was not so remote from that of the Weimar Republic as it might first seem. Württemberg was politically significant in that it had a Committee of Eleven, a democratic assembly with a legal opposition, an institution without parallel anywhere except England. The overthrow of the constitutional government as described in Feuchtwanger's novel resembled the Hitler-Lüdendorff putsch attempt of 1923 to an amazing degree. The emergence of Süss to a position of unique public prominence might be considered as remarkable a phenomenon as the appointment of a Jew as Foreign Minister of the Weimar Republic.

Even Feuchtwanger regarded Süss as personifying a new force in government: that of the power of money and financial expertise seeking an alliance with the traditional authority of inheritance and rank, represented by the Duke. Rathenau's appointment to a post hitherto reserved for the gentile aristocracy might also be seen in these same terms. It was not just that Rathenau simply happened to be a Jew. It was Rathenau as the champion spokesman for German Jewry who had been appointed Foreign Minister.

Feuchtwanger's novel was published in 1925. The dominant theme is how the social outsider comes to terms with a hostile world. Süss makes his mark in the surrounding society despite his background and religion. He neither hides nor parades his Jewishness. Süss' brother was baptized to achieve the same goal but Süss considered this a cowardly way. Yet when he achieves his ambitions, including revenge against Karl Alexander, he realizes that they are meaningless. Thus he becomes passive, and in his passivity he does nothing to avoid being cast as a scapegoat since life has lost its significance for him.

As mentioned, the novel was made into a film in 1932 in England by the Jewish director, Luthar Mendes, and a large cast including Conrad Veidt and Frank Vaspar. According to Hull:

> The film followed Feuchtwanger's novel with some fidelity, and Veidt played the title role of Josef Süss Oppenheimer with satanic brilliance. Indeed with a little editing, the British movie could have been released in Germany as Goebbels' desired project, and he toyed with the idea; he had the film screened many times.[9]

Since Feuchtwanger was Jewish, and the novel forbidden in Germany, the book could not be used by the Nazi screenwriters. They did not consider other literature either, and made their own version of the story. The first film script was written by Ludwig Metzger. Peter Paul Brauer was to have been the director but Veit Harlan replaced him. He compared Süss with the Biblical Joseph of Egypt who supposedly smuggled his "race comrades" *(Stammesgenossen)* into a civilized land against the will of the Egyptian people. He also declared that in his film "the danger of world Jewry would be unmercifully uncovered."[10] Süss was to be regarded as one of the most evil criminals of all time, one who could be considered as "a classical representative of the whole Jewish race."[11]

The supervision of the film dialogue was taken over later by Eberhard Möller who had his own ideas about the story. He said:

We, too, have tried to be objective, but our objectivity is different from the one in the past which tried to understand and forgive everything. We let history talk and it doesn't show that "the Jew is a human being;" on the contrary, history explains that the Jew is a different kind of person than we are, and as far as his behavior is concerned, he lacks our inborn moral control. We are not out to present a wicked demon; we only want to show the abyss between Jewish and Aryan conduct, which even the Duke possessed.[12]

ANALYSIS AND COMMENTARY

The first practical steps in the production of the film began when Harlan went to Poland where he studied several ghettos in the cities. After returning to Berlin, he had 120 Jews brought to be used in the film as extras, a fact not mentioned in the press.

In an interview with *Der Film* on January 20, 1940 Harlan said:

As far as the conviction of the Jew Süss is concerned, the film is in accordance with history. However, the conviction had its problems because Süss Oppenheimer was a lawyer himself; all his dealings, in which he reduced the people to beggary, were so intricate and carefully fixed that no real proof against him was established at first. Finally, he was sentenced according to an old law: If a Jew mixes with a Christian, he is condemned to death. Here we see an interesting parallel to the Nuremberg laws. Süss was sentenced to death for *Rassenschande* [race defiling] two hundred years ago.[13]

In the film, however, the theme of race infamy was emphasized. Harlan's references to the Nuremberg laws could have been questioned by historians because the screenwriters used a supposed "historical truth" (Oppenheimer's execution) to justify Nazi racist propaganda.

There is no doubt that the film served the propaganda aims of Nazism. Our discussion of the film will examine the particular way in which the productional "rhetoric" of the film serves this end. The narrative equilibrium is based on a set of demarcations between Germans and Jews which serves to locate them, and place each side in its designated territory. This is not simply a geographic deliniation, i.e. the place of the Jew is in the ghetto, the place of the Aryan is in the city of Stuttgart. It is a demarcation in a moral and racial sense as well. The Jews of the ghetto in their medieval dress were a favorite visual object for the Nazi propagandists. The historical process of emancipation was labeled by the

148

Nazis as a Jewish ploy and deception. The Jew in the ghetto is within his own world where he plots and schemes to injure the Aryan, but by remaining inside the pale of settlement he enables the Aryan to identify him and to be wary of him.

The Jew's greed, which may turn him into a millionaire, still does not remove him from this sphere. However, the moment he uses his influence and control through the power of money, the Jew transcends the borders of his sphere and constitutes a perceptible threat. This danger is not expressed only by economic achievements or taking bread out of the mouths of the Aryans. The greater danger is the threat of conquering the Aryan woman and polluting her blood, as a result of which the entire race is destroyed. The film traces this process with great simplicity. The Duke Karl Alexander is obsessed with women, and, having squandered his money on debauchery, is in financial need in order to pursue his sexual activities. This makes him dependent on the Jew who never gives anything without demanding something in return.

Scene from the film *Jud Süss*

Old man: Isaac, what do those bloated gentiles want from our Oppenheimer?
Slaughterer: Do you need to ask?
Old man: Oh, you mean money?
Slaughterer: What else?
Old man: But he's lending him the money?
Slaughterer: He is lending him a great deal of money because he has a head on his shoulders. Let him lend him much so that we can take... (laughs and coughs)

The first thing the Jews "take" is the right to leave their geographic area of settlement, an act which enables them later to also depart from the proscribed social sphere and create an opportunity to establish sexual connections with Aryan women. Race is the basis for all these "deviations," the climax of which is Süss' brutal rape of Dorothea, daughter of the Württemberg chief councilor, and newly-married to her betrothed, a blond pure Aryan. The propaganda lesson is clear. The Jew must be returned to his own sphere and in this way the traditional racial harmony of separation can be restored.

The Jew's attempt to deviate from his sphere appears in a symbolic sense immediately at the film's beginning. The music of the opening scene begins with the first notes of the well known 15th century German song "My Thoughts Are With You" (*Alle meine Gedanken, die ich hab', die sind bei dir)*. Intruding on this tune is the harsh-sounding voice of a Jewish cantor. The German song is gentle and soft while the melody of the Jewish prayer grates on one's ears, but it is the German song which triumphs as sung by the couple, Dorothea, a beautiful blond Aryan and her betrothed Faber, who love each other with the purest sentiments and noble qualities as is customary among the German bourgeoisie. Thus, the racial motif at the opening of the film is both visual and musical.

This is followed by a sequence which begins with the accession of Karl Alexander to the throne of the Dutchy. His lust for women is emphasized when one of the guards lining the processional route suddenly tears off the blouse of one of the women in the crowd, revealing her breasts. The Duke's reaction is rollicking laughter, a reaction indicating that he is unfit to be the representative of "a moral and brave people."

The hint that his passion for women will bring the Duke to his ruin is quickly borne out before the eyes of the viewers when the Duke's messenger descends to the dark area of settlement of the Frankfurt ghetto.

The world of the ghetto and the Jewish characters are meticulously interwoven with special emphasis on details. The ghetto inhabitants are dressed in the typical medieval outfit of East European Jews. Their racial characteristics are clearly seen: their black hair, full beards covering almost the entire face, stooped posture and shuffling gait. They are dirty. Their environment is filthy. They speak in a strange dialect, a mixture of Yiddish and German, and accompany their words with gesticulations and a rasping cough.

One of the repetitious motifs of the ghetto Jew in the Nazi films is the portrayal of the home and street as one continuum. Jewish life does not distinguish between them, and both are regarded as areas of livelihood.

The sign over the Duke's palace balcony dissolves into a Jewish sign in the ghetto, thus providing viewers with a clear and ominous indication of the change in environment.

The first meeting with Süss leaves no doubt as to his racial identity. His "Jewishness" is highlighted by his dress, black hair and coiffure. His helper, Levy, opens the door. His body is somewhat stooped and he rocks back and forth while speaking, as if praying. His voice is sharp and rasping, his lips are thick and he speaks in a strange dialect. His eyes never look straight at you. All in all he is a grotesque caricature.

Across the street we see an old bearded one-eyed man. Near him stands his daughter, her hair uncombed, bosom partly exposed, who is moving her lips in an inviting way. In the street we see a butcher hiding a knife in his apron and talking to the old man in the window. All these actors are played, or rather caricatured by one actor, Werner Krauss.

The Jews speak Yiddish, which is made to sound like a corruption of German, and the key word in their conversations is the Yiddish *neiman,* meaning "to take." From their expressions we are given to understand that Süss will know how to take seven times the amount of money from the gentile who has come to see him.

Indeed the amount that Süss requests for a necklace is more than the Duke's messenger is able to pay. The Jew is willing to lower the price but requests permission to enter Frankfurt, which is closed to Jews, so that he can deliver the necklace himself. The dialogue raises the issue of race openly. The messenger declares that even if he had the permission, Süss would not be able to cross the barriers because the visual signs of his race are so obviously apparent.

"I will disguise myself," promises Süss to the amazement of his secretary Levy, who warns Süss not to shave off his beard and sidelocks or remove his skullcap. In response, Süss calms him by insisting that he is not doing this for himself but on behalf of the Jewish People.

From this moment, a guilt falls upon the Duke. He is the first to open the gates and allow the Jew to depart from his proscribed area. Will he be punished for this?

According to Nazi ideology, the Duke is indeed guilty and deserves to be punished because he did this knowingly. In the next scene someone else helps a Jew to escape from his pale of settlement but this time unknowingly. In the following close-up Süss' "Jewish characteristics" disappear. He is smoothly shaven, his hair tied back in the style of the court, and is elegantly dressed in the fashion of the aristocracy. He sits in a carriage hurrying off to the city of Stuttgart.

He cruelly urges the coachman to spur on the horses until suddenly the carriage overturns.

By chance Dorothea Sturm passes by. She is the daughter of the Chief Councilor of Württemberg. She offers Süss a place in her carriage and brings him into town. Her responsibility is now established for opening the gates of the city and allowing him to enter. Due to the fact that she is accompanying him she prevents any suspicion and misleads the guards at the city gate.

Here is a case of the appalling exploitation of a woman's naivite, and in spite of her innocence, she must pay the price for her mistake, according to the Nazi ideology. Her Aryan fiance, who represents the healthy German instinct, discovers the Jew immediately. This healthy instinct cannot be deceived.

In the meantime, the Duke is trying to mobilize funds for his ballet. Since the Dutchy of Württemberg refuses to finance the project, Süss enters the picture. In exchange for his help, Süss again asks for compensation and requests that he be granted the right to collect road and bridge taxes. The Duke agrees. A flood of coins fills the screen, symbolizing the Jew's power. The money jumps up and down and turns into a troupe of dancers in a ring. The Duke receives his ballet and the Jew has increased his hold.

The Jews's hand is felt everywhere. A farmer complains over the heavy taxes, Dorothea complains of the rise in prices, her betrothed Faber reminds her that all this has happened because of "the handsome gentleman" she had brought with her to Stuttgart. Her father begins to have misgivings about the Duke's authority and emphasizes that everything has been done to satisfy his sexual appetite, which has been exploited by the clever Jew.

The Shylock image of the Jew comes to expression in the scene with the blacksmith Bogner. Half of his house "is blocking the direct course of the road." As a result, the street bends around the house. For this bend in the road, the Jew demands payment, claiming that the ground on which the house stands, belongs to him. The blacksmith refuses and half of his house is destroyed. The visual effect of the ruined house resembles that of a house stands belongs to him. The blacksmith refuses and half of his house huge doll house where children play.

The blacksmith cannot pay but the Jew does not relinquish his "pound of flesh." The blacksmith becomes embittered and when Süss, accompanied by his blond mistress, passes by in his carriage alongside the ruined house, the blacksmith attacks him and the police barely succeed in saving Süss.

Süss then decides to hold a ball to which the daughters of Württemberg are to be invited. The nobles at court are ordered to come with their daughters. For the Duke, this is an occasion to choose new girls and for Süss another occasion to meet Dorothea. Their relationship is emphasized by a close-up featuring Süss' face in proximity to Dorothea's large bosom which appears exposed. The lust of the Jew is unconcealed. He is exploiting the power he wields. Although the girl fears his power she is not intimidated. When Süss begins to use his hands, she flees.

At the ball, Süss tells the Duke of the blacksmith's attack. He portrays it not as an attack of the bitter blacksmith against the Jew, but as a rebellion against the Duke's authority. He also requests that the Duke cancel the existing prohibition forbidding the Jews from entering Stuttgart, and that the blacksmith be punished. The Duke, who is an exalted mood after an hour of lovemaking, accedes to Süss' requests.

The blacksmith is executed. Although this is a victory for Süss, it brings in its wake anonymous threats against him. At a council meeting of the representatives of the Dutchy, Colonel Von Röder decides to appeal to the conscience of the Duke, but the latter is imprisoned in the hands of the Jew, and he rejects the recommendations. Instead, the Duke accepts Süss' proposals to replace the Dutchy *Landsmannschaft* with a *Konferenzministerium* (Conference Ministry) in order to gain more power and independence.

Süss also suggests to the Duke that he seek the advice of the astrologer, Rabbi Loew. Accompanied by his black servant, Süss takes the Duke to the Rabbi (also played by Werner Krauss) whom he has already prepared for the visit as part of the general Jewish conspiracy.

The dramatic effect of the star-gazing scene is produced primarily by a long shot of the racially heterogeneous group. Rabbi Loew is shown wearing mysterious garments, long black hair, and a thick beard; the Duke stands by his side and is dressed in Aryan clothes which signify his rank and social status. His excessive fat spills out in front of him. His face is round and full and different from the other Aryans in the film because of his well-known sexual appetite.

Alongside of them stands a Negro boy, the servant. He represents another racial category, inferior but higher than that of the Jew, and he has none of the Jew's shrewdness.

Süss is in the center. His "Jewish characteristics" are disguised, but the viewer knows that he is capable of concealing his origin. The viewer also knows that this is but part of the scheme to topple the Duke and through him the other Aryans who will be caught in a web being woven in the Jewish synagogue.

Indeed the net closes in round the Duke. Süss feels confident of his power and dares to request Dorothea's hand. Her father objects, promising Süss that his daughter will not marry a Jew, and overnight marries her to Faber.

In the meantime, popular feeling against the Jew is simmering and the complaints increase. The people of Württemberg are organizing for an insurrection. Süss suggests to the Duke to mobilize soldiers from the neighboring states, and the Duchess, who is charmed by Süss' flattery, supports his proposal. The Duke, however, begins to suspect the plot being woven around him.

When the citizens gather in the Duke's courtyard and loudly protest, he sees this as a personal affront to his authority and accepts Süss' advice, since it is also accompanied by the promise that the Jews will finance the mercenary army.

Faber wishes to mobilize popular representatives from the neighboring states but is imprisoned by Süss who takes him to the torture chamber.

Dorothea comes to Süss with an appeal to release her husband. Süss refuses to listen. Outside the window, Dorothea can hear how Faber is being tortured. She has the power to stop the torture, Süss tells her, if she submits to his will. Out of fear for her husband's life, Dorothea surrenders to Süss' sexual attack. The rape scene is built around scene changes between Süss and the heroine in his bedroom with the husband being tortured, creating a psychological effect. The appeal to the sexual emotions of the audience is strengthened by the appeal to sadistic feelings against the Jews. The rape itself is not shown on the screen, but the intimation of it arouses erotic fantasies which are even more powerful.

The rape motif has been a favorite source of indignation, reinforcing the popular puritanical feelings regarding sex. These puritanical tendencies were systematically exploited in *Jew Süss*. The viewers are made to feel that sexual appetite is accompanied by all other passions such as the lust for power and greed, all of which are personified in the character of the court Jew, and to a lesser degree in the representative of the Aryan race, the Duke. Although the latter uses force in dealing with young women he is still less disgusting than Süss, and there is no danger of defiling the race.

Furthermore, since the concept of "race shame" was intimately associated with the Jew, it was understandable that rape by an Aryan (the Duke) is not so serious a crime as rape by a Jew, for which there is no possible forgiveness.

In contrast to Feuchtwanger's novel, the film is clear-cut and simplistic, working through pure cliches to depict a consistent semi-fictional world devoid of the uncertainties and complexities of the real world.

Since the aim of *Jud Süss* is propagandistic, in the end good triumphs over evil by means of supernatural intervention. As always in propaganda, evil is punished and, as frequently portrayed in such films, is itself repsonsible for its own downfall.

Instead of the complexity of human relationships, the character of Süss, from the point of view of realism, is reduced to a minimum. Courage is set against cowardice, innocence against corruption, good will and sacrifice against malice and licentiousness. Oddly enough, the chief vehicle of the film's propagandistic message is not Süss, who is portrayed as the embodiment of the ugliness of his race, but the Duke.

Through the Duke's fate, the audience is warned to take heed. Süss not only acts as the procurer for the Duke's sexual appetite, but also arouses new desires and needs in the Duke to satisfy his own lust for power. The Duke, however, a full-blooded Aryan, remains "an enemy of the Jew out of instinct."[14].

The Duke mediates between the Jew and the group of good Aryans. One member of this group is the Duke's comrade-in-arms, Colonel Von Röder, who is concerned about the rights and needs of the people, and finally acts without the Duke's help, on behalf of the citizens.[15] He is a soldier, a warrior, who follows the correct line of thinking. Although he shoots Von Remchingen, "the servant of the Jews" as he is called in the film, he does not lay hands on the Duke, the symbol of authority, but limits himself to admonitions.

The other good Aryan is Dorothea's father, the Chief Councilor Sturm, who, like Röder, is a soldier at heart in civilian clothes. He is not intimidated by threats on his life nor does he change his mind because of Süss' attractive promises. He acts on behalf of the people. In the palace scene, in referring to the death of his daughter, the chief justice turns to Sturm and says: "Speak freely Sturm, because you have suffered the greatest pain, therefore you have the right to judge first."

Sturm, who has a chance to judge Süss personally and thus take revenge, rejects this offer by saying that grief does not qualify one to speak of justice, and an eye for an eye "is not our way of thinking." Instead he makes use of the criminal law of the Dutchy which states that a Jew who has had sexual relations with a Christian must die. This is not revenge. Everything is done according to the law.

The third "good Aryan" is Faber, who burns with hatred for the Jews. He is the first to identify Oppenheimer as a Jew, and in fulfillment of his duty to fight against the Jews, he hardly finds any time for his private life. Due to his concern for his beautiful beloved and his faithfulness to her, he wins the audience's sympathy.

The only important female part in the film is that of Dorothea, daughter of the Chief Councilor. In the film she is pictured as the ideal Nazi woman: passive and patient. Her tragic fate is that due to her being raped by a Jew she is deprived of her goal in life: to be a mother and to preserve the Aryan race. By her death she pays the price for her naive help to Süss, and the sympathy she exhibited toward him at the beginning of the film.

Thus, the propaganda elements of social class, wealth, sexuality, and race were utilized to perfection in this film. While the film suffered from artistic defects, its effectiveness as an instrument of propaganda was considerable. According to Blobner and Helba:

> The impact of the film on adolescents was enormous and devastating. For example, in Vienna an old Jewish man was trampled to death on a public street by a band of Hitler youth just after viewing the film. Special mention must be made of the refined tactics of the authorities which looked the other way when such a film was officially classified unsuitable for young people. The lowest instincts of mankind were appealed to. This is seen in the rape sequence intercut with a torture scene, which was cleverly built up to a climax. Ferdinand Marian acted

superbly and made Jew Süss a personified Satan...The fascination exercised by the film was twice as dangerous, since the insidious intention of the film was fully attained. The film was a great box office hit.[16]

Critical reviews by viewers at that time must be read with caution. Some have been retained in the files of the Security Service. The report of November 28, 1940 by a security agent states:

Among the scenes which were most attentively watched by the people, beside the rape scene, was the entry of the Jews into the city of Stuttgart with bags and baggage. Throughout the scene many in the audience shouted their indignation in an open demonstration against the Jews. In Berlin, there were shouts of "banish the Jews from the Kurfürstendamm! Get the last Jews out of Germany!"[17]

The agent makes the interesting comment:

A large percentage of the audience felt that the Duke was just as guilty as the Jew Süss and that his death was a punishment for his actions.[18]

In terms of traditional propaganda, the hanging of Süss at the end of the film may be construed as a psychological mistake since the situation appears to require an arousal more of pity than hatred. However, in this case the audience who had already chosen the Jews as scapegoats for their national frustration could regard the execution as a symbolic act and derive enjoyment from it as revenge.

At this point, hatred for the enemy found expression in the appeal made to the audience. Nevertheless, according to Harlan, "he did everything possible to minimize the more vicious scenes in the story."[19] He even claimed that Süss was originally given a final speech before his execution which "he hoped would escape Gobbels' eye and give the whole film a somewhat more ambiguous finale."[20]

In the first version of the film, Süss, bound in an iron cage, curses his judges:

You madmen, servants of Baal, judges of Sodom! May your limbs wither as the willows of dry Kidron! May your bodies rot during your lifetime, may the bones of your children and grandchildren be filled with puss. Everyday shall bring you wretchedness, misery, and pain. No sleep shall soothe your eyes; wicked neighbors shall destroy your peace. May your first-born son bring you shame, may your memory be cursed, and may your cities be destroyed by fires from heaven.

No bread shall diminish your hunger, your thirst shall go unquenched with drink. No ear shall hear your pleas, your harvest shall benefit foreigners, all your inheritors, and you shall be forced to deny your own God with your tongue.[21]

According to Harlan, Goebbels, who wanted the death of a cringing Jew, not a tortured and proud martyr, berated him for his insensitivity, and had the scene reshot and edited by someone else.

As already stated, Harlan's film constituted just one small segment of the anti-Semitic propaganda apparatus. However, the interesting point in the Nazi Ministry of Propaganda's dealing with it was the order given to the press not to present the film as an anti-Semitic propaganda film but as an "entertainment film." This singular fact is evidence of the confidence of the Nazi propagandists that it would be understood by the audience without the guidance of the press, and that its effectiveness would be greater if delivered in the form of entertainment.

This aspect has consequences for the level of effectiveness of theatrical entertainment films. The film director has possibilities that, in theory, are unlimited to create any reality he desires. Thus he can both direct and elicit the most elementary emotional responses according to the value judgements he finds appropriate.

It does not seem to me that in 1940 the Nazi film propagandists faced the problem of an audience disgusted by the political objectives of *Jud Süss*. However, when we watch a properly constructed popaganda film, we are liable to find ourselves in an ambivalent situation: a feeling of disgust towards the political message, and an immediate engagement with what is taking place on the screen.

With regards to *Jud Süss* there is no problem of ambivalence. The good and the evil are clear. The conflicts are solvable in only one way. The emotions called forth by the film are bitterness leading to outbursts of emotions, and instincts; and from the propaganda aspect, there is no place for ambivalence on the question of morality.

In order to make the emotional outburst more powerful, the melodrama makes use of eroticism as a catalytic agent to direct the political message. Pure love and loyalty turn the melodrama into something sublime which cannot pardon any affront or heal any wound.

The rape motif has always been a source of embitterment. However, according to Nazi ideology, a mystical bond exists between puritanism, sexual vulnerability, and mental and physical power. *Jew Süss* does not tell the story of the rape of a German girl by a Jew, but the rape of all Germany by the Jews. The rape scene offers the provocation of arousing anger and bitterness, but it also creates a psychological arousal stemming

157

from the rapist's fantasies which turns it into "entertainment," while allowing a projection of the act on to the Jew and to all the acts of the Jews in Germany.

By order of Heinrich Himmler on September 30, 1940, all members of the S.S. and German police were required to see the film. It was also screened before "Aryan audiences" in Eastern Europe in places to be used as transfer points for Jews on their way to the extermination camps.

Outside Germany the film enjoyed little success in spite of winning an award at the fascist-controlled Venice Festival in 1941.

Even today *Jew Süss* is still an active issue of controversy. Harlan himself destroyed the negative in April 1945, but a short time later it became known that a copy of the film had appeared in Beirut and Cairo with an Arabic sound track. Terra, the original production company claimed a percentage of the profits based on their fifty year copyright. A long investigation followed and the embarrassed Bonn government claimed that the film was being openly shown in the Arab states through "Sovexport" via East Germany.[22]

In 1959, another negative was seized in Lübeck from a dealer who intended to sell it for $100,000 to the brother of King Ibn-Saud of Saudi Arabia.[23]

In summarizing the film, I contend that *Jew Süss* had a profound effect on audiences. It is classified by the Federal Republic of Germany as a hate film calling for genocide. Such a classification places full historical responsibility on the German film industry and the role it played in the psychological preparation for the Holocaust.[24]

4

THE ROTHSCHILDS

In order to complete the picture of the major anti-Semitic Nazi films, a few words should be devoted to the film *The Rothschilds*, although it is of lesser importance than *Jew Süss*, and *The Eternal Jew*.

The declared intention of *The Rothschilds* (1940) was to point out the unhealthy influence exercised by international Jewish financiers. At a press conference held on the opening night screening of the film, Fritz Hippler, the head of the Reich Office of Film from 1939 to 1943 (and producer of the film *The Eternal Jew*), announced that he would

> reveal the harmful actions of those powers that have been real
> war criminals for centuries.[1]

the "Judaization of England," an attempt at domination of the world by why the Nazis were fighting international Jewry. This film blends anti-Semitic and anti-British propaganda. For Goebbels, the British were "the Jews among the Aryans." Already in 1940 the British were portrayed as tools in the hands of an internal Jewish conspiracy. The film included such sentences as: "You say Rothschild, I mean England," and concluded with the following announcement:

At the time this film was concluded, the last descendents of the Rothschilds were fleeing from Europe as refugees. The war against their helpers, the British plutocrats, continues.

The plot is based on the history of the years 1805-15 dealing with the Rothschild banking family. As was the custom of Nazi propaganda, it mixed truth with fiction in order to coincide with the regime's goals.

A SYNOPSIS OF THE PLOT

In 1806 William IX, Prince of Hessen, is forced to flee from Kassel before the advance of Napoleon's armies. He takes a part of his treasury, bonds valued at 600,000 pounds sterling, earned by the leasing of Hessian soldiers to the British army, and deposits it in Frankfurt with his Jewish agent, Meir Anshel Rothschild. The money, which was given to him for safekeeping, is used by Nathan, the head of the Rothschild House, to build the foundations of a family empire. At the same time he launches the "Judaization of England", an attempt at domination of the world by the British-Jewish plutocracy. As part of this process he rouses the hostility and jealousy of the city's bankers, epecially Turner and Bering.

Nathan also aspires to be accepted by high society. However, Sylvia, Turner's beautiful wife, whom he loves, does not respond to Nathan's advances or even regard him seriously.

Nathan Rothschild believes he can conquer the heart of his beloved through the money which has been smuggled into England. He enters into a major business venture with his brother James, in Paris in the meantime, and decides to hold a great ball for the high society of London. In contrast to his financial success however, he fails completely on the social scene. The banker Turner, in order to anger him, arranges a party for the ladies and gentlemen of Frankfurt at the same hotel to coincide with Rothschild's. While the peels of laughter and ridicule and the sound of tinkling glasses reach Nathan's ears from the neighboring room, we find him sitting alone at an empty table laden with delicacies of all kinds. He knows, however, how to take his revenge.

The years pass by. Napoleon is defeated and is exiled to the island of Elba. However, for the Rothschild family there is always an opportunity to make money during wartime. It is possible to finance Louis XVIII, the new king of France. However, this step appears to be a major gamble initially, because of the unrest in Europe, but Rothschild is not dissuaded.

Napoleon succeeds in escaping from Elba, raises his army once again, and sets out to war against England, Prussia, and Austria. Nathan senses that his time has come. He and his army are deployed for battle against the enemy at Waterloo. Rothschild reckons that the results of the battle will decide the fate of Europe and its future commerce. Victory must be a victory of gold, the Rothschilds, and the Star of David.

Wellington's victory over Napoleon is manipulated by Nathan Rothschild for the benefit of his own personal interests. He spreads rumors that Napoleon has triumphed on the battlefield. Panic reigns and the stock market collapses. Nathan exploits the panic to make an enormous profit by acquiring shares offered at very low bids. By doing so, he not only strikes at the English bankers, but also destroys the investments of "the people." The following dialogue from the film between Anschel Rothschild and Meir Hirsch reveals the nature of his conspiracies: When asked about money, Rothschild replies.

Anschel Rothschild: There is blood on every one of these bills.
Hirsch: Blood pays for itself.
Rothschild: Remember, one can always make a lot of money by spilling a lot of blood.

160

COMMMENTS

Erich Waschneck, the director who was chosen for this film, had a considerable reputation from the silent film era. With the assistance of his cinema background, he strove to have the script written properly and supervised the selection of the crew. Nevertheless, the film is full of anti-Semitic cliches, both verbal and visual. The direction is heavy, totally lacking in charm and relief.

Once again we are told that the ghetto is the natural home of the Jews, and that the Jew is unable to liberate himself from his surroundings. Although some of the family reside in London, they are connected to the ghetto in Frankfurt. The sons of the wealthy Rothschild family are portrayed dressed as rag pickers. They act in a miserly way with the intention of cheating the gentiles. Even Anschel Rothschild lives in a poorly lit room resembling a basement in which the rats are constant guests. Anschel's courier, Meir Hirsch, is the link in the chain between the Rothschilds of the Frankfurt ghetto and the wealthy family in London. He is represented as possessing an evil appearence with a swollen face, meager hair, long and thick sidecurls, and he walks about without any clear sense of direction. His head is bowed and he speaks with his eyes cast down to the floor.

He is sent by Anschel to his son, Nathan, in London, and of course is warned not to travel on the Sabbath. We meet Nathan Rothschild for the first time in the film while he is standing in front of a mirror, dressed in a prayer shawl and wearing a skullcap. He says that he negotiates with everyone, including God: "During the week, I am an Englishman, but on the Sabbath, I am a Jew, and do business with God."

Nathan is shown as a brutal man, fat and uncultivated, with deeply set eyes that move incessantly, and a forehead covered with curly hair. He has no sensitivity at all, and this provides the director with many opportunities to portray the Jews as materialistic and lacking in charm. We observe this in the public confrontation with General Wellington who has gotten himself involved financially with Nathan.

When Nathan tries to court the wife of his most difficult rival and competitor, the banker Turner, nothing deters him from attempting to sneak inside her house, neither her unhidden contempt nor the sharp comments of this pure-bred beautiful Irish woman. Only a vicious dog is capable of keeping him at a distance from the. house.

Although Nathan is portrayed as evil, it is the deviousness of the Jew in money matters that serves as a warning to the viewers that the Jewish danger remains extant as long as the Jews exist. They are part of a worldwide plot to destroy the states where they have become citizens with the help of the one and only true Jewish weapon – money.

The commercial ties among Jews are portrayed in the film as a world conspiracy, in the scene where Nathan Rothschild stands before a map and connects lines which form a Star of David. In this way he indicates the Rothschild family's area of activities.In the continuation of the dialogue we hear the following which makes the thesis clear.

And what's that there?
Jerusalem.
Do you also want to open a branch there?
On the contrary, we are the branches of Jerusalem.

Only the Aryan, who opposes the egotistical striving after money, and thinks of the good of society as a whole, is capable of opposing the Jew. However, since this conclusion does not receive visual treatment, it is considered a failure. Its appeal is indirect, and the viewer needs to draw the desired conclusion. The writers of the script did not understand that, according to the psychological concept of Nazi propaganda, it was incorrect to let Nathan win. The majority of the Nazi film critics not only analyzed Nathan as a historical figure, but also tried to point out the Jewish traits common to Nathan, the recent immigrant to England, and to the Jews who had lived in Germany for a long time. The hope was that the viewer who frequently read the criticism in the press, would be able to see in every Jew a kind of disguised Nathan.

Nathan's secretary, Samuel Bronstein, although resembling the Jewish figures in his appearance and in the motions of his hands, is exceptional in that he does not want to assimilate, i.e., he knows his place as can be discerned from the following dialogue:

When will Nathan Rothschild finally admit that no one can erase the fact that he was born in the Jews' Alley in Frankfurt? I say to you, no matter how high he climbs, even if it is to the very summit in England, he will still be no more than a Jew from the Frankfurt ghetto.

The concern of the Nazis that the differences in appearence between the Jews and the Aryans may disappear, is reflected in Nathan's answer:

Bronstein, look at yourself, you look like a ragamuffin. Your clothes are old and dirty, but your son will call himself a gentleman, and your grandson might be a lord of this country and achieve everything in it."

As previously mentioned, the film is also anti-British. British high society is portrayed as a hypocritical group of people who deceive themselves. As a result of its preoccupation with unbridled materialsm, it

162

is quickly conquered by Nathan after only a short resistance. Lord Wellington serves as an example of the moral breakdown of this society due to his weakness for beautiful and spendthrift women.

This is revealed by a scene in which the Prussians, who have suffered heavy defeats, attempt to convince Wellington to abandon the beautiful women at the party, and return to join his army on the battlefield. Only after considerable efforts is he convinced to leave the ball. When he achieves victory at Waterloo, we are given to understand that this is not the result of his conduct, but of the heroism of the Prussians who have brought the victory.

In spite of this, in comparison to the Jews, the description of the British characters is relatively sympathetic. They are portrayed as those who have been led astray. They have no leader who can liberate them from the domination of the Jews.

At the end of the film a Star of David appears burning in fire over the map of England. The true victor at Waterloo is Nathan Rothschild, representative of an ugly and disgusting nation who has joined another unpleasant people in their striving to dominate the world.

The heaviness in the film was felt not only in the direct propaganda, but also in the direction and one-dimensional acting which contributed to the general boredom. Therefore, there was little interest in the film and it was shown to almost empty movie theaters.

5

SUMMARY AND FINAL WORD

This study of the propagation of anti-Semitism in the Nazi cinema of hate brings clearly documented examples of the purposeful, continuous, and controlled use of film propaganda in the Third Reich.

Joseph Goebbels was well aware of the limitations of direct propaganda, and recognized the value of entertainment and drama in the process of influencing public opinion. He understood that an audience that knows that it is being saturated with propaganda, will be on its guard. Nevertheless, when the Nazi films were produced, and especially when the Jewish theme was dealt with in the cinema, that rule was almost completely forgotten.

Instead, the Nazis served up an orchestrated and organized substitute: social realism full of allegories and symbolism that was edited by a process of de-historification, and blended with a nationalistic and completely militaristic present. This was propaganda in all its nakedness that exploited cinematic techniques in order to present a glorification of the Teutonic Knights, the S.A., the S.S., death and blood, as well as a pantheon of good German virtues: working families (of farmers), mothers, worship of power, racial purity, together with magnificent architecture, processions and military pageants that were fashioned with great care.

All the "pure" arts were harnessed to this need, purified of any hint of "degeneration" and directed by the "super-Wagner" of propaganda, Joseph Goebbels.

The image of the Jew in the Nazi films represented the Nazi interpretation of Jewry. From the point of view of public opinion, this was not any ideological novelty. The novelty was in the possibility of strengthening the opinions of the viewing audience by providing visual proof, by means of the cinema, to their world outlook.

As Fritz Hippler, the producer of *The Eternal Jew* noted: "In the cinema .... the viewer must know whom to hate and whom to love."[1] The cardinal theme of the Nazi film was racial superiority and its antithesis: the inferiority of the Jew. In this way anti-Semitism became the war cry of the regime as the trumpets of Nazi propaganda energized all the frustration, anger, and despair that had accumulated and intensified in Germany since the First World War. In the midst of this turmoil, the producers of these films made a notable contribution to the psychological climate in which the extermination of the Jews by the most terrible means was accomplished, by a people who had long been considered one of the most cultured in Europe, and who were yet capable of such atrocities and even boasted of them.

After the facts of these horrors became known to all, it was important for the future of humanity to reveal, as far as possible, how this hellish drama could take place. In other words, it became necessary to deal with the problem not as a specifically German one, but as a problem related to the basic questions of human behavior as such.

The question has already been dealt with in a number of ways, but, in my opinion, without sufficient depth, and by the continuing search for scapegoats. This seems dangerous to me not because it is improper to accuse individuals (of course many of them were guilty and their guilt arouses horror), but because of the unstated hint that if only others had taken their places, everything would have been fine as we should naturally expect.

This view was prominent in a class discussion that was held in a German school in 1982. The pupils who participated in the discussion were asked what should be done with the Nazis still living in Germany. Their answer was clear and unequivocal:

The Americans killed Indians, the French killed Algerians, and we had the Jews and Auschwitz. There is no people that does not have a skeleton in the closet, and we are not the only ones.[2]

It is possible to see in the above answer an attempt at self-justification, and dissassociation from the Nazi past. However, this answer is symptomatic of the general atmosphere in Germany. Much more shocking and revolting is the letter of a professor of education who visited Israel at the head of a group of German students. He summed up his tour in the following words:

The Jews want to hold the Arabs by their throats, to take the tourists' money, and to go to bed with them. They [the Jews] are all alike from the manual worker to the professor. We [the Germans] continue to think in humanitarian terms of honor and truth, but these two concepts are unknown among the Jews.[3]

It would be difficult to assert that this honest anti-Semite excels in a fruitful imagination, he was merely repeating the same charges that his

165

predecessors hurled at the Jews in past generations. Nevertheless, there is something monstrous in this audaciousness, for according to this logic, where there is no truth or honor, the Jew can be blamed for everything.

The traditional, religious bases of hatred for Israel have not disappeared either in the post-Holocaust world. The Jews are still accused of the crucifixion of Jesus, and the Holocaust is regarded as nothing more than punishment for the sins of the fathers. The Passion plays, the roots of which are found in the Middle Ages, are still presented in Germany and other countries.

In today's anti-Semitic phenomena the sense of the need for defensiveness or a feeling of guilt have disappeared among the young generation of Germans. One should not be surprised therefore by the logic of the extreme right in Germany which is still angry over the murder of their messiah by the Jews, this time not by crucifixion but by his death on a funeral pyre in a Berlin bunker. Also, among leftist German intellectuals one can detect fascist indications which find expression in anti-Zionist declarations. The bearers of the flag are students from the University of Heidelberg (Goebbels' university), who have declared their support for the Arabs (representatives of equality and democracy), against Israel, representing the imperialist and capitalist monopolies. Then there is no feeling of guilt and no will to make amends.

A faithful representative of the attempt to abolish the sense of guilt is found in the play written by Reiner Werner Fassbender, a German, born after the Holocaust, one of the generation that did not know Hitler. He later became a film genius, and died from drug use. The name of the play is *Trash, City and Death.*

One of the figures in the play is a wealthy Jew, portrayed as a blood sucker, speculator, murderer, dirty old man, who, in addition, is driven by the desire for revenge. In the play, the same figure is described in the following terms: "The Jew sucks our marrow, drinks our blood, and makes us into the responsible ones because he is a Jew and we bear the guilt...and that is the Jew's guilt because he has turned us into the guilty ones because he is here. If he had stayed in the place where he came from, or if they had finished him in the gas chambers, I could sleep better today."

In another place, he says: "They forgot to poison him with gas. I rub my hands when I think of the air emerging from his body in the gas ovens."

To our great surprise, not only the Jew of Fassbender, but the Jew of Gunther Grass, former Wehrmacht officer in the Second World War, and among the greatest German writers of our time, would not embarrass any anti-Semite.

In his book, *The Tin Drum,* Gunther Grass describes the Jew Feingold, a survivor of the Treblinka extermination camp, who arrives in the city of Danzig after the war. Feingold reveals himself as egotistical and money mad. This is even apparent from his name. He is deceitful. His goal is to inherit German property which does not belong to him. He is not satisfied with plundering the property, but also desires Maria, a daughter of the Aryan race.

In this case, the Israeli critic and author Shamai Golan claims that even an author of the stature of Grass, in approaching the description of a Jewish character, does not succeed in liberating himself from anti-Semitic propaganda, and completely ignores the former concentration camp inmate Feingold.[4] If this is the case regarding Gunther Grass, what can we say about those of Hitler's generation who participated in a study conducted in Munich, regarding the film *Jew Süss?*

The film was shown before this group, and the audience was asked to light up a red bulb each time it seemed to them that the film contained a hint of anti-Semitism. When the red bulbs failed to light after a while, the investigator asked why. He was told "there isn't any anti-Semitism here. The Jew is exactly like that."

If we assert that there is a reawakening of anti-Semitism, then there is an additional aspect regarding the anti-Semitic movement we must not ignore. Anti-Semitism does not only effect Jews, but is a direct result of a crisis of civilization. It represents a social, economic, political, and educational crisis in culture and religion, and perhaps more than anything else, it is a reflection of the personal and emotional crisis in the psychological make-up of man.

The Christian Church as well, whose responsibility for the traditional anti-Semitic image does not require proof, understands this. At the episcopal conference in Rome in 1982, the Pope decreed that an objective image of the Jew, free from all insults and superstitions, be presented in religious education at all levels. This was done not primarily out of love for Israel, but from a recognition that hatred and violence endanger the psychological stability of the individual, of children and parents, of the family, society, the state and church. Such instability promotes access to drugs, alcoholism, prostitution and murder.

Here there is a consideration of anti-Semitism not as a partial, however important, problem of attitudes towards the Jews, but as a general issue indicating a problem of the anti-Semitic society. In this there is a sobriety which is a significant contribution in the war against anti-Semitism.

In this context it is of significance that today's Germans no longer speak of Nazism but of fascism. Nazism has therefore changed much of its historical weight. We meet this shocking phenomenon more and more

167

today. It was described in Saul Friedlander's eye-opening book, *Reflections on Nazism – An essay on Kitsch and Death*.

> At the end of the war, Nazism was the damned part of western civilization, the symbol of evil. Everything the Nazis had done was condemned, whatever they touched defiled...By the end of the sixties, however, the Nazi image in the West had begun to change. Not radically or across the board, but here and there, and on the right as well as the left, perceptibly and revealingly enough to allow one to speak of the existence of a new kind of discourse; the fascination with the magic and the myth of the Hitler movement.[5]

In the face of all this, I would like to believe that this study was not conducted only for the sake of history and an analysis of propaganda rhetoric of the Nazi films, but also for the light it sheds on the dimensions of the problem. The issue is not solely the evil of propagandists and the producers of the Nazi films or the entire German people. There is also a reflection on the failure and breakdown of human values which we have not yet completely absorbed. It is my hope that the more we understand and the more we struggle with this fundamental question, the more we will be capable of preventing a repetition of this phenomenon.

We must continually be on guard. It turns out that we have been living in a kind of strange euphoria and have not paid attention to the renewed and stirring animosity under our noses. Unfortunately, the lesson of the Holocaust, and the creation of the State of Israel were unable to kill the anti-Semitic bacteria, as in the closing words of *The Plague* by Albert Camus:

> The bacillus never dies or disappears for good; it can lie dormant for years and years in furniture and linen chests; it bides its time in bedrooms, cellars, trunks and bookshelves... until quite probably the day comes when to the calamity of mankind, it rears its ugly head...[6]

APPENDICES

APPENDIX A

"THE ETERNAL JEW"

Production: The Office of Film of the Third Reich
Director: Fritz Hippler
Idea: Eberhart Taubert
Photography: Albert Endrejat
Music: Frantz R. Friedl
Film Editors: Hans Dieter Schiller, and Albert Baumeister
Censorship Passed: 4/11/1940. 1,820 meters
Premier Performance: 2/11/1940 in Berlin
Remarks: Of political and artistic value; in abridged version-recommended for youth.

Introduction:

The civilized Jews that we know in Germany only give us an incomplete picture of their racial character. This film shows genuine shots of Polish ghettos. It shows us the Jews as they really are, before they conceal themselves behind the mask of the civilized European.

ACT I

The war in Poland has given us the opportunity to get to know Jewry at its swarming den. Nearly four million Jews live in Poland, although you would seek them in vain among the peasant population. Nor have they suffered from the chaos of war, as has the native population. They remained in their ghetto, untouched by events, and within an hour of the German occupation they had resumed their money dealings.

We Germans had an opportunity 25 years ago to cast a glance into the Polish ghetto. This time, however, our eyes have been made keener by the experiences of the last decades. We no longer see, as in 1914, merely the grotesque and strange elements in these questionable figures of the ghetto – we recognize that here lies the source of a plague spot that threatens the health of the Aryan peoples. Richard Wagner once said: "The Jew is the evil force behind the decay of man!" And these pictures confirm the accuracy of his statement.

The home life of the Jews shows a marked lack of creative ability. To put it plainly, the Jewish houses are dirty and neglected.

One must bear in mind that these Jews are not poor by any standard comparison. After decades spent in trading, they have hoarded up enough money to be able to create for themselves and their family a clean and comfortable home. But they have lived for generations in the same dirty, bug-ridden holes. There too, careless of the profanity of their surroundings, they say their ceremonial prayers. The bowing down movements of the upper part of the body are part of the ritual, belonging to the reading out of the Jewish scriptures.

The main part of Jewish so-called community life takes place in the streets.

Rarely will you find Jews engaged in useful work. Even then it does not happen willingly. The German Military Government has employed them in salvage work. You can easily see that they aren't used to hard work and don't like it either. But that isn't helplessness, which could be pitied, that is something quite different – these Jews don't want to work, they would far rather be out bartering, where they are in their best element.

It is not the case, as the innocent say to excuse them, that the Jews are forced into trading because other occupations and professions are forbidden to them. Quite to the contrary. They rush into trade because it is in accordance with their character and inclination.

The innocent spectator will first feel inclined to view these haggling children as a sign of great poverty. But to the person who watches them for some time, it soon becomes clear that they are proud of being able to behave like grown-ups. These children see no ideals before them like our own children do. The egoism of the individual is not put by them into the service of higher common goals. On the contrary, the Jewish racial moral proclaims, in contrast to the Aryan morality, that the unrestrained egoism of each Jew is a divine law. His religion in fact makes a duty out of treachery and usury. In Deutoronomy it is written, for instance: "Unto a foreigner thou mayest lend upon usury, but unto thy brother thou shalt not lend upon usury: that the Lord thy God may bless thee in all that thou puttest thine hand into." In other words: for the Jews, business is a kind of holy activity. For non-Jews this is something completely incomprehensible. The Aryan attaches a conception of its value to every activity.

The Aryan wants to create something worthwhile. Food or clothing, machines or works of art, or anything else that is of value to us, is a matter of complete indifference to Jews.

The first trade goods are usually worthless rubbish and scraps of all kinds. Jews start small. Soon they reach the point where they can set themselves up with a tray, and soon they gather together a complete stock in trade. Not long afterwards, they own a proper stall. And the particularly cunning among them are soon owners of a little shop. And then a bigger shop.

And the most cunning, i.e. the most unscrupulous, eventually set up department stores and big banks and live in the most splendid houses and villas of the towns, provided they don't crowd each other, as in the narrrow ghettos of the East. That is why they leave their nests to seek their fortunes in rich lands among rich peoples. They need other people because they need goods with which to carry on business. Those things which are valued by the creative Aryan peoples have been reduced by the Jew to a level of a mere piece of merchandise, which he buys and sells, but cannot produce himself. He leaves production to the laborers and peasants of the people upon whom he has imposed his presence.

The Jews are a race without farmers and without manual laborers, or workers; a race of parasites.

Whenever a sore shows itself on the body of a people, they settle themselves firmly and feed on the decaying organism. They find their business among the diseases of the people, and for this reason do their utmost to increase and perpetuate every form of sickness. This is the case in Poland – and how it once was in Germany. It has always been so with the Jews, in the whole course of their history. They bear the age-old features of the eternal parasite on their faces – the features of the eternal Jew, who, throughout time and throughout his world-wide wanderings, has always remained the same. There is no difference between the Jews in Poland and those in Palestine, although many hundreds of miles separate them.

Palestine is the spiritual center for international Jewry, even though numerically the Jewish population there today plays no important role. Here at the Wailing Wall, the Jews gather and lament the fall of Jerusalem.

But their homelessness is of their own choosing, and in accordance with their whole history.

Four thousand years ago their Hebrew forefathers were already on their travels. They left the Land of the Two Rivers (Mesopotamia), wandering down the coast towards Egypt, where, for a while, they carried on a flourishing trade in grain. When the local agricultural population showed resistance towards the foreign usurers and speculators, they emigrated once more and set out on their looting raid into the Holy Land, where they settled, and pitilessly destroyed the lawful and culturally more advanced inhabitants. Here, in the course of centuries, there developed the final mongrolized Jew from the oriental Near Eastern races with

Negroid admixture – differing from us Europeans, coming as we do from quite different racial elements, in body, and above all, in soul. In all probability we never would have had much to do with them, if they had remained in their Eastern homeland. But the cosmopolitan empire of Alexander the Great, which stretched from the Near East across half of the Mediterranean, and, of course, the limitless empire of the Romans, gave the first main impetus to their trading and migratory instinct. And they had soon spread over the now easily accessible Mediterranean area. While groups of them settled in the large towns, trade and communication centers of the Mediterranean, other groups migrated still further through Spain, France, Southern Germany, and England. They are disliked everywhere.

The people of Spain and France rose against them in the 13th and 14th centuries, and they travelled on further, mainly to Germany. From then on they follwed the culture-bearing creative ways of German colonization of the East, until finally they found a gigantic new untapped reservoir. The 19th century with its vague idea of human equality and freedom, gave the Jews a powerful new impetus. From Eastern Europe now, in the course of the 19th and 20th centuries, they had spread like an irresistible tide, flooding the towns and nations of Europe, indeed the whole world.

ACT II

Comparable with the Jewish wanderings through history are the mass migrations of an equally restless animal, the rat. This beast followed mankind from its beginnings. Its home is Asia. From there it migrated in vast hordes across Russia and the Balkan states towards Europe. By the middle of the 18th century they are already spread across the whole of Europe. In the middle of the 19th century,as a result of the growing shipping trade, they also take possession of America and likewise Africa, and the Far East.

Wherever rats appear they bring ruin, they ravage human property and food stuffs. In this way they spread disease, plague, leprosy, typhoid, cholera, dysentry, etc. They are cunning, cowardly and cruel, and are found mostly in large packs. In the animal world they represent the element of craftiness and underground destruction – no different from the Jews among mankind.

This Jewish race of parasites perpetrates a large part of international crimes. Thus in 1932, the part played by the Jews, who represent only a small percentage of the world population, was 34% in the entire drug trade of the world; in robberies it was 47%, in international crime orginizations it was 82% and in prostitution 98%.

174

The professional terminology of international thieves' dialect does not originate without reason from Hebrew and Yiddish. These physiognomies refute impressively the liberal theories of the quality of all those who bear a human face. Of course they change their outward appearance when they leave their Polish nests to go out into the rich world. Earlocks and beard, skullcap and caftan are the distinguishing characteristics of the eastern Jews for everyone. If he appears without them, then it is only the more keen-eyed among us who recognize his racial origins. It is an intrinsic characteristic of the Jew that he always strives to hide his parentage when he is among non-Jews.

A group of Polish Jews – still wearing caftans, and now ready to steal into Western civilization. Of course, these ghetto Jews don't know at first how to behave themselves correctly in their fine European suits. These Berlin Jews are a bit better at it. It is true that their fathers and grandfathers still lived in ghettos, but there is no trace of that left now in their external appearance. Here, in the second and third generation, the Aryanization has reached its zenith. In all superficialities they attempt to imitate their hosts. And people lacking in intuition allow themselves to be deceived by this mimicry, and regard them as being in truth their equals. Therein lies the dreadful danger. For even these "civilized" Jews remain foreign bodies in the organisms of their hosts, no matter how much their outward appearance may correspond to that of their hosts.

Even those aristocrats with old Jewish names, who, after generations of marriage with the Aryan nobility, belong to the uppermost circles of European so-called society, and have completely assumed the manners of their aristocratic surroundings, have remained foreign bodies and are to be assessed as such.

Here we show an excerpt from the film which depicts the history of the House of Rothschild. American Jews produced it. Obviously, in order to create a monument to one of the greatest names in Jewish history. They honor their hero in typical Jewish manner, and take delight in the way old Meir Anschel Rothschild defrauds the state which made him welcome.

Insert: The House of Rothschild, 1934, by Alfred Werker.
Translation of the German sub-titles:

(Meir Anschel Rothschild, his wife Gizelle, and his children are at home. We hear knocks on the door. The wife takes out a duck from the oven and gives some to one of the children. The child hides in the cellar, the floor of which is covered by a carpet. All those in the room change their luxurious clothes, replacing them with worn and padded clothes.)
Gizelle: (to two of her children) Are you hungry?

Son: Not very much, mama.

Gizelle: So, pretend you are hungry.

Children: (laughingly) We are hungry.

Meir Anschel Rothschild: (helps the child hide in the cellar) Stay there! Sit down with your sewing. Nathan, take your hands out of your pockets.

Tax Collector: Open! Open! Jew! (the door opens and the Tax Collector, accompanied by soldiers, enters the room.)

Meir: Ah, my good friend, the tax-inspector.

Tax Collector: Fetch your ledger out.

Meir: (to his wife) This is my friend the tax collector. Of course, I was just looking at it. Times are very bad. That is my good friend, the tax-collector. I've never had such a bad month. I've not seen a single guilder for 5 days. Our customers come, yes, but they don't buy anything. My exchange-trade is less than nothing. I'll starve to death soon.

Tax Collector: But there's a lovely smell in here.

Meir: My neighbor's probably got a roast. (to his wife) Go and shut the window.

Tax Collector: What do you take me for?

Meir: I don't understand you, sir.

Tax Collector: Your business is more prosperous than anyone else's. Twenty thousand guilders tax.

Meir: 20,000 guilders? You may kill me, but I could scarcely raise 1,000.

Tax Collector: Search the house. Upstairs.

Meir: Perhaps I could manage the thousand guilders.

(The tax collector then discovers the secret trapdoor to the basement).

Meir: Perhaps two thousand?

(Here the scene ends and a new one appears on the screen. Meir is lying on his deathbed. His sons are gathered around him.)

Rothschild: Unity is power. You must always be united. No one brother must be allowed to fail when another succeeds. Our five banking houses will rule Europe. One firm, one family, – The Rothschilds! This will be your strength. When this power is in your hands – remember the ghetto!

Narrative: At this point it must be noted that transfer of money by cheque was not an invention of the Jews, nor was it cultivated by them for the good of mankind, but simply to serve them as a means of obtaining international influence over and above the heads of their hosts.

Nathan goes to London and becomes an Englishman, Jacob goes to Paris and becomes a Frenchman, Salomon goes to Vienna and becomes an Austrian, Carl goes to Naples and becomes an Italian, but Anschel stays in Frankfurt and remains a German. And yet, of course, they all remain Jews. So that when, during the priod of the French Revolution, the Jews were recognized as rightful enfranchized citizens of their respective countries, they suddenly belonged to two nations simultaneously.

And it is not for nothing that they have blood relatives at all the European courts, and accordingly, confidential knowledge of all events in these courts and their countries. Thus, in this industrious century of technical progress, Jewish business blooms as never before. The House of Rothschild is only one example of these machinations of the Jews, to spread the network of their influence over the working man. The same tactics are pursued by the House of Warburg and other Jewish banking families.

At the beginning of the 20th century they squat everywhere at the junctions of the world's money business. They are an international power. Although only a small percentage of the world's population, with the help of their capital they terrorize the world's stock exchanges, world opinion and world politics.

Today, New York is the centre of Jewish Power, and the New York Stock Exchange, the financial center of the world, is ruled by the Jewish banking houses – Kahn, Loew, Warburg, Hanauer, Wertheim, Lewisohn, Seligman, Guggenheim, Wolf, Schiff, Kraus, Stern, etc. These kings of finance love to keep to themselves in the background and let their power dramas take place behind the scenes.

In appearance they have adapted themselves to their host nation. They look almost like genuine Americans: Bernard Baruch, the Jewish financial adviser and friend of the American president, in the mask of a smart Amercian citizen. Otto Kahn, Jewish Wall Street banker flatters himself in the pose of an Anglo-Saxon Lord. The Jewish banker, Felix Warburg, the Jewish banker, Mortimer Schif, the Jewish lawyer and Germanophobe, Samuel Untermeier, Professor Felix Frankfurter, the Jewish legal adviser to the American president, Herbert Lehmann the Jewish governor of the state of New York, La Guardia the half-Jewish mayor of New York; Henry Morgenthau, the Jewish Secretary of the Treasury in the U.S.A., the Jew Leon Blum, the former Prime Minister of France-he holds himself almost like a true Frenchman. Millions of French workers honored him once as their party head. The Jew Hore-Belisha, the former Secretary of State for War in England. English soldiers saluting their Jewish commanding officer.

But the Jew remains a rootless parasite, even when he is in power. His power does not come from his own strength, it only lasts as long as misled people are prepared to carry them on their backs.

Let us remember those vile days when Germans lay stretched

defenceless on the ground. It was then that the Jews seized their chance. They came to the forefront, as if, like faithful citizens, deeply disturbed about the fate of the German people.

Thus they hurried to the so-called National Assembly in Weimar, where Germany's future was to be decided. The Jewish representative Landsberger, on his left Scheidemann. The Jew Hirsch, Prime Minister of Prussia. The Jew Theodor Wolf, editor-in-chief of the *Berliner Tageblatt*. The Jew Georg Bernhard, head of the Ullstein publishing house. The Jew Hugo Preuss, creator of the German republican constitution. The Jew Walter Rathenau, Foreign Minister of the German Republic. The Jew Hilfferding, German Minister of Finance. The Jew Bernhard Isidor Weiss, Assistant Chief of Police of Berlin.

Other Jews, whose task it was to represent the radical line, proclaimed in the meantime against every form of public order. Masquerading as selfless public benefactors, they promised great things and incited the masses to break the bonds of civil order. Unchecked personal freedom and enjoyment of life to the full for the individual, rejection of all obligations to an ideal, and denial of all higher values. Recognition of the lowest material life of pleasure, unrestrained criticism of the most sacred things, revolt in fact, against everything that existed, incitement of youth, stirring people up to class-war and terrorist acts. It is no accident that this false doctrine, which disrupts nations, sprang from the brain of a Jew.

ACT III

Karl Marx, son of the rabbi and lawyer Marchoche in Treves. The founder and first organizer of the German Social Democratic party was the Jew Ferdinand Lasalle-Wolfson. The Jewess-Rosa Luxemburg – whose real name was Emma Goldmann, one of the most notorious communist agitators. The Jew Nissen, the man most responsible for the brutal shooting of the hostages in the Munich Soviet Republic.

For every thousand struggling Germans there were ten Jews, who always united in one common aim in all genuine or pretended rivalry- mutual exploitation of the Germans. Now the enterprising Jews crowded into the cities. But not to work there they left that to the Germans. For every 1,000 artisans in Berlin there were only two Jews. On the other hand, at the beginning of 1933, there were 15 Jews out of every 100 state prosecutors in Berlin. Of every 100 judges, 23 were Jews. Forty-nine out of every 100 lawyers were Jews. 60 in every 100 doctors were Jews. The average income of the individual German stood at 810 marks, the average income of the Jew stood at 10,000 marks. While millions of native Germans were unemployed and in distress, immigrant Jews had, in a few years, gained fantastic fortunes.

Not by honorable work, but by usury, swindles and fraud. We only remind you of names like the Sklareks, who relieved the Berlin Treasury of 12.5 millions. The Jew Kutisker, who swindled Prussia of 14 millions, the Jew Barmat who defrauded the same state of 35 millions. The inflation profiteeer, Mendelssohn, the Jewish shares racketeer Katzenelnbogen, and all the others.

Jews, however, are most dangerous where they are allowed to meddle in the people's holy of holies, in its culture, in its religion and art, and to give their presumptuous judgments on it. The Northerner's concept of beauty is, by nature, completely incomprehensible to the Jew and will always remain so.

The rootless Jew has no feeling for the purity and neatness of the German idea of art.

What he calls art must titillate his degenerate nerves. A smell of fungus and disease must pervade it. It must be unnaturally grotesque, perverted or pathological. These pictures, fevered fantasies of incurably sick minds, were once foisted upon the German public by Jewish art theorists as the highest artistic manifestations. Nowadays we find it difficult to believe that such pieces were once bought up by nearly all the state and city galleries – indeed had to be bought by them because Jewish art dealers and Jewish artists extolled them as unique modern works of art. A wave of vulgarization and bastardization swept through all fields of German cultural life – plastic and graphic arts, architecture, literature, and music – all suffered in the same way. For more than a decade the Jews have wielded their pernicious power here as art dealers, as music publishers, editors, critics; they determined what art and culture were in Germany.

The Jew Kerr, the pontiff of art in the Weimar Republic. The Jew Tucholsky, one of the sickest pornographers, coined these words

> ... treason is an honor and the heroic ideal is the most stupid of all ideals.

The Jew Hirschfeld propogated homosexuality and sexual perversion. Under the cloak of ingenious or even learned discussion they tried to turn the healthy urges of mankind on to degenerate paths.

The "relativity" Jew Einstein, who hid his hatred of the Germans behind his obscure pseudo-science. The Jew Kestenberg had the control of German music in the Prussian Ministry of Culture.

The El Dorado of the Jews was the German theatre. Here they ruled unchecked, and degraded the classical tradition by their unrestrained appeal to the lowest instincts. The Jew Haller and his revues, likewise the Jew Nelson. The Rotter family, who possessed a monopoly of 7 theaters in Berlin, and finally, leaving behind debts of several million marks, decamped. The Jewish revue director, Robert Klein. The Jewish stage director, Max Reinhardt.

Jews were to be found as producers in most theaters. Here are the Jewish comedians Ehrlicka and Morgan, and in films it was no different. The Jewish film director, Richard Oswald, the comedian Gerron. The presentation of all that is disreputable and repellent by the Jews as a particularly fertile subject for comical effect. The Jewess Rosa Valetti.

The Jew Kurt Bois enjoys a particularly perverted role. Fritz Kortner-Cohn, who glorified a depraved officer who did not shrink back even from murder. (Excerpts from Fedor Ozep's film *Dimitri Karamasow-Murderer,* 1931.) Narrative: The Jew is interested instinctively in everything abnormal and depraved. Here he noses out ways of disrupting the healthy judgement of a race. The Jew Lorre in the role of a child murderer. Following the notion that it it is not the murderer but his victim who is guilty, an attempt is made to twist the normal judgment, and, by presenting the criminal in a sympathetic way, to gloss over and excuse the crime.

Film: *M* by Fritz Lang, 1932

"I can hear it, yes, it burns within me. I must go the way that I am driven. And run, run, into the main streets. I want to go away, go away. And with me run the ghosts of the mothers, the children. They won't leave me alone. They are there, always, always...always, until. Until I do it, until I...until I... Than I am conscious of nothing more...Then I stand in front of a poster and read what I have done, ... read. I did that? But I don't know anything about it. But who will believe me? Who knows what is going on inside me? How I have to do it, not want must. And then there is a scream. And I can't listen to it any more. I can't. I can't, I can't."
Narrative: A disproportionally large number of Jews were considered outstanding people, and were presented to the German public by their Jewish cronies in newspapers and newsreels as German artists and representatives of German culture. The Jew Richard Tauber – his departure from New York was mourned as an a alleged loss for German art.
Interview: Richard Tauber at the airport sings "You are My Heart's Delight."
Narrative: The Jew Ernst Lubitsch was hailed as a German film producer.
Lubitsch: I am extremely happy to be back in Germany and especially in my home town, Berlin.
Narrative: The Jew Emil Ludwig-Cohn was honored as a German writer.

Emil Ludwig-Cohn: I believe that an author today can do nothing better than to carry the German name abroad with honor.

Narrative: The Jew Chaplin was welcomed by an enraptured mob when he visited Berlin. It cannot be denied that at that time a portion of the German public applauded unsuspectingly the foreign Jew, the deadly enemy of their race. How was that possible? A mendacious dogma of human equality had dimmed the healthy instinct of the people.

Several hundred years of religious education has taught the European Christians to see in the Jew a fellow countryman, the author of the Christian religion. High-minded German painters and poets had projected their conceptions of the ideal into the Biblical figures of the Hebrew tribal history. Abraham, Isaac, and Jacob were considered as pillars of a particularly high standard of morality and ideals of noblest humanity.

In the meantime we have learned to use our eyes, and we know that the Hebrews of Biblical history could not have looked like this. We must correct our historical picture. This is what genuine Hebrews looked like.

The following scenes show a Jewish Purim festival, taken by the Warsaw Jews themselves for their own use as a cultural film. Moreover, it must be pointed out that this harmless looking family celebration is in memory of the slaughter of 75,000 anti-Semitic Persians, which was perpetrated 2,500 years ago by the Biblical forefathers of our present day Jews. The Bible gives details about the victory celebration: "And on the next day, the Jews rested and made the day a day of feasting and joy and gave one another presents, and they decided that these two days, named Purim, should not be forgotten, but kept by their children's children, from generation unto generation."

The German educated class, with its prudent and objective spirit of tolerance, is inclined to regard such tales as a piece of original folklore and an example of strange customs. But that is the race of Israel which is seen here rubbing its hands and celebrating its feast of vengeance; underneath Western European clothing they conceal their Eastern character.

ACT IV

In order to be sensible about the gravity of what lies behind all these things, it is necessary to take a closer look at the moral laws and teachings of the Jewish race. The Jew is brought up in the moral laws of his race.

As the Jew grows older, he receives lessons in Hebrew. And the rabbis, these masters of the art of hypocrisy, are not peaceful theologians, but political distorters. The politics of a race of parasites must be made in secret. And, at the same time, their designs are not necessarily known to the individual ghetto Jew. It is enough if, from youth on, he is impregnated with their ideas.

What does the ancient law of the Talmud teach? Always be cunning in fear, answer gently, and sooth even the anger of the stranger, so that you will be beloved above and found pleasing here below. Join yourself to him on whom fate smiles. Five things did Canaan recommend to his sons: love each other, love pillage, love excess, hate your master, and never speak the truth.

The further develompent of the Jewish inner life is undertaken by the synagogue. They count on the fact that people do not understand their language and thus the secret ambiguity of their symbols. Therefore they agree to appear before the cameraman even while at worship. The black boxes on the heads of the faithful contain passages from the law.

Carrying on petty dealings during the service is no disrespect for the Israelites, since according to the law, he who honors the Torah will prosper.

The Torah roll, which contains the five law books of Moses, is taken out of the so-called Holy Ark.

On its way to the pulpit, they kiss the Torah roll to ask forgiveness for their sins. The Torah scroll is rolled to the place where it is to be read out. What are the pieces of wisdom which the Torah preaches? Let us hear a few excerpts from it.

Orah Haim, Verse 290. The Sabbath blessing runs as follows: "May you be praised, oh Lord, you who have made a difference between the holy and the common people, between Israel and other races. The heathens, who do not keep your law and have gone over to your enemies, will be destroyed. God's anger is on the heathens and He says: Even the best among the heathens I will kill, and I will not be good to the peoples of the world, for they are nothing but blasphemers, but all the sons of Israel are righteous."

Or, in another place: Hahida, Verse 1: " And the Lord said to the Israelites: You have made me the one God of the world, therefore I will make your people the only rulers of the world." Orah Haim 126, Verse 1: "Glory be to the eternal God, you who destroy the enemies of your people, crush and humble them, so that the earth may belong to you alone and to your people."

That is no religion, and no religious service, that is a conspiracy against all non-Jews, by a cunning, unhealthy and contaminated race, against the health of the Aryan peoples and against their moral laws.

182

(Titles appear on the screen.)

Title: One of the most instructive customs of the Jewish so-called religion is the slaughter of animals. The following pictures are genuine. They are among the most horrifying that a camera has ever taken. We are showing them in spite of this, without regard for objections on the grounds of taste. Because more important than all objections is the fact that our people should know the truth about Judaism.

Title: Sensitive compatriots are advised not to look at the following pictures.

Narrative: Seemingly, their so-called religion prevents the Jews from eating meat butchered in the ordinary way. Therefore they let the animals bleed to death. This cruelty is described by the Jews themselves, in order to deceive innocent non-Jews, as the most humane type of slaughter.

European science has long affirmed the cruelty of this type of slaughter. As long ago as 1892, as a result of a referendum, it was forbidden in Switzerland. The Jewish law books have no sense for the considerations for Germanic respect and love for animals. They even forbid that a suffering animal should be put out of its misery.

The National Socialist movement has fought with all its might against this cruel torture of defenseless animals from the very beginning of its struggles. In nearly all the provincial diets and in the Reichstag they moved that this type of slaughter should be forbidden. But the entire Jewish and Jewish-controlled press treated this fight as a disgrace.

(Newspaper cuttings in quick succession)

Berliner Tageblatt: Anti-Semitic Move to Forbid Jewish Ritual Slaughter. In the Landtags of Baden, Bavaria, and Thuringia, the National Socialists have proposed the motion that this form of animal slaughter should be forbidden, as unworthy of a civilized nation. It seems that the Nazis, in their hate-filled anti-Semitism, do not shrink from interfering in time honored religious customs. Unbiased, objective experts, on the other hand, have long proved that this form of slaughter is one of the most humane that exist anywhere.

Vossische Zeitung:
The battle against kosher meat. An objective study by Rabbi Dr. Engelbert – in reply to the many queries from all circles as to whether the slaughter of animals according to Jewish rites is really a form of cruelty to the animals, "I should like to say following. With this form of slaughter it is a question of....."

183

Tempo:
Nazi Fantasies About Ritual Slaughter. Explanations by Rabbis of Germany.

Acht Uhr Abends:
Stormy Meeting of the Landtag. Scientists Against Nazi Lies.

Vorwärts:
Assault on the Constitution Fails.

Die Rote Fahne:
Nazi Motion Fails.

Narrative: The Jewish press was able to write this because scarcely any German ever had an opportunity to witness kosher butchering. It would also have been inconceivable, considering the well-known German love of animals, that the Jews, until recently, were able to perpetrate unpunished their cruel tortures on innocent and defenceless animals.

These pictures are unequivocal evidence of the cruelty of this form of slaughter. At the same time they reveal the character of a race that conceals its crude brutality under the cloak of pious religious practices. Jewish butchers tie the animals so that there are no movements to betray their agonies. But it is also customary, to some extent, for unbound animals to be slaughtered in this way.

Immediately after the Führer had assumed power, a law was passed by the government of the Reich on the 21st of April 1933, which prohibited the Jewish form of slaughter, and directed that all warm-blooded animals should be given an anaesthetic before slaughter.

And, just as it has dealt with this cruel slaughter, so will the Germany of National Socialism deal with the whole race of Jewry.

Hitler at the Kroll Opera House. January 30, 1939: "There is sufficient living space in the world, but the idea that the Jewish people were specifically chosen by God Almighty to create a certain percentage of beneficiaries on the body and productive work of other races should finally be dispensed with. Jewry will just have to adapt itself to the idea of performing some respectable, constructive activity,as other races do, or sooner or later, it will succumb to a crisis of inconceivable magnitude....

"If the Jews of international finance in and beyond Europe were to succeed in hurling the people into another world war, then the result will not be the bolshevization of the earth, and consequently the victory of Judaism, but the destruction of the Jewish race in Europe."

The eternal law of nature, to keep the race pure, is the legacy which the National Socialist movement bequeaths to the German people in perpetuity. It is in this spirit that the association of German peoples marches into the future.

Law of the 21st of April 1933, Concerning the Slaughter of Animals

The Government of the Reich has passed the following law which is herewith made known.

Paragraph 1.

1) Warm-blooded animals intended for slaughter are to be anaesthetized before blood is drawn.

2) The Reich Minister of the Interior can decide that the order under 1 above can also be applied to other animals.

Law Relating to German Nationality Rights, 14th of November, 1935.

Paragraph 4.

1) A Jew cannot be a citizen of the Reich. He has no right to vote in political affairs; he cannot hold an official post. Jewish blood and the Jewish way of thinking will never again contaminate the German people.

Law Concerning the Protection of German Honor and German Blood, 15th of September 1935.

Filled with the knowledge that the purity of the German race is the prerequisite for the continuance of the German race, and inspired by the firm intention to ensure the future of the German nation forever, the Reichstag has unanimously passed the following law, which is herewith made known:

Paragraph 1.

1) Marriages between Jews and nationals of German or related blood are forbidden. Marriages contracted in spite of this are null and void, even when, in order to evade this law, they are performed abroad.

2) The plea of nullity can only be lifted by the state prosecutor.

Laws Concerning An Act of Expiation By Jews of German Nationality, 12th of November, 1938.

The hostile attitude of Jewry towards the German people and the Reich, which does not even shrink from cowardly acts of murder, calls for determined resistance and strict atonement. I have therefore, determined, by virtue of the decree of the 18th of October, 1936, concerning the execution of the Four Year Plan, the following:

Paragraph 1. Jews of German nationality are to pay a total contribution of one billion Reichsmarks to the German Reich.

Under the leadership of Adolf Hitler, Germany has raised the banner of war against the eternal Jew.

"JEW SÜSS"

Note: The script has been prepared on the basis of a copy of the film found at the Harry Karren Institute for the Analysis of Propaganda, Herzliya, Israel.

Fade In

1. Opening
The titles appear in white on a black background; music with Jewish themes is heard mixed with the German song *"All' meine Gedanken, die ich hab', die sind beir Dir"* (All My Thoughts Are With You) which during the film becomes the leitmotif of Dorothea, Sturm's daughter and the heroine of the film. A Star of David and a seven-branched candelabrum appear on the screen.

Titles:
Jew Süss
A film of Veit Harlan (studio Terra Filmkunst).
Script: Veit Harlan, Wolfgang Eberhardt Möller, Ludwig Metzker
Music: Wolfgang Zeller
Scenic Decorations: Otto Hunter, Karl Paul Bersht
Camera: Bruno Mundy
Sound: Gustav Sellers
Actors: Friedrich Marian, Kristina Söderbaum, Heinrich Georga, Werner Krauss, Eugene Kulpepper, Albert Floret, Malta Yeger, Theodor Loss, Hilda Von Sthultz, Else Alstater, Walther Verner, Jakob Teitke, Otto Henning, Emile Hess.
Production Company: Otto Lemmen.
Subtitles: The events of the film are based on historical facts.

2. The Dutchy of Württemberg.

(The date 1733, appears in Gothic script on the background of a picture of the Dutchy of Württemberg. The camera comes in for a **close up** of a sign "Stuttgart")

3. Interior. Meeting Hall

(Members of the local parliament are gathered together in the company of the Duke. On the wall is a picture of the late Duke, predecessor of the present one. The camera pans across the faces of those present, among them, **Sturm,** The Lord Chairman of the Assembly of Württemberg who holds in his hand a copy of the oath of allegiance. In the background the peal of bells is heard)

Duke: After the tragic death of my cousin, the Duke Aberhard Ludwig, control over this blessed land has passed to my hands, and at this moment I would like to swear an oath before my people. I request from this gathering that the oath be read. (He rests his fist on the constitution placed before him on the table.) I place my fist on the constitution of this state as a symbol of my oath.

Sturm: (Holds the book containing the oath before him and reads aloud) I, Prince Karl Alexander, Duke of Württemberg, Imperial General and Fieldmarshal, and former General Governor of Serbia, with the aid of divine grace, hereby swear in the name of God Almighty to act on behalf of the welfare of all our citizens and to increase it. With fatherly concern we intend through our princely oath to ensure that our princely government act without any deviation in all areas according to the ancient Württemberg principles of loyalty and honesty. And we especially obligate ourselves to be faithful to the constitution (closes the book of the oath and turns his gaze to the duke) to administer the matters of state together with the representatives of the Assembly in accordance with the constitution.

Duke: I swear.

4. Exterior. The Marketplace

(On a balcony facing the square, a line of trumpeters is arranged. They let out a trumpet blast. The sound of bells is heard. The square is full of people. All salute the duke who passes by in his royal carriage. Lines of soldiers stand along the route of the carriage's procession and prevent the crowd from bursting through to approach the duke. A young woman tries to get close to the carriage. The soldiers grab her and rip her blouse off. The woman tries to cover her nakedness. The duke sees the scene, enjoys it immensely, slaps his thigh in pleasure and laughs loudly. The carriage continues along its way and the crowd closes in after it)

5. Interior. Sturm's House

(**Faber,** Sturm's secretary, is sitting by the harpsichord. The camera moves back to reveal Dorothea, Sturm's daughter. She is standing near Faber. He begins to play)

Dorothea: (sings) All my thoughts are of you. You are my only and chosen sweetheart, you will always remain with me. Please, think of me, if all my wishes were to come true....(her voice is silenced)

Faber: (completes the song)...in reality.

Dorothea: (continues to sing) I do not wish to be separated from you. (speaks) I thank you. (They kiss)

Faber: Dorla! (a noise is heard from the direction of the door)

Dorothea: Father!

Sturm: (enters in haste) Hurry Dorothea! Quickly, quickly, the food! In another hour I must be at the palace. (approaches Faber sitting with the harpsichord) A new book of notes? All My Thoughts Are With You. How nice. (Reads) "To my beloved bride Dorothea Sturm, on the oath-taking day of our beloved Duke Alexander. With Love and Loyalty. Faber. Hail Württemberg!"

6. Interior. Around the Sturm Table

(Sturm, Dorothea and Faber sit down at the table)

Dorothea: Quickly, the goose is almost burned. It was too long in the oven because you made us wait. This beautiful goose...

Sturm: Don't be angry Dorothea. It was a solemn royal event. Our household routine can be changed a little because of it, certainly. So, you can begin to serve. Give some to your groom, and for yourself take the drumstick, and for me lots of stewed apples. Ah! This crisp skin. This is a Sunday meal after my heart. To whose health shall we drink?

Dorothea: May I suggest, to Faber?

Sturm: Faber? Your Faber isn't so important. None of us is so, important. So to whose health shall we drink?

Dorothea: To us?

Sturm: (in amazement) Dorothea! Today!?

Dorothea: (embarrassed) To the health of our duke.

Sturm: (raises a glass and toasts with it) Alexander. May God enable him to succeed in the works of his hands.

7. Interior. Great Hall in the Palace

(The hall is full of guests, among them the Dutchess and her entourage. The camera pans across the Duke approaching the Dutchess)
Duke: Dutchess! You will receive your present later. You have a poor husband. Come, your people call you. (They go out on the balcony)

8. Exterior. The Palace Balcony

(The Duke and Dutchess and their entourage look out over the balcony upon the throng of cheering people)
Duke: (in excitement) My people! My country!
Sturm: Württemberg, the most blessed land under the skies of Germany.
(The camera pans across the Ducal emblem)
Dissolve

9. Exterior. The Jews' Street in Frankfurt

(A Hebrew sign "Exchange." **Von Remchingen** stands beside his carriage. Music with Jewish motifs is heard)
Von Remchingen: (to the coachman) Wait up on Hermerberg. I don't want you to stand here in the Jews' street.
Coachman: Yes, sir.
(The door of Süss Oppenheimer's house opens and **Levy** appears)
Von Remchingen: I need to see Herr Oppenheimer.
Levy: Süss Oppenheimer awaits your honor. (they enter)
(The carriage moves off. A slaughterer enters the picture; an old man and his daughter appear at the window of a neighboring house)
Old man: Yitzhak! What do those high and mighty *goyim* (gentiles) want with our Oppenheimer?
Slaughterer: Why do you need to ask at all?
Old man: Ahh, you mean money?
Slaughterer: What else?
Old man: But he won't part with any.
Slaughterer: He will loan him a lot because he has a good head on his shoulders. When he gives a lot, we'll be able to take more. Seven folds. (laughs and coughs)
Old man: (to his daughter) Get dressed, Rivka!
Dissolve

10. Interior. Süss' House

(Süss opens an iron chest before Von Remchingen)

Süss: I believe that Württemberg is rich.

Von Remchingen: Yes, Württemberg, yes, but not the Duke.

Suss: Good, I'll think it over. (Opens a chest of jewelry)

Von Remchingen: Fabulous!

(Süss shows him a crown encrusted with pearls)

Von Remchingen: Fabulous, quite fabulous, but too large for us.

Süss: Too large for the Dutchess?

(returns the crown and shows him a pearl necklace)

Von Remchingen: Fabulous, (laughs) wonderful! I dare not ask the price.

Süss: 50,000.

Von Remchingen: I have already told you that my Duke does not have so much money.

Süss: Very well, ten thousand.

Von Remchingen: And the remaining forty thousand?

Süss: We'll find a way to come to an agreement.

Von Remchingen: When and where?

Süss: In Stuttgart.

Von Remchingen: Jews may not enter Stuttgart. You know that!

Süss: Tell the Duke that if he needs me, he should make it his business that I get permission to come to him.

Von Remchingen: If you will be in Stuttgart, perhaps I can help you, but you won't be able to get in with your passport.

Süss: If that's the case, then cancel the prohibition against the Jews.

Von Remchingen: How? Do you expect me to cancel it? Even the Duke cannot cancel it without the approval of the Assembly, and the Assembly does not allow any Jew to enter the capital city.

Süss: If His Royal Highness is interested in doing business with me, then His Highness will find a way to get me a passport that will remove all the obstacles at the border.

Von Remchingen: Suppose I do send you a passport like that, but everyone would still recognize immediately that ...

Süss: (cutting him off)I am a Jew because of the earlocks, beard, and skullcap.

Von Remchingen: Isn't that so?

Süss: Don't let His Highness worry about that. I'll take care of my external appearance. Will you see to the passport? The Duke will get his jewelry (Süss and Von Remchingen get up), but only on condition that I bring them to him.

Von Remchingen: All right, but it is urgent, the Duke needs the jewels!

Süss: Depend on Süss Oppenheimer, Sir. (Von Remchingen exits).

Levy: (to Süss), Joseph, Have you gone mad? Do you want to shave off your beard and sidelocks? Will you no longer wear the skullcap? ... Are you not afraid of the Rabbi?

Süss: You are a fool; I am opening the door for all of you! Perhaps tomorrow or the day after, but it will come!

11. Exterior. On the Way to Stuttgart

(Süss, who is cleanly shaven, is travelling in a carriage. The coachman whips the horses onward. He passes by Dorothea's carriage which is also bound for Stuttgart. The horses stumble from the great speed and the carriage overturns on its side and falls into a ditch at the edge of the road. Süss rises completely shaken)

Süss: Oh, I feared this, this was what I was afraid of. You call this a road?

Coachman: (stands and looks at the overturned carriage) Madness!

Süss: (removes his suitcase from the carriage), Yeah, yeah, no more of that, I must be in Stuttgart this evening.

Coachman: If we had travelled more slowly, we would probably have arrived there.

(Dorothea's carriage approaches and stops besides the scene of the accident)

Dorothea: (from a distance) Are you hurt?

Süss: No, not at all young lady, thank God, no. (approaches Dorothea)

Dorothea: My God! How did it happen?

Süss: (smiles) The roads are in terrible condition, what is the distance to Stuttgart young lady?

Dorothea: By carriage it is another hour.

Süss: An hour! Would it be impolite on my part to ask the young lady to take me in her carriage?

12. Interior. The Assembly Hall

(Members of the Council of Eleven are met in the Assembly Hall, seated around the table. Sturm sits at the head)

A: What does the Duke need a ballet for? What does he need an opera for? or a palace bodyguard? No one is threatening him.

Sturm: Gentlemen, I am also of the opinion that the requests made by the Duke at the last meeting of the Council are not feasible. I also believe that we Württembergers are used to a life of simplicity and that the people who have chosen us will not understand if we give in to the Duke's wishes. But, gentlemen, we do not wish to be petty either. The Duke is a great general and loves to have soldiers around him. Therefore let us approve the bodyguard.

192

Ferdinand Marian as Jew Süss

The Alley of the Jews in Frankfurt, in the film *Jew Süss*

Süß

50/x279

TERRA
FILMKUNST

üß A Jew and His Immoral Daughter in Jew Süss.

TERRA
FILMKUNST

Jud Süß

Jud Süß

Top: Frivolous ball arranged by the Jew Süss, at which the bureaucrats'
daughters a debauched
Left Above: Süss displays his treasures before Von Remchingen, the
Duke's emissary
Left Below: Heinrich George, as the Duke Karl Alexander, fondles the
prima ballerina of his ballet troupe

Jud Süß

Above: Werner Krauss as Levy, Süss' Secretary
Right Above: The Duke's Ballet Troupe, acquired with the Jew Süss' money
Right Below: Ferdinand Marian as the Jew Süss, courts Kristina Söderbaum, as Dorothea, the Assembly Chairman's daughter

Jud Süß

Jud Süß

The Jew Süss plays cards at the Duke's Place. At his side is his German mistress

üß

TERRA
FILMKUNST

The Procession of Jews enters the gates of Stuttgart

Süß

Jud Süß

Above: Werner Krauss as Rabbi Loew in the film *Jew Süss*
Right Above: The blacksmith Bogner attacks the carriage of the Jew Süss
Right Below: Jew Süss and Rabbi Loew conspire in the Synagogue

Jud Süß

Jud Süß

The Duke's Guard, in the film *Jew Jüss*

Süß

TERRA
FILMKUNST

Jud Süß

Jud Süß

Jud Süß

bove: Jew Süss and Dorothea at the beginning of the rape scene
eft Above: Jew Süss and His secretary Levy
eft Below: Levy sitting at the head of the Interrogation Committee of the
hairman of the Assembly

Jew Süss Influences the Duke to abolish the Assembly and become an
absolute ruler

Jew Süss and Dorothea in the rape scene

Jew Süss at his trial

Jew Süss being led to the hanging cage

Jew Süss begging for mercy from the hanging cage

The judges at the execution of Jew Süss

B: Alright, let's approve the bodyguard, but under no circumstances the ballet or opera!

C: I must emphasize that only because of our great love for the Duke, and against our conscience, did we approve all his requests which he made at the first session of the Assembly. We haven't achieved anything as a result except that his requests grow grander all the time. If we comply with his request, we will only make our own road unnecessarily more difficult. I also oppose the bodyguard, on principle!

Col. Von Röder: (contemptuously dismisses the words of the last speaker) Oh, you have no sense of humor.

Sturm: Faber, take the ballot box and collect the stones. Gentlemen, my opinion is known to all of you. Let us now vote.

13. Exterior. The Stuttgart City Gate

(A soldier checks Oppenheimer's passport. He is sitting inside Dorothea's carriage)

Soldier: Herr Oppenheimer from Frankfurt?

Dorothea: (in surprise) Herr Oppenheimer?

Süss: (with an apologetic smile) Yes, Oppenheimer.

Soldier: The passport is in order. (The barrier is lifted and the carriage passes through the gate)

14. Exterior. A Street in Stuttgart

(Dorothea and Süss sit inside the carriage which passes along the city streets)

Dorothea: Oh, how I would like to travel, most of all around the world. You probably have travelled a lot ... isn't that true?. Have you already been to Paris?

Süss: Yes.

Dorothea: In Versailles?

(Süss nods his head in agreement)

Dorothea: Oh, how I envy you. Where else have you been?

Süss: Oh, London, Vienna, Rome, Madrid.

Dorothea: (sighing) My goodness.

Süss: Lisbon.

Dorothea: My God, that is almost the whole world. Where was it the most beautiful. I mean where did you feel yourself most at home?

Süss: At home? Everywhere!

Dorothea: Everywhere? Don't you have a homeland?

Süss: Yes, the whole world!

Dorothea: Nonsense, in some particular place, you must have felt most happy.

Süss: I think that I have never been so happy as right now, here in Stuttgart, by your side, young lady.

Dorothea: Oh!

15. Interior. The Duke's Bedroom

(Von Remchingen is leaning against the open door)

Duke: What? They refused?

Von Remchingen: Yes, Your Royal Highness. Seven votes against four.

Duke: (angrily) You mean I won't get the opera?

Von Remchingen: No, Your Highness, and not the ballet either.

Duke: No ballet and no opera! They probably won't give me the guard either?!

Von Remchingen: No, your Highness.

Duke: In Belgrade, where I was just a minor governor, they treated me better.

Von Remchingen: The Assembly believes...

Duke: (cutting him off) Oh really, the Assembly indeed!

Von Remchingen: The Assembly is of the opinion that your higness' ancestors had no need for a guard.

Duke: They had no sense of grandeur, my ancestors.

Von Remchingen: Nevertheless, according to the the constitution ...

Duke: Constitution! (throws himself on the bed) Let them run matters as they see fit.

Von Remchingen: Perhaps it would be possible to negotiate with them one more time. I would be willing to try.

Duke: The Assembly, the Assembly! As an advisor I would be better off with a donkey that shits ducats (covers himself with a blanket, insulted).

16. Interior. The Entrance Parlor to the Sturm House

(Faber looks at Süss Oppenheimer, accompanied by Dorothea)

Faber: But this is the Jew, Herr Oppenheimer from Frankfurt!

Süss: (To Sturm) If you should ever need my help, I would be happy to assist you, in return for the cordiality of your charming daughter, the young lady.

Dorothea: Nonsense, they let him pass at the city gate without problems.

Faber: I am not mistaken. He is a Jew! (approaches Süss) Sir, I would like to recommend to you not to miss the next carriage out of town.

Süss: Why? I am not in a hurry. I have business in Stuttgart. On the

contrary, I was about to ask you if you could recommend a good inn.
Faber: In Stuttgart, the capital, there are not any hostels for Jews.
Süss: (lowers his glance) My congratulations on your sagacity, sir...(to Sturm), but I thank the charming young lady who will certainly understand that I am obligated to repay her in a fitting manner.
Dissolve

17. Interior. The Duke's Workroom

(Süss, the Duke, and Von Remchingen are in the room. The Duke is examining a pearl necklace)
Duke: (to V.R.) So, ask him how much it costs.
Süss: Your Highness need not worry about the financial side of matters. I would be happy to serve His Royal Highness.
Duke: (surprised) Well, yes, but one does have to pay sometime.
Von Remchingen: The Jew will wait.
Duke: Yes?...is that so? (smiles) Can the Jew be more generous than my lords of the Assembly?
Süss: The gentlemen apparently don't know how to deal with a great nobleman.
Duke: (sarcastically) But you do?
Süss: I think that I know how. For example, I do not understand how the Assembly can refuse his Royal Highness a ballet. I simply can't fathom it. Your Royal Highness (approaches the Duke flatteringly), I would be truly happy, if I might be allowed to make a small arrangement whereby His Highness would nevertheless get the ballet. I don't know but I would be happy if I could say of myself that I am a faithful servant of my master! (empties a purse full of money on the table. The camera zooms in on the rolling coins)
Dissolve

18. Interior. Banquet Hall, The Duke's Palace

(Ballet dancers are prancing coquettishly in a circle. The Duke looks down in enjoyment from the interior balcony. Von Remchingen and Süss are standing at the side. The Duke signals to Von Remchingen to approach him)
Duke: (points out the prima-ballerina) Stop the rehearsal for a moment and bring that pretty little brunette up to me. (The prima balerina sends a kiss to the Duke)
Duke: Süss!
Süss: (in readiness) Your Royal Highness.

Duke: I need something simple.

Süss: (removes a ring from his finger) I don't have anything on me right now, Your Royal Highness. (Von Remchingen appears with the prima ballerina. They enter the Duke's private quarters. Süss and Von Remchingen close the door after them)

19. Interior. The Duke's Quarters

(The Duke places Süss' ring on the prima-ballerina's finger, draws her near to him and kisses her passionately)

20. Interior. Corridor in the Palace

(Süss and Von Remchingen stroll through the corridor. The camera zooms in on them)

Von Remchingen: One day you will certainly present the bill.

Süss: Herr Remchingen. Why are you getting excited as if it were impossible to withdraw a penny from Württemberg, a country so blessed? In Asia they would pale, if they could but sip from the springs of plenty which flow from Württemberg.

Von Remchingen: God, he just doesn't understand.

Duke: (joins the two) Who doesn't understand what? (Süss approaches the Duke) So speak at once!

Süss: With your leave, Royal Highness. I simply can't understand why it is impossible to withdraw money from 400 villages and 70 towns.

Duke: (laughingly) What money does he wish to withdraw?

Süss: Not for myself, Royal Highness, perish the thought!

Duke: For whom then? For me? What interest do you have in it?

Von Remchingen: Does Your Highness know how much money he owes to the Jew? 342,000 thalers, to be exact.

Duke: (to Süss) All right, so you want to squeeze me?

Süss: Your Royal Highness, I haven't requested anything.

Duke: What you ask for, you shall of course receive. Do you think that I will allow a Jew to give me presents?

Süss: Of course not. An honest man knows it is unwise to ask for something at a time when he knows he will not be able to get it. I am not a blackmailer.

Duke: (laughingly) You can place a lien.

Süss: (also laughs) A lien?...No, (mumbles) I wouldn't know.

Duke: I beg your pardon?

Süss: What exactly is your collateral?

Duke: You insolent man, my collateral is Württemberg.

Süss: So, is that so bad, Württemberg?

Duke: Oh, so it's Württemberg that you want, and I will be a dealer in jewels?

Süss: That was only a joke, that His Royal Highness give me... After all, Your Highness, I am only a Jew; you can also hang me.

Duke: What should I give you?

Süss: The roads of Württemberg.

Duke: The roads of Württemberg? What do you want with the roads of Württemberg?

Süss: Give me the rights to the roads of Württemberg for ten years. Give me the administration. They are in terrible condition. It's about time that someone took care of them and repaired them. I demand for myself the road and bridge tax, and give to Your Highness the city gate tax, for the roads pass through the city gates.

Duke: Just a second, slowly, slowly.

Süss: In this way His Majesty does away with his obligations, I get my money, and no one interferes with the other.

Duke: A road tax, a bridge tax? Slowly, slowly! What would my Swabians say about that?

Süss: What do the Swabians have to say in the matter. Why, such a bridge and road cost money! That is good money, Your Highness.

Duke: Hmmm. If you weren't a Jew...

Süss: Why? Doesn't the Emperor Leopold in Vienna have his Jew to make money for him, his own Isaac Oppenheimer? And doesn't he have power? The power of money?

21. The Stuttgart City Gate

(The farmer Miller arrives with his horses and wagon at the customs barrier)

Miller: You could go crazy! Until now I have paid the transit tax in four villages and the bridge tax on two bridges. All in all six thalers. And now you want the seventh from me. All my goods are only worth twenty thalers. Tell me how far I'll get, ha?

Customs Agent: (points out Levy who approaches with his wagon and a constable) Please turn to him. He's coming right now. If you don't like it, see the one responsible. I didn't invent the customs and the bridge tax.

Levy: What is it?

Customs Agent: The man is complaining. They are all complaining.

Levy: Why is he complaining if nothing is damaged?

Miller: The flour costs me seven thalers more now.

Levy: Don't shout. You don't know arithmetic. How much extra can you take for your wheat?

Miller: Fifteen from a hundred.

Levy: (sarcastically) Fifteen from a hundred. Speak German! Fifteen percent! So listen, until today you were taking fifteen percent profit on these twenty thalers?

Miller: Ahh. Yes, three thalers.

Levy: Today you can take fifteen percent on twenty-seven thalers, right?

Miller: Uhh...

Levy: Uh, uh, uh, twenty four and a half, that is today an extra thaler and a quarter for you. For every taler that the Duke adds, you gain twice as much. So go to the Duke and thank him!

Miller: But...

Levy: Oh, there is nothing more to be said. Pay! Pay! Learn how to do arithmetic.

22. Interior. Sturm's Workroom

(Sturm and Faber are sitting at their desks. Dorothea enters)

Dorothea: Father, meat has again increased in price; vegetables, too; almost everything!

Sturm: Is that so?

Dorothea: Yes, I once paid one pfenning for a head of cabbage. Today I pay three pfennings for two cabbages!

Sturm: First meat, and then bread. Great God.

Dorothea: And then eggs, and who knows what else?

Faber: You, Dorla, brought him to Stuttgart, the one we all owe thanks to for this.

Dorothea: Please don't speak to me like that, Faber.

Sturm: (approaches Faber) The Duke exceeds his authority. The Assembly did not approve the money for his orgies so he is taking it by force. I love the Duke, but there is a limit to everything. This won't end well.

Dorothea: (frightened) It frightens me, the way you speak.

Sturm: I am afraid of the Jew, Dorothea.

Faber: Yesterday I saw how a Jew named Levy went by carriage from gate to gate, from bridge to bridge, and how he checked each bridge and each customs house and how he collected the money. And how he put the Württemberg farmers' money into his dirty pockets.

Sturm: (reassuringly) So, so, take it easy my son. There is no wisdom in this. The Jew bought even the Duke's bodyguard, and the guard is stronger than you, my son. We must be wise.

Faber: We will never be as wise as the Jews.

Sturm: Wiser. We must be a lot wiser. The Jews are not wise, only shrewd.

23. Interior. Süss' Workroom in the Palace

(Süss sits at his desk. Levy stands at his side. The blacksmith, **Bogner**, stands before the table, his wife, with a child in her arms, stands by his side)

Süss: The road is mine. I bought it from the Duke and even paid for it.

Bogner: The house doesn't stand on the road, the road detours around it.

Süss: That's right! Pardon, do allow me. (points to the area on a map) The road detours because of your house. In essence the road goes straight. Does the road detour because of a river in the way? No, but your house is in the way, and therefore the road must detour around it. Why does your house have to stand in the middle of the road, of all places?

Bogner: The workshop has always stood on the road.

Levy: No, not on, alongside! Alongside the road. But from my point of view, it can just as well stand on the road but then that part of the road must belong to you, right? And if it doesn't belong to you, then you have to buy it, so?

Süss: Well, all right Levy. But I am not selling the road to the blacksmith. I just wanted no more than to act towards him generously and in a friendly way so I offered it to him for sale. But no one understands generosity properly around here.

Bogner: That's generosity?

Süss: Blacksmith, what stands on your land is yours. Is that not so?

Bogner: Of course.

Süss: And what stands on my land, whose is that?

Bogner: What do you mean?

Süss: That means that the part of your house that stands on the road belongs to me. And I am getting rid of it because I don't want a house on my road.

Bogner's wife: (she and her child approach Süss) Sir, that half of the house that stands on the area that your secretary determined is our workshop, our room, it is our livelihood!

Süss: Pardon me madam, then he should have thought of that before, the rebel.

Dissolve

24. Exterior. The Blacksmith Bogner's Workshop

(One sees rows of stones; half of the house is demolished. Soldiers stand on the remaining half. An angry crowd is gathered by the house. The blacksmith and his wife stand by the ruins of their house and workshop. Süss and his mistress arrive in the carriage)

Mistress: Half a house, like a toy, like a dollhouse. How cute.

Süss: This sweet dollhouse will remain here for a full year so that people will begin to wonder whether it is permissible to object to the Minister of the Treasury, even if his name is Süss Oppenheimer.

Mistress: How clever you are, but cruel.

Bogner: Are you enjoying the scene?

(The angry mob halts the carriage. A soldier tries to push them back)

Süss: What happened? Forward!

Coachman: The people are in front of the horses!

Süss: Run them down.

(The blacksmith throws his hammer and shatters the carriage's partition. The mistress screams in fear)

Süss: (to the soldiers) Arrest the murderer immediately! (to the mistress) pull yourself together, you little fool. (to the coachman) Go!

25. Interior. In the Parlor of the Feibelkorn Family

(Feibelkorn, Mrs. Feibelkorn and their daughter Mina are sitting at the table)

Herr F: (shocked) Imagine ordering all the clerks to appear with their adolescent daughters!?

Mrs. F: Is that what you call an honor?

Mina: I am not a little girl. I already know how to behave.

Herr F: Shut up and don't be so smart!

Mrs. F: Oh, don't ruin the children's happiness. You know it isn't everyday that they get to be invited by the Duke.

Herr F: By the Duke...They were invited by the Jew! The Jew is once again organizing a meat market, this time in the palace, and our girls are good enough to constitute the merchandise.

26. Interior. The Palace Ballroom

(Couples are dancing the polonaise. The master of ceremonies is among the dancers)

Master of Ceremonies: The ladies on the left, continue forward.

Duke: (looking at the dancers from the balcony. Süss is at his side) For primitive souls, this may be quite amusing. But for me....too bourgeoise, too bourgeoise, too moral. For this reason I didn't have to send my wife to Ludwigsburg. Where is your idea Jew?

Süss: Your Royal Highness, be so kind as to look at the arrangement. The old ladies from behind, the young people in front and opposite them your guard, your Royal Highness.

Duke: Ha?

Süss: Patience, Your Royal Highness. Don't spoil the surprise for me and yourself. (In the hall the dancers continue dancing with masks on their faces. Levy enters the ranks of the dancers in panic)

Levy: (to the servant) Close the door!

Servant: I beg your pardon?

Levy: Close the door, you jackass!

Süss: (walks with the Duke over to the other side of the balcony) I thought that instead of the boring thorns of the courtyard, I would bring the flowers of spring in from the fields to Your Royal Highness.

Duke: (to himself) I wonder what the bastard has hit on now.

Süss: Just as God divides the lambs from the sheep, so I too divide the daughters from their parents.

Süss: (watches the dancers together with Faber and a member of the Assembly) Keep calm Faber. We are at court.

Faber: A pigsty, this is not a court!

Member of the Assembly: You are endangering your life.

(The young girls are led off during the dance to a side hall)

27. Side Hall

(The Duke examines the girls. Süss is at his side)

Süss: (presents a girl to the Duke) The young lady Tauzend. (The girl curtsies before the Duke and removes the mask from her face)

Duke: They should have named her "Thousand times more beautiful." (They approach the Feibelkorn daughters)

Süss: Fredericia and Minchen Feibelkorn, both not more than 18 years old.

Duke: (impressed) Two roses, heh?

Süss: Minchen, why are you so shy, and hiding when everyone is jealous of you. Show the Duke your legs.

(One of the girls lifts the hem of her skirt. She is crying)

Duke: Don't cry, Minchen. Don't cry. Do you wish to teach your old master how to dance? (leads her aside)

Süss: (approaches Dorothea) May I invite the Mademoiselle?

Dorothea: I don't dance, Herr Minister of the Treasury.

Süss: Oh, you don't wish to come to your Duke?

Dorothea: To the Duke?

Süss: Who else?

Dorothea: (makes herself agreeable) Please.
(Levy closes the door after Süss and Dorothea)
Levy: (to the servant) Stand before the door!

28. Interior. A Small Sideroom
(Süss and Dorothea are dancing)
Süss: You probably didn't expect to see me so soon, and in these surroundings.
Dorothea: No I didn't.
Süss: Oh, why is this beautiful mouth so serious? In fact I expected to see you laugh again as you did in the carriage.
Dorothea: You wanted to dance!
Süss: Burning lips, a cold heart. Isn't that what they say? Oh, can your heart fulfill what your lips promise? (kisses her on the back of her shoulder)
Dorothea: (angrily) Stop!
Süss: Does Mademoiselle wish to dance?
Dorothea: No not anymore! (slips out of his hands and runs toward the door)

29. Interior. Side Hall
(Dorothea bursts in. Süss catches up to her)
Süss: Mademoiselle, where are you running?
Dorothea: I am looking for my father.
Faber: (comes towards Dorothea and draws her near to him) The next dance is mine!
Süss: Pardon, will Mademoiselle do me the honor of having dinner with me?
Faber: No, she won't.
Sturm: (approaches) My child is going home.
Süss: (to Sturm): So, you allow yourself to be insolent or you don't tolerate your daughter enjoying entertainment?
Sturm: I beg your pardon. I am leaving.

30. Small Sideroom
Duke: (bends down toward Mina) What is your name, my little one?
Mina: Mina Feibelkorn.
Duke: (amorously) Hmmm. Minshen, are you afraid of me?
Mina: (shaking) No. (tries to get up)

Duke: (pushes her back) Don't be boring Minchen, you can't stay like this forever.

31. Interior. Gambling Room

(Süss is playing with those around the table. Next to them sit Faber and a friend, both in masks)

Von Remchingen: I am going with you.

Süss: The king has the upper hand.

Mistress: I am bringing you luck, my angel.

Süss: I need it for you, my greedy one. (She laughs. Süss gives her money and she leaves)

Faber: Did you win all this money you give away by honorable means?

Süss: My native son, why are you breaking your head.

Faber: I am not your native son!

Von Remchingen: (throwing out a card) Yes, I'm with you.

Süss (bangs on the table) The prince has the upper hand. Double!

Faber: You are playing with this money so serenely, as if you don't know how much honest men have sweated for it.

Süss: Money does not stink. The Romans already knew that. Should I be more righteous than the Roman Emperor. Ahcch! So jack, queen, king, triple (rakes in the coins). Thank you very much.

Friend: A pretty pile. You are choking in money.

Faber: (shouts aloud) It is blood money, native son!

Friend: What?! Blood money, and a Jew is playing with it?

Faber: He is playing with Württemberg. The Jew plays with your daughters, and the Duke controls the bank!

Süss: (pounces on Faber) You are attacking the Duke. It will you cost your life!

(The friend holds on to Süss, and Faber struggles free and escapes)

Süss: Take off your mask, rebel!

Friend: It is the freedom of the masquerade, Hebrew!

32. Exterior. Palace Stairs

(Faber and his friend escape)

Faber: That was well done.

Friend: My heart is pounding in my throat.

33. Interior. The Duke's Workroom

(The Duke and Süss enter, the Duke sits and Süss serves him a drink)

Süss: Whoever insults me, insults the Duke.

Duke: (in contempt) So, no great matter. There is still a small difference. Don't get so worked up. Swallow it.

Süss: Your Royal Highness. I request that you think for a moment of your welfare. As long as the prohibition exists against the entry of Jews into Stuttgart, any vagabond can insult his Royal Highness' minister.

Duke: Well then, you'll get what you want. I abolish the prohibiton against entry of the Jews into Stuttgart.

Süss: (somewhat surprised) Will that become law?

Duke: It is the law if I say so.

Süss: Thank you, your Royal Highness, but if I am to serve His Highness loyally...

Duke: (cuts him off) That's still not enough for you?

Süss: Your Royal Highness, I wish nothing for myself. I wish the success of Your Highness, and I need a power of attorney.

Duke: A power of attorney?

Süss: Yes, Royal Highness, a power of attorney that will declare that all my actions are for the benefit of His Royal Highness and according to his will, and that in any situation I am under the patronage of His Royal Highness.

Duke: Well, that is the greatest arrogance I have ever encountered!

Süss: If that is so, is Your Royal Highness of the opinion that a citizen of Stuttgart can threaten His Highness' Minister of the Treasury with a blacksmith's hammer?

Duke: Who did so?

Süss: The blacksmith Hans Bogner.

Duke: The blacksmith Hans Bogner will be hanged!

34. Exterior. The Marketplace

(The blacksmith Bogner is hoisted inside the hanging cage. The crowd looks on. Süss and his mistress are watching the scene from the balcony. Levy is at their side)

Mistress: Aren't you afraid, Süss?

Süss: You needn't be afraid. I have a power of attorney from the Duke. Nothing can happen to us.

Man A: (shouts) You whore of the Jews!

Levy: (in a whisper) Did you hear Reb Yosef?

Man B: Watch out you dirty Jew, you are next!

Süss: Arrest him!

Levy: I have enough enemies, Reb Yosef.

228

Süss: (points out the cage) They can't hang me higher than that anyway.
Guild Head: (to Süss) That's what you think, My Lord Minister of the Treasury:

35. Exterior. The City Gate
(A convoy of the Jews' wagons, loaded to overflowing, passes through the city gate. At the head of the procession, a Jew is singing in Hebrew)

36. Interior. The Assembly House
(The Council of the Eleven is meeting)
Faber: (angrily) The Jews are entering the town by the hundreds. The people are bitter.
Sturm: Like locusts, they are falling upon our country. Herr Oppenheimer is already determining the taxes. The Jew controls the silver, salt, beer, wine, and even the grain.
A: (rises) And even our wives and daughters!
Von Röder: Easy now, you have already submitted a complaint.
B: The Duke has forbidden written complaints.
Von Röder: The Duke cannot forbid us anything. He swore on the constitution. Furthermore, he will soon hear what our veteran officer has to say.
B: You will burn you mouth, sir.
Sturm: It is preferable that we burn our mouths, and not our blood. The mouth belongs to us, but the blood belongs to our children, and to our children's children.

37. Exterior. Steps of the Palace
(Von Röder and a delegation of the Assembly climb the stairs)
Von Röder: To the Duke!

38. Interior. A Hall in the Palace
(The head of the delegation, Neufer, stands at the entrance)

Neufer: Now?
Von Röder: Announce my arrival!
Neufer: His Highness is sleeping.
Von Röder: So wake him!
(Von Röder and the delegation pass by Neufer and approach the Duke's

bedroom door. **A Mameluke** stands before it. Neufer follows them)
Mameluke: Your Highness.
Von Röder: Let me enter.
Neufer: It's forbidden.
Von Röder: (to Neufer) I saved his life at Petrordine. Don't make yourself so important. (to the Mameluke) Do you still remember it?
Mameluke: How could Mula el Hassan ben Omar ever forget, Your Highness?

39. Interior. The Duke's Study

(Von Röder enters and the entourage follows. The Duke rises from his place)
Duke: My friend Röder. Ah. How good it is for you to visit your old general.
(to Neufer), Ah, Neufer, bring some wine. (to Röder) Come, sit, Röder. What is the matter?
Von Röder: (approaches the Duke excitedly) I come in the name of the Assembly. The Assembly has sent a commission regarding the abolition of the prohibition forbidding Jews to enter the city.
Duke: And so? What do my Schwabians say?
Von Röder: My general, I stood at your side in the thick of the fire at Petrordine, and I am used to being direct. I must tell you exactly what I think. Expel the Jews, and stand at the side of our Schwabians.
Duke: Do you stand with the renegades? Huhh?
Von Röder: (in resignation) With all my heart, Your Highness.

40. Interior. Süss' Workroom

(Süss sits at the table. Levy is by his side)
Levy: He sides with the renegades and has succeeded in arranging an interview with the Duke.
Süss: That's not so.
Levy: He is in his room.
Süss: I would like to see that. (They rush out)

41. Interior. Hiding place

(Süss and Levy go up the stairs to the hiding place and look through a crack in the wall into the Duke's room)
Duke: Nonsense, gossip! Gossip! Once and for all. The Assembly does not exist in order to rule over the Duke or cancel his will.
Sturm: If His Highness no longer upholds the constitution ...

230

42. Interior. The Duke's Study

(The Duke and the Assembly delegation are in the room. Süss and Levy are eavesdropping through the hole in the wall)

Sturm: (continues) Let the Duke at least follow the advice of Luther who said: "Christian, know that apart from the devil you have no more venomous enemy than a true Jew. I would like to give you my loyal advice, that you first burn their synagogues, their schools,..."

43. Interior. Hiding place

(Süss and Levy are eavesdropping through the hole in the wall)

Sturm: (continues, outside the picture) "Secondly that their..."

44. Interior. The Duke's Study

Sturm: (continues and reads aloud) "books of prayer and the Talmud, in which they teach all manner of idolatry and lies, be taken from them ... third, that all ..."

Duke: (interrupts him angrily) I don't give a damn about your Luther!

Von Röder: As a veteran soldier, I am of the opinion that if the Jew wishes to carry out his disgusting designs on our wives and daughters, then you, my Duke, must stop him.

Duke: (boiling) Röder, do you have complaints to bring against me? I will put you in prison! (takes a step towards the delegation)

Sturm: Let His Royal Highness place the entire population of Württemberg into prison!

Duke: (shrieking) I can do just that! You rebels! I can forget who I am if I keep on looking at you ... Get out!!

45. Interior. Hiding place

(From the viewing point of Süss and Levy, through the hole in the wall)

Duke: (continues) Get out! (The camera moves backward. Süss and Levy are revealed)

Süss: Come, Levy. (They go)

Duke: (exhausted) Neufer, my pipe. Call the Minister of the Treasury, Oppenheimer.

46. Interior. Süss' Workroom

(Süss and Levy return to the room.)

Levy: May God enlighten him, so that he'll destroy them with fire and the

sword. (Knocking of the door. Enter Neufer)
Neufer: Your Highness, (Süss gets up, starts towards him) His Majesty
wants to see you.
(Süss leaves with Neufer. Levy murmurs a prayer)

Duke: (turns to face Süss who enters) You have got me into a mess with
your Jews. What should I do with my Assembly now?
Süss: If your Royal Highness asked me, I would say destroy them!
Destroy them with fire and the sword.
Duke: Destroy?
Süss: Dissolve the Assembly. Establish a ministry of loyal followers; stuff
the mouths of those who cry out, especially that Sturm.
Duke: (paces back and forth) Süss, Süss, you are suggesting dangerous
methods.
Süss: Everyone must believe in his own star, Your Royal Highness.
Duke: Do you understand the stars?
Süss: (draws near to the Duke) I know someone who does. If your Royal
Highness were to command, he would reveal your fortune, and then Your
Royal Highness could be reassured. I know that the position of the planets
is positive.

47. Interior. Süss' Bedroom
(A magnificent bed decorated with the Star of David; Süss approaches
accompanied by Rabbi Loew)

Süss: The location of the stars is favorable, Rabbi, because it must be
favorable.
Loew: It is possible to say that they must be favorable, but is it possible to
determine their position as one likes? I ...
Süss: One cannot determine the paths of the stars, but can one not
determine the paths of men if one leads them to believe that the stars are
with them.
Loew: My son Yosef, God is looking at you too, and sees that you have
become vain and proud like a peacock. God's punishment is hard if the
Jews forget who they are.
Süss: What must I do Rabbi?
Loew: Don't you have a palace like that of King Solomon's? (strikes Süss'
book case with his cane) Don't you have a wall full of books which are
forbidden to be read? (feels the cloth of the curtain) Didn't this
damascene cloth cost at least twelve thalers?
Süss: But, Rabbi ...

232

Loew: Look, the Lord wishes His people to serve him in sackcloth and ashes, and be dispersed so that they can secretly dominate the peoples of the world.

Süss: How can I rule if I don't show myself to the people?

Loew: If you wish to rule the gentiles, first rule over their money! But don't get involved in the disputes of princes.

Süss: If I rule over the prince, then I rule over his people.

Loew: The people will pardon a prince, but hang a Jew.

Süss: God's will cannot prevent me from turning Württemberg into a holy land for the people of Israel! It is already spread out before us. I simply have to catch it in my hand. I can already see how the milk and honey is flowing for the people of Israel. Can it be that now it is God's will to prevent me from casting my hands over the Jordan? ... Can this be God's will?

Loew: You interpret God's will as your will.

Süss: One must interpret God's will as Israel's will. That is the will of the Lord, Rabbi.

Loew: What should I do, lie?

Süss: You don't have to lie. Tell him the other truth according to our way. Lead him to our password, Attempto.

Loew: What does Attempto mean?

Süss: The one who dares.

48. Interior. The Telescope Room

(Loew is at the telescope. The Duke and Süss enter)

Duke: Sit. Well, what do you see?

Loew: ... the sky. Mars intertwined with the sun in a square with Jupiter; Jupiter in a positive transition to the rising star. The Lord is great, and magnificent are his signs.

Duke: How do you see the future?

Loew: How can my eyes see what God hides? He allows the stars and the moons to turn in such a way as to brighten our paths, or to threaten us, but only He knows the meaning of these things

Duke: Let me see my star.

Loew: (rises from his place and the Duke sits down at the telescope) May God bless the eye that can find what it is looking for among millions. Is it good like that? ...

Duke: What is the name of my star?

Loew: What a question, Duke. Why, it is Mars!

Duke: And what do you call that red one there on the horizon?

Loew: Venus, in opposition to Mars.

Duke: (rubbing his eyes) It is hopping up and down in front of my eyes, a thing of the devil. Tell me clearly: Should I dare, or do the stars object?
Loew: (consults a book and leafs the pages) The stars are not favorable or hostile. But it is written that they respond to the one who dares. It is written here.
Duke: To the one who dares, that is my motto – Attempto. It is good then. I will dare. Come, Süss, you will create this ministry for me.
(The duke goes. Süss kisses the Rabbi's coat)
Dissolve

49. Interior. Süss' Workroom

(Sturm is waiting. Levy appears at the door of the waiting room)
Levy: His Royal Highness bids you enter. (Sturm enters)
Süss: Oh, my friend. I thank you for coming. Please sit down. We are alone, so let's drop all the formalities. You have confidence in me, and I will pay you back for that confidence. Our ruler plans to gather men he can trust around him, and he has thought first and foremost of you.
Sturm: I don't know why.
Süss: I have therefore asked you to come. The Duke is weighing the possibility of creating a ministry and wants you to lead it.
Sturm: I can't accept it. I swore before the Assembly.
Sturm: You gave your oath to the Duke as well.
Sturm: I only do what is correct.
Süss: And so does the Duke. My friend, don't you want to help him in this?
Sturm: I don't trust his advisor.
Süss: (rises and approaches Sturm) I know that from a reliable source. You understand? But why should we be enemies when we could be much more than just friends? You have a charming daughter.
Sturm: What does that have to do with anything?
Süss: You will undoubtedly understand if I tell you that I have decided to take a wife.
Sturm: You mean my daughter?
Süss: Legally, My Lord Chairman of the Assembly.
Sturm That is not possible. No, I am sorry, no.
Süss: You won't say no, you will say yes and yes again if you really think it over well.
Sturm: There is nothing to think about. My daughter is already promised to somebody.
Süss: Is that so? I will give you time to think the matter over, until tomorrow.

234

Sturm: Until tomorrow.

50. Interior. A Church

(Faber and Dorothea kneel, organ music is heard in the background, the musical theme is "All My Thoughts," a ring is placed on Dorothea's finger)

Priest: I entwine your hands in the eyes of God. Your love will be as pure as gold. Your faithfulness will be forever like these rings. Be man and wife before God in heaven until death do you part. Remember, nothing without holiness is worthwhile, and only a life without illusions is true.

51. Interior. Sturm's Workroom.

(Süss is led in by the servant girl)

Süss: I have the honor, Lord Chairman of the Assembly.

Sturm(rises from his place) Lord Minister of the Treasury.

Süss: The period of deliberations is over.

Sturm: My decision was final and did not change in the course of one night. You know well that my daughter was promised to my secretary, Herr Faber.

Süss: You can use your fatherly influence!

Sturm: Even if I could, I wouldn't do it. My daughter will not bring little dirty Jews into the world.

Süss: Is that so?

Sturm: I see we have understood each other.

Süss: It would be dangerous to refuse a man in my position. I ask you to think about it.

Sturm: I have nothing more to think over. My daughter is already married.

Süss: Since when?

Sturm: Since last night.

Süss Where do you get the courage for such arrogance?

Sturm: (approaches Süss in a threatening manner). Damn it, I stand here in my capacity as Chairman of the Assembly, and in so doing I ask you, where do you get the audacity to burst into my family tranquility in the same manner as you violated the tranquility of this land?

Süss: In your place...

Sturm: (cuts him off) Where do you get the impertinence to advise the Duke to act against the constitution? Yes, where do you get such impertinence, you scum! (shakes Süss by the collar) To sow hatred between the Duke and his people?!

Süss: I thank the Lord Chairman of the Assembly for his frankness.
(Süss exits. Sturm hurries to open the window)
Sturm: Clean air!

52. Interior. Süss' Workroom

(Süss enters in anger. Levy sits down at the desk)
Süss: Write!
Levy: What is the matter, Yosef? Why are you shouting at me?
Süss: Write! According to documented eye-witness testimony, it has been proved that he is involved in a plot against Your Royal Highness, the Duke, a plot which is based on rebellion ... and therefore the Ministry of the Treasury orders that procedures against him begin immediately.
Levy: (while writing) Against whom?
Süss: Against the Chairman of the Assembly.
Dissolve

53. Interior. Investigation Room of the Ministry of the Treasury

(Levy and the clerk Metz are interrogating Sturm)
Levy: Ha, where is the answer?
Sturm: I don't recognize you as a judge or this room as a court.
Metz: My Lord Chairman of the Assembly, we are sitting here as agents of the Duke.
Sturm: There is no meaning to it. If Jews judge Württembergians, then that is against the constitution and Württembergian honor.
Metz: Sturm, I am convinced that you did not violate the law.
Levy. Really, you are convinced, Lord Clerk. So, to the matter. Did you not plan on Sunday afternoon, on the 27th of last month, an assassination attempt against the life of His Royal Highness, the Duke?
Sturm: Now it is beginning to be funny. Continue with your text.
Levy: Did you not say on that certain Sunday in the home of Wisneze in the presence of witnesses whose reliability is unimpeachable: "What happened to the blacksmith Bogner was criminal murder?..."
(Sturm is surprised)
Levy: (continues) Did you or didn't you say it?
Sturm: (angrily) Yes, I said it. So what?
Levy: Don't pretend. If there was a murder, then who is the murderer? Obviously the one who sentenced him. And who was it who sentenced him? Who signed the death warrant? The Duke, of course. Therefore in your opinion the Duke is a murderer.
Sturm: Ah, that's what you're getting at?

Levy: Yes, and what does one do with a murderer for whom there is no repentance, even if he is His Royal Highness, the Duke.

Sturm: Even if it were the Emperor, I would still call him before a judge if he had acted contemptuously against the law.

Levy: Even His Royal Majesty the Emperor isn't holy in your eyes. I have the desire to rip my clothes off my body in mourning. Well, are you still of the opinion that the charge of treason is not appropriate?

Sturm: If there is anything that degrades His Royal Highness, the Emperor and the Duke's name, it is your dirty and stinking malicious gossip.

Metz: Sturm, Sturm, you are getting more deeply involved.

Sturm: But Herr Metz, can't you feel how they are distorting things in order to find a reason to eliminate me? Are you lending a hand to an act created by this Talmudic Jewish mind?

54. Dorothea's Room

(Dorothea changes the sheets. Faber stands in the doorway, approaches and helps her)

Dorothea: Enter. Why are you afraid? You will sleep in my bed today and I will sleep downstairs in the salon.

Faber: But Dorla, you don't know if your father will agree.

Dorothea: Come already and help me hold the ends. I can't manage by myself. Why should he object? After all, we are husband and wife.

Faber: But one must get used to it, ... oh, Dorla.

Dorothea: You are already sighing. I have got used to it. I have yearned so for this day, Faber.

Faber: I imagined my wedding day differently.

Dorothea: So did I, I think Father also regrets it.

Faber: You mean, because of the Jew.

Dorothea: Most of all because of the rush in which everything had to be arranged. Oh, from the day I first remember myself, there has never been an evening when I did not sit together with Father. But believe me Faber, in spite of everything, we are happy. You are my husband, my shield, and that is my happiness.

(They kiss, the servant girl appears at the door.)

Servant girl: Excuse me.

Dorothea: You always come at the wrong moment.

Servant girl: (curtsies) Pardon me. Colonel Röder is below and wants to see madam.

Dorothea: Does he want to see me or my father?

Servant girl: No. You and Master Faber.

55. Interior. Entrance to Sturm's House

(Von Röder is waiting. Dorothea and Faber descend the steps quickly)

Dorothea: Good evening, Herr Von Röder. You are bringing us congratulations. Is that not so, Herr Von Röder?

Von Röder: There is no time for that. Your father has been taken by force, and imprisoned in the palace.

Dorothea: (frightened) Why?

Von Röder: I don't know.

Dorothea: The Jew?

Von Röder: I myself am bringing the summons to the Assembly because I didn't want anyone else to inform you of the imprisonment. In another hour a special session of the Assembly will meet.

56. Interior. The Assembly House

(The members of the Assembly are being heard)

Faber: Lord Advisor to the assembly, Phillip Heinrich Wisneze,

Wisneze: Here.

Faber: My Lord, The Mayor of Tübingen.

Mayor: Here.

Faber: (continues) Konstadt!

Konstadt: Here.

Faber: From Ludwigsburg?

Ludwigsburg: Here.

Faber: From Wissenburg?

Wissenburg: Here.

Faber: From Berkenheim?

Berkenheim: Here.

Faber: (continues) The blacksmith and Guild Head, Peter Eugen? (Peter Eugen raises his hand)

Faber: (continues) Damsler!

Damsler: Here.

Faber: (continues) All are here except for one.

Von Röder: All of you in this hall know, of course, where the missing one is.

Member A: Release him!

Von Röder: Patience. That is not so easy. You know exactly who arrested him, and he is sitting more securely than ever before. As long as the Duke listens to him, it may be that the Assembly will have nothing further to say here in Württemberg.

Wisenze: What do you mean by that?

Guild Head: It means that the Duke is acting against the constitution.

Faber: He wants to create a government and abolish the Assembly.
Von Röder: That is a blow against the constitution.
Wisneze: He would never dare to do that.
Von Röder: It would not be the first time. It has already happened several times in our history that someone has violated the constitution.
A: What arrogance!
B: I suggest we prevent the creation of this government, by force if need be.
Guild Head: And demand the release of the Chairman of The Assembly, Sturm.
Von Röder: All those who agree, raise hands. (They all raise their hands) **Dissolve.**

57. Interior. A Great Hall in the Palace

(The Duke is speaking before a group of people. Süss is at his side. Behind them are the guards)
Duke: As a result of the grave events against the government and against me, I have decided, gentlemen, to call you to form a government which will be responsible to me alone. It has become known to me that during the night a special session of the Assembly was held in the Assembly House. As my advisor, Herr Oppenheimer has informed me that it was decided to arrest me. For my own security I have decided (shouts) to dissolve the Assembly immediately. This law has already been placed in Herr Oppenheimer's hands. I thank you. (He leaves, the guards salute)

58. Interior. Palace Corridor

(Neufer leads Von Röder through the corridor. On their way they meet The Mameluke; Neufer continues but Von Röder stops)
Von Röder: (to the Mameluke) Mula, from now on I want to know everything the Jew says to the Duke.
Neufer: (to Von Röder) His Royal Highness will receive you in his workroom.

59. Interior. The Duke's Study

(The Duke enters accompanied by Von Remchingen and Süss)
Duke: Ah, Herr Von Röder...
Von Röder: Your Highness, please pardon this interruption, the Assembly has designated responsibility to me to announce to His Royal Highness...

Duke: (cuts him off) I already know, Herr Von Röder. I don't always have to wait until you come to bring me up to date.

Von Röder: Your Royal Highness, allow me to show you my diligence, and how much the welfare of His Royal Highness is important to me. Your Highness' welfare is in serious danger but it is not yet too late.

Duke: (strikes his scepter on the table in anger) Not too late! The people are being incited against the Duke, rebels and traitors like Sturm are in league together, they are making decisions, threatening with arrest ... what in hell would you call that?

Von Röder: A public rising for the benefit of His Royal Highness.

Duke: (sits in his chair) So what? As a soldier, what do you have to say?

Von Röder: Always the same thing, my Duke, get rid of the Jew.

Süss: If I am the stumbling block, His Royal Highness would...

Duke: (cuts him off) I want to tell you something Herr Von Röder. (rises and threateningly) Your Assembly has been conferring in secret. Even the best soldier knows about as much about ruling a country as a bull does about playing the piccolo. But my Minister of the Treasury is a genius. He brings me money, profits, gives me advice, he brings me...

Von Röder: (cuts him off) Enemies!

(The Duke sits back again in his chair, dismisses Von Röder's word with a wave of his hand)

Von Röder: (continues) Only enemies.

Duke: I will run you down, Herr Von Röder. I have nothing to add. Get Out! Out! Out!

(Von Röder leaves, the Duke appears feeble in his chair)

Duke: (continues) The man is right, unfortunately. You are creating an opposition greater than I can overcome.

Süss: There are examples of a prince overcoming opposition if he has friends he can rely on.

Duke: But I have no friends.

Süss: I will arrange it, Your Royal Highness, I will go find powerful friends for you.

Duke: What do you mean?

Süss: I have already begun negotiations with Wurtzburger. Let not His Royal Highness underestimate the solidarity among princes. Wurtzburger has soldiers one may rent.

Duke: :(doubtful) Rent soldiers? Rent soldiers? (amusingly) That is a Jewish idea, like it is written in books.

Von Remchingen: But a good idea, Your Royal Highness.

Duke: Von Remchingen come closer! (Remchingen bends over towards the Duke.) What do you advise me Remchingen if open hostilities break out between me and my Swabians. You yourself are a Swabian,

Remchingen. So is your Duke. But for the Jew, to be a Swabian means nothing.

Duchess: (enters the room) You have problems, Karl Alexander?

Duke: You were listening again, ha?

Duchess: You spoke in such a loud voice that I did not need to eavesdrop. (points to Süss) Do what he asks for.

Duke: What do you understand about politics, my child?

Duchess: (approaches the Duke, bends over towards him) Little or nothing, but I understand men. Depend on your Minister of the Treasury.

Duke: Do you love me at all?

Duchess: Yes, Karl Alexander. And I would love you even more if you were daring like...

Duke: Like your friend, Oppenheimer?

Duchess: (strokes the Duke) Like you were before Belgrade and Petrordine.

Duke: I was young then.

Duchess: You can be young again, today. Listen to your friend.

Duke: Are you really my friend?

Duchess: I think so.

Duke: (to Von Remchingen) Remchingen, leave me alone with my wife.

Duchess: (goes toward the door) No, no, I will leave you alone here. I am holding my fingers crossed, Karl Alexander. (departs and throws a kiss in the air)

Duke: I am no longer free in my decisions.

Süss: But Your Royal Highness, why not?

Duke: You think that if I listen to you now, then I will have to listen to you in the future? Don't you? If I want to or not ... You have also stolen the heart of the Duchess ... only her heart?

Süss: I do not understand.

Duke: (shouts) I ask if it was only her heart?! (approaches Süss in a threatening way)

Süss: (retreats) What do you mean, Your Royal Highness?

Duke: I mean that nothing is sacred to you, not even your Duke's wife, you dirty Jew, only your interests, your profit!

Süss: Apparently Your Royal Highness doesn't believe me.

Duke: Right, I don't believe you.

60. Exterior. The Square In Front of the Palace

(Crowds are seen running toward the palace)

Crowd: (screaming) Sturm! Sturm! Sturm! Sturm!

61. Interior. Corridor in the Palace

(The Duke, Von Remchingen and Süss go towards the window)
Süss: This is the way revolutions generally begin.
Von Remchingen: If a bullet is let loose, there will be panic.
Süss: The palace guard, a thousand men. It will be a bloody massacre if His Royal Highness doesn't decide in time. Against the people one has to demonstrate power that will intimidate them.
Duke: Is it true that the Wurtzburger used an army by the Pfalzneuburg?
Süss: Absolutely true, Your Royal Highness. Von Remchingen can confirm it.
Duke: Remchingen, is that true?
Von Remchingen: Documented, your Royal Highness.
Duke: You mean a revolt!
Von Remchingen: This, Your Royal Highness, will make you an absolute ruler.
Süss: Like the king in Versailles.
Duke: How much does it cost to rent soldiers, how much does it cost?
Süss: Ahhem..How much does His Royal Highness need?
Duke: I estimate four or five thousand soldiers.
Süss: Four or five thousand soldiers are needed to hold the position, that is to say for three or four months. His Royal Highness' treasury is in any case not...but the Jews His Highness allowed to enter Stuttgart are indebted to His Royal Highness. I will see what can be done.

62. Interior. Synagogue.

(Jews are praying in festive holiday dress
Rabbi Loew is seen with the Torah Scroll. Süss is at the entrance)
Süss: (to Rabbi Loew) Rabbi, Rabbi!
(Rabbi Loew goes out to meet Süss while the others continue praying)

63. Interior. Corridor

(Loew approches Süss)
Loew: You are disturbing the holy ritual. Can't you wait?
Süss: No, Rabbi. There is no time. You must speak for me to the congregation.
Loew: Why are you in such a hurry? Whoever does not have enough time for prayer will fall on his way.
Süss: Time is fine Rabbi, but everything at its proper time. But now I need from the community five times 100,000 thalers.
Loew: From the community, five times ... Have you gone crazy?

242

Süss: Listen, I came to you in the synagogue because everyone is together here. The Assembly wants to expel the Jews from Stuttgart but the Duke would be willing to abolish the Assembly with one blow. I have led him to that decision. He will become an absolute ruler and then his hand will protect the Jews.

Loew: What do you want, for the Jews to become soldiers?

Süss: No, only that they pay. Soldiers cost money.

Loew: Süss, do you want to fight against the gentiles? Do you want to be Mordechai who killed approximately 75,000 of them for Esther the queen. Then you must take off the clothes of the gentiles and become a son of Israel.

Süss: Rabbi, Rabbi. You don't see the necessity of the hour but I do, because I sit at the source. If the Jews give 500,000 thalers today, then I will see to it that the Duke never forgets that the Jews gave him the money that placed him on the throne, but if they are stingy and hide behind clever Talmudic passages, then they will lose everything, including, maybe, their lives.

Loew: Come, pray with us. You and your ideas will find favor in the eyes of the Lord and the brethren will see you standing at my side. Afterwards, we will talk to them.

64. Interior. Syngagogue

(The Jews are praying. Loew and Süss approach several of them and speak. A congregant closes the Holy Ark)

65. Interior. Sturm's Music Room

Dorothea: (sings sadly) All my thoughts are of you, my chosen one. (weeps)

Servant girl: Dorothea, it will be all right.

Dorothea: I was in church. I ran through the streets. I was at my mother's grave. I prayed but it didn't help me, nor does my singing. This is already the third night that I haven't heard anything from Father. And my husband has no time to spend with me. (sobs. Faber arrives)

Faber: Dorothea.

(They embrace)

Dorothea: I cannot get up. I am in shock because you are here. It is good that you are here, Faber. You mustn't leave me alone. You must never leave me alone! They were here today and went through all the closets and drawers.

Faber: They won't find anything against your father. They can look wherever they want. But I cannot stay with you, Dorothea.

Dorothea: Where are you going?

Faber: Don't ask where I have been or where I am going.

Dorothea: Are you going again? To the Assembly House?

Faber: The Assembly House. The Assembly House is closed and a guard stands watch over it.

Dorothea: Why?

Faber: The revolution has begun.

Dorothea: And Father?

Faber: We will free him.

Dorothea: Must you go already?

Faber: I came so you would know that nothing has happened to me.

Dorothea: And if I never see you again Faber, if this is the last time I hold you in my arms, Faber?

Faber: But Dorla, I am sure that...

Dorothea: Don't speak, I want to hear the beating of your heart.

66. Interior. The Ministry of the Treasury

(The clerks, Metz and Hollweg are sitting at the table. Sturm is nervously pacing up and down)

Metz: Yes, My Lord, Chairman of the Assembly, the papers testifying to your treason were found in your house, in your desk drawer, and in your own handwriting.

Sturm: How many times do I have to tell you: everything is forged by that treacherous dirty Jew.

Süss: Beware, Lord Chairman of the Assembly. In Hanufein there are cells from which you won't be able to see the sun or the moon.

Sturm: You won't be able to silence me in prison.

Süss: Just my signature, and you are a hanged man.

Sturm: I am not afraid of death.

Süss: So, you are a hero, eh? It is never too late to learn. Well, all right. I want to be alone. The guard may also leave. (they leave)

Süss: (continues) Sturm, I want only what is good for you. I will not touch a hair on your head, and will even free you tonight; just agree to be a minister. Well, really, in your situation, I would only be too glad if someone made me an offer like that.

Sturm: I prefer to hang and not break my oath.

Süss: I don't understand you Sturm. I offer you position, power, a title; I offer you as much honor as you could want.

Sturm: And what do you know of honor?

Süss: Don't be obstinate like this. I need your good name for my government.

Sturm: Ah, hah!

Süss: You will be the guarantee for bridging conflicts. So, isn't that something?

Sturm: For you, not for me.

Süss: Is that your last word?

Sturm: Certainly!

Süss: All right, but all the responsibility rests on you. What I am offering is for your own good and the good of your daughter.

Sturm: (cuts him off) Please leave my daughter out of this dirty game.

Süss: Why? Why leave her out of it? Why not ask her? Perhaps her father's suffering will touch her heart?

67. Interior. A Beer Cellar

(The members of the Assembly are meeting in secret. Von Röder and Faber enter)

Von Röder: A Jobian development, comrades. The Duke wants to disperse the Assembly with the help of foreign troops.

Faber: That's civil war.

A: He wouldn't dare to do that!

Von Röder: I know it for a certainty from the Duke's Mameluke servant. The Jew arranged the whole affair. The Jews are financing the Duke's war against his people.

Faber: Unless we beat him to it!

Von Röder: Von Remchingen wants to act within three days.

Faber: In three days?

Von Röder: If so, then in another two days, we need to be ready. All the people must arm themselves. I will see to it.

B: The Assembly's instructions must be made known this very night.

Von Röder: If you can. There is a double watch on the city gates until the evening.

Faber: I will pass as the Duke's messenger.

Wisneze: Why are you in such a hurry? Without the password, no one will pass by the guard.

Von Röder: The password is Karl Alexander.

Dissolve.

68. Exterior. The City Gate

Faber: (approaches the gate, mounted on a horse) A special messenger of the Duke. Open!

Guard: The Password?

Faber: Karl Alexander.

Guard: In the name of the Duke, you are under arrest! (The guards take him off his horse by force)

Faber: What does this mean?

Guard: The password from midnight is "Attempto". You are not a messenger. Take him immediately to the palace of the Minister of the Treasury, by his order.

Dissolve

69. Interior. A Corridor in Süss' Palace

(A Soldier of the guard goes up the stairs with Süss and hands him papers)

Soldier: These are the secret orders we found on him.

70. Interior. Süss' Workroom

(Faber is held by the soldiers. Süss joins them)

Süss: Ah, it is the husband of Dorothea Sturm. Her Christian husband. (to Faber) For whom are these orders meant?

Soldier: (To Faber) Turn around.

Süss: For whom are these orders?

Soldier: (strikes Faber) Speak!

Faber: (against his will) To Württemberg.

Süss: To Württemberg, so? Give me the names of the participants! Who is supposed to be ready within two days? Who is to be ready for the action?

Soldier: Open your mouth!

Süss: So, who are the plotters. Who wants a civil war?

Faber: You

Süss: I? Interesting.

Faber: You want a revolt. You advised it to the Duke, didn't you?

Süss: I am the one who asks the questions, not you, and it will be a lot less pleasant for you.(To the soldier) Torture him on the rack without mercy until he talks.

71. Interior. The Drawingroom in Sturm's House

(Dorothea paces the room, weeping and distraught; sad music: Dorothea's motif)

246

72. Interior. The Duke's Study

(The Duke is sitting between Süss and Von Remchingen)

Duke: What is written here?

Süss: That the Assembly wants to act in two days.

Duke: Is that so? And what about us?

Süss: If we don't want to lose everything, Your Royal Highness, we must act sooner. There's just another two days left.

Von Remchingen: Everything depends upon us surprising them tomorrow night.

Duke: With whom?

Süss: I won't be able to bring the Wurtzburgers by tomorrow. We must use our own army!

Duke: You really are a dirty Jew! Do you know what you are advising me? For a Württemberger to shoot a Württemberger?

Von Remchingen: Your Royal Highness does not have to be present.

Duke: No! I won't cooperate.

Süss: All right, Your Royal Higness wishes then to be the faithful servant of your Assembly.

Duke: Shut up, you bastard!

Süss: I wish to resign my office.

Duke: (grabs hold of Süss' chin) So you want to get out of this, hah? Now you want to leave by the back door. Take heed. Remchingen, see to it that this Jew bastard remains close by.

Süss: Does His Royal Highness wish to hear my advice in these circumstances?

Duke: Go ahead and speak.

Süss: The banquet that Your Royal Highness is arranging to honor the representative of the Emperor, can be a proper setting. Your Royal Highness is travelling tomorrow as a constitutional Duke to Ludwigsburg, and will return the day after tomorrow ... as an absolute monarch.

Duke: As an absolute monarch? Within a day and a night? All honor to you! That's what I call a turn-about.

Süss: It's a revolution, Your Royal Highness!

Duke: Good, I am going to Ludwigsburg. Inform the Duchess.

73. Interior. The Torture Chamber Opposite Süss' Window.

(Faber is in the chamber together with an interrogator and a torturer)

Interrogator: To the seat! For ten minutes! But ·wait for my signal.

Torturer: (leads Faber to the torture instrument, seizes his hand) Look, here we put the fingers. You see, don't you want to take off your ring? Oh, it's a wedding ring, leave it then! Look, a horseshoe, isn't it? They say a horseshoe brings good luck, no?

74. Interior. A Room in Süss' Palace
(Dorothea enters. Süss is seated and is eating breakfast)
Süss: Only the Duke may pardon the traitors ... you should know that.
Dorothea: But the Duke is in Ludwigsburg. I beg you, Your Royal Highness, help me. (shows the paper in her hand) I have recorded everything. Here, here is the request.
Süss: What will the Duke do with the request? (closes the door after Dorothea) He will rip it to pieces just as I am doing. (tears up the paper and then sits on the couch) He will execute the traitors.
Dorothea: Mercy....have you no heart?
Süss: I had a heart. I was always merciful, young lady – pardon, madam...
(Dorothea looks at her hand)
Süss: (continues) A lovely ring, from your husband? In this case it will be very difficult to help (sighs).
Dorothea: Do you want the ring? It is a real gem (gives him the ring).
Süss: A small ring for a small hand. Do you want to see a ring? Look at this. Do you still think you can buy me with your small ring? Do you want this? (Süss comes from behind her and shows her his ring. Dorothea objects to his embrace and pushes him away. He falls and gets up in anger) Do you want to free your husband? You are doing a fine job of it! If a hunter frees a bird from the cage, then he needs another one to take its place. Do you understand that? (places a handkerchief on the window)

75. Interior. The Torture Chamber
(The interrogator looks at the high skylight)
Interrogator: The handkerchief is outside, let's go! (The torture applies the rack. Faber cries out in pain)
Interrogator: (continues) So, do you like that?

76. Interior. Room in Süss' Palace
(Dorothea is at the window and hears Faber's screams. Süss stands behind her)
Süss: Well, is that a familiar voice?
Dorothea: God in heaven!
Süss: Lift the handkerchief a moment, lift it. (She lifts the handkerchief and the screams cease) Do you still hear something? I mean... (places the handkerchief back and the screams begin again)

Dorothea: (understanding) Faber! (lifts the handkerchief. The screams cease)

Süss: Now, return my handkerchief to me. (Dorothea runs to the room and hides the handkerchief. Süss attempts to be passionate with her.)

Dorothea: No!

Süss: No? All right. So be it.

Dorothea: Our father, who art in heaven.

Süss: What, go ahead and pray, pray to your God. Pray. But it is not only you Christians who have a God. We Jews have one too. And He is the God of revenge. An eye for an eye. A tooth for a tooth. Thank your father.

Dorothea: Let me go!

Süss: Do you want me to see to it that the traitors are not taken out to be executed?

Dorothea: Don't touch me!

Süss: Don't be shy. Afterwards, you can return to your clerk. (Drags her to the bed. She screams. He pulls her down to the bed and falls on her)

77. Interior. The Torture Chamber

(Levy quickly goes down the stairs. Faber is sitting in the torture seat)

Levy: Stop! Stop! Free him immediately.

Interrogator: Why? He hasn't confessed yet.

Levy: Minister of the Treasury orders you to release him at once.

Interrogator: Who can understand this? (to Faber) Be on your way.

Faber: Where to?

Torturer: (pushes the weakened Faber) Go home!

Faber: Home? (He sways to and fro)

Torturer: Here's your pipe.

Faber: Whom must I thank for my release?

Torturer: Your beautiful young wife personally requested it from the Minister of the Treasury.

Faber: That can't be true!

Levy: Yes, yes, yes.

78. Exterior. The Bank of the River

(Dorothea runs in panic; her clothes are in disarray)

79. Exterior. A Street In Front of Süss' Palace

(Faber arrives exhausted and bearing the marks of torture. He knocks at the door. A servant comes out)

Servant: Yes?

Faber: Is the daughter of Assembly Chairman Sturm at home?

Servant: No she is not with me.

Faber: Don't avoid the question.

Servant: Well, there are many people who come and go. What do you care what they do? They all look the same when they leave here.

Faber: Was she with him?

Servant: Do you mean the young lady who wept so? That could be.

Faber: Where did she go?

Servant: Neckar Street. Go after her!

80. Exterior. The Bank of the River

(Small boats are sailing on the river, flaming torches; Faber stands on one of the boats and carries Dorothea in his arms. She has drowned. The boat arrives at the river bank and Faber gets off)

81. Exterior. Street In Front of Süss' Palace

(Faber carries Dorothea's body. He arrives at Süss' palace. The crowd follows behind him)

Faber: Jew! Jew!

(Levy appears at the window and looks down upon the mob. Von Röder and the Head of the Blacksmith's Guild approach Faber. Faber lays Dorothea's body on the steps of the palace)

Faber: (continues) Excuse me. The Jew is responsible for her death. Leave her.

A: Forward!

B: Kill the defiler!

C: Down with the Jew

Von Röder: Down with the Jew!

Mob: Yes, yes! (begins to assault the palace)

2. Interior. Süss' Workroom

(Levy retreats in panic from the window. The door is broken down, Levy attempts to hide. The people rush into the room. Levy closes his eyes in fear)

83. Exterior. The Palace Gate

(Von Röder and a delegation of the assembly mounted on horseback approach)

Von Röder: We want to got go to Ludwigsburg, to the Duke!

Von Remchingen: (approaches them with a drawn pistol) Colonel Von Röder, in the name of the Duke...

(Von Röder shoots him. Von Remchingen falls. The soldiers point their rifles at Von Röder)

Von Röder: Lower your rifles! Don't shoot, comrades!

Faber: He deserved it. The servant of the Jews!

Von Röder: We do not wish a civil war, but if you shoot now, no one will be able to prevent it. In the name of the Assembly, I demand that you open the gate! We need to get to Ludwigsburg, to the Duke!

Corporal: Open the gate!

84. Interior. The Grand Ballroom in the Ludwigsburg Palace

(The ball is at its height. Fireworks. The ambassador and the Duchess are seen together. The Duchess invites Süss to approach her)

Duchess: Well, Oppenheimer, sit.

Süss: Thank you.

Duchess: Well, whom are you looking for!

Süss: His Royal Highness, Duchess.

Ambassador: Please, Your Royal Highness.

Duchess: (whispers to Süss) I'm afraid the Duke has drunk too much. Go and tell him that Count Felpi is waiting for him below. Go!

85. Exterior. Fields.

(The delegation headed by Von Röder is riding hard towards Ludwigsburg)

86. Interior. A Room In the Palace of Ludwigsburg

(The Duke is lying in bed. Süss is at his side)

Duke: It's nothing Süss. It's just that I don't feel well. Bring a doctor to me tonight. Hasn't a messenger arrived yet?

Süss: Tomorrow, Your Royal Highness.

Duke: When? When?

Süss: Tomorrow at the very latest.

Duke: What are you saying? I thought he should be here any moment.

Süss: A joke, Your Highness?

Duke: (tries to rise) Stop with your jokes. (Süss and the Mameluke help him to sit) I am not in the mood for jokes. I don't understand anything. I don't understand. I don't understand where they are. I don't feel comfortable at all! Since Petrordine I haven't felt such a uneasiness in my body. (screams) Champagne!

87. Exterior. Fields
(A lone rider)

88. Interior. A Room in the Palace of Ludwigsburg.
(The Duke and Süss are sitting on the couch. The Mameluke serves champagne)
Duke: This is the best medicine. Champagne! (to Süss) Well, why aren't you drinking to my health? Ha? Why aren't you gulping it down, Jew!?
Süss: Wouldn't it be better if Your Royal Highness went down to the ball?
Duke: Fireworks, rockets, lighting, women, always the same thing. What lies behind it all? What is supposed to be behind it all? Always the same thing, Süss. Yes I have seen man in all kinds of situations, on the battlefield, on the dance floor and in bed, but today, it seems to me that it has always been the same. How you are looking at me, as if your face was taking pity!
Süss: What's the matter with you?
Duke: Take off your mask my friend.
Süss: What mask?
Duke: The last one, the last one! Oh how you look, how do you really look?
Süss: How should I look?
Duke: (spills champagne in Süss' face) Yes, yes, a joke. If you joke with me then you must know how to accept jokes.
Servant: (enters) Messengers would like to speak with the Duke.
Duke: Where are they? Let them enter. I have been waiting for them.
Servant: Down below in the garden. They do not wish to come up.
Duke: Bastards! My wig! (puts on his wig)

89. Interior. Reception Hall in the Palace of Ludwigsburg
(The Duke approaches the delegation, the Duchess tries to stop him)
Von Röder: In the name of the Assembly, Your Royal Majesty. Here are the demands of your people.
Duchess: Alexander!

252

Duke: Demands, demands?

Duchess: Alexander!

Duke: Who has the audacity to make demands of me?

Duchess: Alexander!

Duke: (pushes his wife aside) Go! Women have nothing to do here!

Duchess: Stop the music!

Von Röder: We know of your plans, Your Royal Majesty, and the Jew's advice. Therefore, we demand...

Duke: (cuts him off) You demand!? I think it is my turn to demand!

Süss: Nothing has changed, Your Royal Highness.

Von Röder: Not yet. The oath that Your Royal Highness gave to the Württembergian people is still in force, and we are asking you if it is your intention to keep your oath, or is the Jew dearer to you than your people?

Duke: My advisors are chosen by me and by no one else!

Faber: Your advisor is a murderer.

Süss: A lie!

Faber: He brought about my wife's death.

Süss: A libel! (attacks Faber, the two of them fall) A dastardly libel!

Duke: What!? You dare brawl before me (draws his sword), I'll hang you, you dogs! I'll hang the lot of you.

Duchess: Alexander!

(The Duke collapses, the Duchess kneels over him)

Alexander, Alexander, Alexander! Help! Doctor! Fetch a doctor!, Alexander, Alexander, Alexander. What is the matter with you?

Von Röder: (kneels over the Duke with his ear next to the Duke's heart) He is dead!

(The Duchess bursts into screams. Süss tries to escape)

Faber: Halt! (falls upon Süss and holds him. Von Röder also holds on to him) Herr Oppenheimer!

Von Röder: After the death of the Duke, the executive authority passes to the Assembly until the election of a new Duke. (To Süss) In the name of the Assembly, I arrest you!

Dissolve

90. A Courtroom

(Süss without a wig, his wild looking· beard has grown back. The courtroom is full)

Chief Judge: Here he sits, this Jew. During months of sessions he has not managed to bring any evidence on his behalf except lies, lies and more lies. His whole defence is based on the power of attorney given to him by the Duke and releasing him of all responsibility.

Süss: What are you accusing me of? I did nothing except at the will of my Duke (the audience laughs contemptuously). It is written in the power of attorney. You must read it. I was only the faithful servant of my ruler!

Audience: Foo!

Süss: Yes! Foo!

Chief Judge: (silences the audience) Decide in the end if this piece of paper obtained from the Duke by trickery can wipe out the list of crimes. Weigh and judge according to the law. We now will pass verdict.

Guild Head: Jew! The Head of the Blacksmiths' Guild is speaking to you. Does not your conscience torture you now?

Court Clerk: Acch, leave him be.

Guild Head: Did you not once say that it would be impossible to hang you higher than the member of our guild? The blacksmith Bogner?

Court Clerk: Be silent until the judges return with the verdict.

91. Interior. Judges' Office

(Among those present is also Sturm)

Chief Judge: After an examination of months, we find all the accusations correct. You know them: blackmail, provocations, corruption, sexual licentiousness, procurement, treason ... but the guilt of the Jew appears to me to be even greater if we take into account the shame, harm, and suffering which our people has had to bear because of him, and therefore, I am of the opinion that he who has been most insulted and injured should speak.

Sturm: Not revenge, only what he deserves.

Chief Judge: Speak freely, Sturm. You bore the worst suffering and therefore you have the right to judge.

Sturm: (Hands the book of laws to the chief judge) Suffering does not make justice! An eye for an eye and a tooth for a tooth is not our way. Look in the ancient code of criminal justice. There it is written forever... if a Jewish man and a Christian woman....

Chief Judge: If a Jew and a Christian woman become one flesh, he will lose his life on the gallows.

Dissolve

92. Exterior. The Marketplace

(Süss stands in the hanging cage next to the executioner. The square is full of people)

Chief Judge: (reads aloud) If a Jew and a Christian woman become one flesh, he will lose his. life on the gallows. To him – the punishment he

deserves; to others – as a deterrent and warning. (A drum roll, the executioner pushes Süss into the cage which is hoisted slowly upwards)
Süss: (screams and pleads) I was just a faithful servant of my ruler! (Snow begins to fall) What am I guilty of, if your Duke was a traitor? Take my money but spare my life! I ask for mercy. I am innocent. I am an unfortunate Jew. Spare my life! (The judge gives a sign to the hangman)
Süss: (continues) I want to live!
(The hangman pulls on the rope)
Süss: (continues) I want to live!
(The bottom of the cage falls out. Süss' legs fall through)
Süss: to liv ..... (his scream is interrupted by his death. Quiet music. Dorothea's motif)
Sturm: The Assembly expresses, through me, the will of the Württembergian people. All the Jews must leave Württemberg within three days! From now on there will be a curfew on the Jews throughout Württemberg! Declared in Stuttgart on the Fourth day of February one thousand seven hundred and thirty-eight, in order that our descendants keep this law so as to prevent great suffering to their property, lives and the blood of their children and their children's children.
Fade

THE END

FOOTNOTES

PART 1
1. The Art of Propaganda

1. *The American College Dictionary* (New York: Random House, 1970.)
2. Edmund Burke, *Thoughts on French Affairs, III* (London: Bohn Library, n.d.), p.356
3. John Hargrave, *Words Win Wars* (London: Gardner, Tarton and Co., 1940), p.77
4. Ibid., p.2.
5. Ian Harvey, *The Technique of Persuasion* (London: The Falcon Press, 1951) p.149.
6. Vance Packard, *The Hidden Persuaders* (New York: Pocket Books Inc., 1958), pp.6-7.
7. Clark Leavitt, "Advertising Marketing Communication and Consumer Choice," in *Communication and Behavior,* eds.: Gerhard J. Harmerman and Wm. J. McEwen (Reading: Moss Addison Wesley Pub. Co. Inc., 1975), p. 285.
8. Jacques Ellul, *Propaganda, The Formation of Men's Attitudes* (New York: Knopf, 1965), p.76.
9. J. Driencourt, *La Propaganda* (Paris: Nouvelle Force Politique, 1950), p.18.
10. *Bulletin of the Propaganda Analysis Institute* 1, no.1. October, 1937, p.1.
11. H.L. Childs, *Introduction to Public Opinion* (New York: John Wiley and Sons, 1948), p.244.
12. Leo C. Rosten, "Movies and Propaganda," *Annals of the American Academy of Political and Social Science* 254 (November 1947): 118.
13. Leonard Doob, *Public Opinion and Propaganda* (New York: Henry Holt and Co., 1935) p.240.
14. H.D. Lasswell, D. Carey, and B.L. Smith, *Propaganda and Promotional Activities* (Chicago: University of Chicago Press, 1969). p.39.
15. L. Fraser, *Propaganda* (London: 1957) p.3.
16. Robert Merton, *Mass Persuasion* (New York: Harper Bros, 1946), pp.3-4.
17. J.A.C. Brown, *Techniques of Persuasion; from Propaganda to*

Brain-washing. (Harmindsworth, 1963) p.21.

18. Hardy Forsyth, ed., *Grierson on Documentary* (New York: Harcourt, Brace and Co., 1947). p.265.
19. John Hohenberg, *The Professional Journalist* (San Francisco: Rhinehart Press, 1969), p.330.
20. Lewis Mumford, *Values for Survival* (New York: Harcourt, Brace and Co., 1954), p.39.

2. Film As An Instrument of Propaganda

1. *Lenin on the Film Industry* (Moscow: Isskustvo, 1973). p.11.
2. E. Lesier, *Deutschland, Erwache! Propaganda in Film des Dritten Reiches* (Reinbek bei Hamburg, 1968), pp.40-44.
3. Jean Benoit-Levy, *The Art of the Motion Picture* (New York: Coward-McCann, 1946), p.xi.
4. Gloria Waldron, *The Information Film* (New York: Columbia University Press, 1949), p.8.
5. Ernest Lindgren, *The Art of the Film* (Hempstead, England: Allen and Unwin Ltd.), 1956. p.2.
6. Joseph M. Boggs, *The Art of Watching Films* (Menlo Park, Cal: Benjamin Cummings Publishing Co., 1978), pp.4-5.
7. Doob, *Public Opinion,* pp.525-26.
8. Michotte Van den Berck, "Réalité des Projections Cinematographiques," *Revue Internationale de Filmologie,* (October 1948) pp.3-4.
9. Siegfried Kracauer credits the cinema with having a very strong feeling of "being present," and says that film can give the spectator a sense that the events presented are like life. *The Nature of Film* (London: Denis Dobson, 1961), p.2.
10. Doob, *Public Opinion,* p.525-26.
11. Kracauer, *Theory of Film,* p.160.
12. Amos Vogel, *Film as Subversive Art* (New York: Random House, 1974), p.10.
13. Kracauer, *Theory of Film,* p.7.

3. Art and Propaganda in Nazi Germany

1. Hellmut Lehman-Haupt, *Art Under Dictatorship* (New York: Oxford University Press, 1954), p.xviii.
2. *Film-Welt,* 5 May, 1935.
3. George L. Mosse, *Nazi Culture* (New York: Grosset and Dunlap, 1966), p.135.

4.   Karl Eberlin, *Was ist Deutsch in der Deutscher Kunst?* (Leipzig: Verlag E.A. Seemarm, 1933), p.56.

5.   George L. Mosse, *Nazi Culture,* p.136.

6.   Hans Volz, ed. *Von der Grossmacht zur Weltmacht* (Berlin: Junker und Dunnhaupt Verlag, 1938), pp.416-26.

7.   Adolf Hitler, *Mein Kampf* (New York: Reynal and Hitchcock, 1941), p.237.

8.   Ibid., p.237.

9.   Ibid., p.239.

10. Ibid., p.234.

11. Adolf Leschnitzer, *The Background of Modern Anti-Semitism* (New York: International Universities Press, 1956), p.162.

12. Louis P. Lochner, ed., *The Geobbels Diaries* (Garden City, N.Y.: Doubleday and Doran, 1948), p.56.

13. H. Rauschning, *Hitler Speaks: A Series of Political Conversations with Adolf Hitler on His Real Aim* (London: T. Butterworth, 1939), pp.208-212.

14. George Sadoul, *Le Cinèma Pendant la Guerre 1939-1945* (Paris, 1954), pp.7-14.

15. H.H. Woolenberg, *Fifty Years of German Film* (London: Falcon Press, 1948), p.40.

16. Franz Neumann, *Behemoth: The Structure and Practice of National Socialism 1933-1944* (Oxford University Press, 1949), pp.436-39.

17. *The Attorney General Against Eichmann* (Jerusalem: Center for Information, 1961), p.11.

18. Lucy Davidowicz, *The War Against The Jews 1933-45* (Harmondsworth, Middlesex: Penguin Books Ltd., 1975), p.56.

19. Shlomo Aharonson, "Monologues With The Devil," *Yediot Ahronot,* April, 1983.

20. Jacob L. Talmon, *"Teuda ve' Edut"* [Documentation and Evidence] in Hebrew, in – *The Universal Significance of the New Anti-Semitism; The Holocaust of the Jews of Eastern Europe* eds. Israel Gutman and Livia Rothkirchen, (Jerusalem, 1973), p.124.

21. Yehuda Bauer, *HaShoa; Hebetim Historiim* [The Holocaust: Historical Apects] in Hebrew, (HaKibutz HaArtzi Publishers, 1982), p.53.

22. Talmon, p.142.

23. David Stewart Hull, *Film in the Third Reich* (Berkeley: University of California Press, 1969), p.10.

24. *The New York Times,* 16 April, 1933 Section IV, p.2, and G.W. Kelnisch, *Die Entwicklung des National Sozialistischen Filmmonopols von 1933-1940* (München: Rutten und Loening

Verlag. G.M.H., 1954), p.37.

25. P. Glaesser, "Filmkunst und Erziehung Zeitschrift für Pädagogische Psychologie, etc.," *Psychological Abstracts* 10. No. 7 (July, 1936), p.399.

26. Paul Rotha and Richard Griffith, *The Film Till Now* (London: Vision Press Ltd., 1949), p.588.

27. Louis Marcorelles, "The Nazi Cinema 1933-1945," *Sight and Sound* 25, No. 2 (Autumn, 1955): 67.

28. *Catalogue of Forbidden German Features and Short Films.* Film Section, Information Services Division, Control Commission for Germany. Hamburg, 1951.

29. Joseph Goebbels, *Erkenntnis und Propaganda* (Munich. F. Eher Nachf, 1934), p.28.

30. "Jewish characteristics" were generally derived from cartoon caricatures that were regularly featured in the daily press. In Julius Streicher's *Der Stürmer,* Jews were portrayed with an immense expanse of body, crooked short legs, colossal flat feet, ape-like posture and long hairy arms and hands. The head was thick with bloated and furrowed features, protruding eyes, huge ears and distended lips.

31. John Altman, "Movies' Role in Hitler's Conquest of German Youth," *Hollywood Quarterly* 3 No. 4 (Summer, 1948): 382.

32. Gregory Bateson, "Cultural and Thematic Analysis of Fictional Films," *Transactions of the New York Academy of Sciences* Series II, 5, No.4 (February, 1943), pp. 72-78.

33. *The New York Times* 10 October, 1933.

34. Personal Interview with Dr. Theo Dürstenau, July 27, 1979.

4. Ideology and Propaganda

1. Aldous Huxley, "Notes on Propaganda," *Harper's Monthly Magazine* vol. 174 (December, 1936), p.34.

2. Peter Pulzer, *The Rise of Political anti-Semitism in Germany and Austria* (New York, 1964).

3. Talmon, p.115.

4. Adolf Hitler, "My Political Testament" *NCA 6 Doc. 3569-PS* pp.258-63.

5. Robert G.L. Waite, *The Psychopathic God: Adolf Hitler* (New York: Basic Books, 1977), p.85.

6. For a further discussion of this point see Tzvi Bachrach, *Anti-Shemiyut Modernit* [Modern Anti-Semitism] Ministry of Defense: 1979), p.17.

7. For a further discussion of this point see Nili Mirski *"HaYehudi HaNitzhi: Tikvot HaOlam"* [The Eternal Jew; The Hopes of the World] HaAretz, 19 August, 1983.

8. Robert Waite, p.288.

9. Gordon A. Craig, *The Germans* (New York and Ontario: New American Library, 1983), p.128.

10. quoted in Robert Waite, p.288.

11. quoted in Robert Waite, p.289.

12. Erik Erikson, *Young Man Luther* (New York: W.W. Norton and Co., 1962), p.105.

13. Dietrich Echard, *Der Bolshewismus von Moses bis Lenin* (n.p., n.d.).

14. G.B. Roberts, *Anti-Semitism* (Jerusalem: Keter Publishing House, 1948), p.23.

15. Shmuel Ettinger, *Shorshey HaAnti-Shemiyut Bezman Hehadash* [The Roots of anti-Semitism in Modern Times; The Holocaust of the Jews of Europe,] p.23.

16. Louis L. Snyder, *Hitler and Nazism* (New York: Bantam, 1967), p.132.

17. Robert Waite, p.315.

18. Talmon, p.131.

19. Friedrich Nietzsche, *Philosophy of Nietzsche.* (New York: Random House, 1968), p.452.

20. Alfred Rosenberg, *Friedrich Nietzsche, Commemorative Speech of October, 1944 on the 100th Anniversary of Nietzsche's birth* (Zentral Vorlag, NSDAP. Munich, 1944), p.14.

21. Karl Dietrich Bracher, *The German Dictatorship,* trans. Jean Steinberg. (New York: Praeger, 1970), p.28.

22. Friedrich Nietzsche, p.457.

23. Gordon A. Craig, *The Germans,* p.136.

24. Heinrich von Treitschke, *Politics* (Leipzig: 1899), pp.299-302.

25. Hannah Arendt, *Anti-Semitism* (New York: Harcourt, Brace and World, 1968), p.87.

26. C.W. Grattenauer, *Erklärung an das Publikum über meine Schrift: Wieder die Juden* (Berlin, 1803), pp.32-36.

27. Lucy Davidowicz, *The War Against the Jews, 1933-45* (London: Penguin, 1975), p.56.

28. Quoted in Hans Kohn, *The Mind of Modern Germany* (New York: Harper and Row, 1965), p.88.

29. George L. Mosse, *The Crisis of German Ideology* (New York: Grosset and Dunlap, 1976), p.4.

30. Karl Dietrich Bracher, *The German Dictatorship* (New York:

Praeger Publishers, 1970), p.33.

31. Peter Gay, *Freud, Jews and Other Germans: Masters and Victims in Modernist Culture* (New York: Oxford University Press, 1979), p.218.
32. The reference to Ahashuerus was probably to the folk legend of the Wandering Jew.
33. These two and Brunhild and Hagen are the ancient heroes and heroines with whom many modern Germans identified themselves.
34. William F. Shirer, *The Rise and Fall of the Third Reich* (Greenwich, Conn.: Fawcett Publications, 1960), p.149.
35. Houston Steward Chamberlain, *Foundations of the Nineteenth Century,* vol. 1 (London: John Lane, 1911), p.265.
36. Chamberlain, vol. 2, p.206.
37. Werner Sombart, *The Jew and Modern Capitalism* (Glencoe, Ill.: Free Press, 1951), p.2.
38. Karl Marx, A World Without Jews (New York: Philosophical Library, 1959), p.41.
39. Ibid., p.41.
40. Ibid., p.40.
41. Ibid., p.37.
42. Ibid., p.vi.
43. Alex Bein, "Sheelat HaYehudim Besifrut HaAntishemit HaHadasha KeHahsharat HaDerech el "HaPitron HaSofi," *Shoat Yehudei Europea* ["The Jewish Question in the New Anti-Semitic Literature as Preparation for the Final Solution;" The Holocaust of European Jewry], p.140.
44. Gordon Craig, *The Germans,* p.140.

5. Propaganda and Stereotype in the Anti-Semitic Film

1. *The International Encyclopedia of the Social Sciences* (New York, 1968) vol.15. pp.259-60.
2. Ettinger, *The Roots of Anti-Semitism in Modern Times,* p.15.
3. Yeshayahu Nir, *Mivneh HaKarikatura Ha Sovietit 1967-1973* [The Structure of Political Caricature; The Arab-Israeli Dispute in Soviet Caricatures 1967-73] in Hebrew (Tel Aviv, 1976), pp.12-18.
4. Mosse, *The Crisis of German Ideology,* p.140.
5. Quoted in Mosse, *The Crisis of German Ideology,* p.143.
6. Bein, p.66.
7. *Bulletin of the World Jewish Congress,* December 1939, quoted in Bauer, *The Holocaust: Historical Aspects,* p.53.
8. *Hitler's Speeches* (New York: Oxford University Press, 1942), p.12.

9. *Mein Kampf,* p.82.
10. *Hitler's Speeches,* p.59.
11. Adolf Hitler, *Mein Kampf,* p.325; for a further discussion of the problem of Hitler's incest from a clinical psychological point of view, see Waite, p.424.
13. Uriel Tal, "Antishemiut Antinozrit," [Anti-Christian Anti-Semitism] in *The Holocaust of the European Jewry,* p.103.
14. Eric Goldhagen, *The Sources of the Final Solution (2) Patterns of Prejudice* (The Institute for Jewish Affairs in London: World Jewish Congress) Jan-Feb. 1978.
15. Quoted in *The Black Book,* (published by the Jewish Black Book Committee, United States, 1946), pp.49-50.
16. Quoted by Mosse, *The Crisis in German Ideology,* p.128.
17. Quoted by Alfred Leschnitzer, in *The Modern Background of Anti-Semitism* (New York: International Universities Press, 1956), p.111.
18. Cited in Mosse, *The Crisis of German Ideology,* p.46.
19. Gay, p.185.
20. Gay, p.187.
21. For further discussion see the chapter on *Jud Süss.*
22. Leon Poliakov, *The History of Anti-Semitism* (New York: Schocken Books, 1976), p.273.
23. For further discussion of the modern urban character of European Jewry see below.
24. Norman Cohn, *Warrant for Genocide: the Myth of the Jewish World Conspiracy and the Protocols of the Elders of Zion* (New York: Harper and Row, 1969),
25. Jacob R. Marcus, *The Jew in the Medieval World* (New York: Jewish Publication Society, 1938), p.47.
26. Arendt, *Anti-Semitism,* p.36.
27. Ibid., p.30.
28. Ibid., p.37.
29. Mosse, *The Crisis in German Ideology,* p.142.
30. Hitler, *Mein Kampf,* p.344.
31. Goebbels, *Erkenntnis und Propaganda,*
32. Zvi Bachrach, *Gaz'anut BeSherut HaPolitika,* [Racism – The Tool of Politics; From Monism Towards Nazism] (Jerusalem: The Magnes Press, The Hebrew University, 1985), p.67.
33. Hitler, *Mein Kampf,* p.751.

PART 2

2. The Eternal Jew – The *Mein Kampf* of the Anti-Semitic Nazi Cinema.

1. Two early pioneers of cinematic techniques at the end of the nineteenth century.
2. Kracauer, *Theory of Film,* p.56.
3. Robert L. Snyder, *Pare Lorentz and the Documentary Film* (Norman: University of Oklahoma Press), p.3.
4. Hull, *Film in the Third Reich,* pp.173-174.
5. In French he is frequently called Issa Lequedem, corrupted Hebrew for "Isaac the Old" or "From the East." In the German connotation, he appears in a distinctly anti-Jewish light, referred to as the "Eternal Jew" (German-*Der Ewige Jude*), which in English and French versions became the "Wandering Jew" *(Le Juif Errant).*
6. The legend has obvious affinities with other tales of eternal wanderers, primarily Cain, with whom the Jewish people as a whole are identified by Christian homilists beginning with Terulian (150-230). See L. Neubauer, *Die Sage Vom Ewigen Juden,* 1893, and J. Gaer, *Legend of the Wandering Jews,* 1961.
7. Entitled *Kurtze Beschreibung und Erzehlung von Einen mit Namen Ahasuerus.*
8. A euphemism for Jew, then popular through familiarity with the Purim plays.
9. G.B. Roberts, pp. 105-106.
10. *Der Film* no. 48 (30 Nov. 1940).
11. Ibid.
12. Hippler capitalized on the success of the former by incorporating a large segment of it in his film. The film *Jud Süss* is discussed in detail in the following chapter.
13. *Der Film,* 30 November, 1940.
14. Ibid.
15. *Der Film,* November 1948.
16. Hippler's first major project was the film, *Feldzug in Polen* [Campaign in Poland], a documentary he put together in time for release in February, 1940. In the film he represented the Poles as weak and deceitful.
17. Waschnek's film, *The Rothschilds,* was introduced with a map showing the expansion of one single Jewish family in Europe.
18. *Der Angriff,* no. 288 (29, November 1940).
19. *Der Völkische Beobachter,* no.335 (30, November 1940).
20. Ibid.

21. The most macabre example is the Nazi film about Theresienstadt, *The Führer Gives the Jews a New Town,* 1944.
22. Erwin Leiser, *Nazi Cinema* (New York: Collier, 1974), p.87.
23. Bernard Goldstein, *Die Sterne Sind Zeugen* (München: Deutsche Verlagsanstalt, 1965), p.86.
24. Leiser, p.87.
25. The Russian cinema developed a full iconography of detestable capitalistic attributes to be linked with the enemy: obesity, umbrella, gloves, cigarette holders, and bowler hats.
26. Leif Furhammars & Folke Isaksson, *Film and Politics* (London: Studio Vista Publishers, 1968), p.101.
27. This premise is also stated in the film's opening title "The Jews Such as We Know in Germany," and provides a picture of their racial characteristics.
28. *Meldungen aus dem Reich* no.115 (20 January, 1941).
29. *Der Film* 30 Nov., 1940.
30. *Meldungen aus dem Reich* no.115 (20 January, 1941).

3. Jud Süss

1. David Steward Hull, *Film in the Third Reich* (Berkeley: University of California Press, 1969), p.160.
2. Curt Elwenspolk, *Jud Süss Oppenheimer* (Stuttgart: W. Hüdecke, 1929), p.158.
3. Selma Stern, *Jud Süss, ein Beitrag zur Deutschen und zur Jüdischen Geschichte* (Berlin: Akademie-Verlag. 1929), p.64.
4. Quoted in W.E. Yuill, *Leon Feuchtwanger: the Man, His Ideas and His Work* (Los Angeles: Hennessey and Ingalls, 1972), p.116.
5. Yuill, p.117.
6. K.S. Pinson, *Modern Germany* (New York: Macmillan, 1966), p.405.
7. Craig, *The Germans,* p.142.
8. Craig, p.143.
9. Hull, p.161.
10. *Licht Bild, Bühne,* no.164 18 July 1939.
11. Ibid.
12. Joseph Wulf, *Theater und Film im Dritten Reich* (Gütersloh: Sigbert Mohn Verlag, 1964), p.398.
13. *Der Film* no.3 20 January 1940.
14. *Das Reich,* no. 19 29 April 1940.
15. *Berliner Börsen-Zeitung,* 25 September 1940.
16. Helmut Blobner and Herbert Helba, "Jackboot Cinema," *Film and*

Filming 8, no.3 December 1962.

17. *Security Service,* AKTE no. R 58/156.
18. Ibid.
19. Hull, p.167.
20. Ibid.
21. *Filmpress,* no.27a 22 July 1950: p.8, quoted in Hull, pp.167-68.
22. *Variety,* 7 April 1958.
23. *Variety,* 12 December 1959. The same dealer offered it to Martha Feuchwanger, the wife of the writer of the novel. *Jud Süss,* which appeared in the United States under the name of *Power.*
24. Hull, p.169.

4. The Rothschilds

1. For a full discussion of Hippler's approach, see Part 2 Chapter 2.

5. Summary and Final Word

1. For a full discussion of Hippler's approach see Part 2, Chapter 3.
2. Heinrich Broder, *Jerusalem Post,* December 1982.
3. Ibid.
4. Shamai Golan, *Yediot Ahronot,* 16 April 1982.
5. Saul Friedlander, *Reflections on Nazism; An Essay on Kitsch and Death* (New York: Harper and Row, 1984), pp.11-12.
6. Albert Camus *The Plague (London: Penguin Books. 1987),* p.252.

RECOMMENDED
FILM BIBLIOGRAPHY
IN ENGLISH AND GERMAN

Albrecht, G. "Korrektur zum Nazifilm." *Film* (Hannover), (October 1963): 46f.

Altenloah, E. *Zur Soziologie des Kino.* Jena: 1914.

Altman, John. "Movies' Role in Hitler's Conquest of German Youth." *Hollywood Quarterly* III, No.4, 379-386.

------."The Technique and Content of Hitler's War Propaganda Films. Part I: Karl Ritter and His Early Films." *Hollywood Quarterly*, IV Summer 1950 385-391.

------."The Technique and Content of Hitler's War Propaganda Films, Part II: Karl Ritter's Soldiers' Film." *Hollywood Quarterly* V, Fall 1950 61-72.

Bächlin, P. *Der Film als Ware*, Basle, 1945.

Baird, J.W. *The Mythical World of Nazi Propaganda 1939-45.* Minneapolis, 1974.

Barr, Alfred H. Jr. "Nationalism in German Films." *Hound and Horn* 7, 1934, 278-283.

Barsam, R.M. *Filmguide to Triumph of the Will.* Bloomington, Indiana, 1975.

Bateson, G, "An Analysis of the Nazi Film Hitlerjunge Quex," in Mead, M., and Métraux, R. eds., *The Study of Culture at a Distance.* Chicago, 1953.

Belling, C. *Der Film im Dienste der Partei*, Berlin, 1937.

Bramsted, E.K. *Goebbels and National Socialist Propaganda* 1925-45. London: 1965.

Brentano, B. von, *The Cabinet of Dr. Caligari.* London, 1972.

Brunner, Carl. "Das Wort aus Stein." *Film Woche* (Berlin) 17, May 24, 1939. p.644.

Bukhartsen, Demitri. "Nazi Movies Through Russian Eyes." *The Living Age* (originally published in Izvestia), 347, November 1934: 270-271.

Burden, Hamilton T. "The Celluloid Image," pp.92-99 in *The Nuremberg Party Rallies: 1923-39.* New York and London: Frederick A. Praeger, 1967.

Cheronnet, Louis. "The German Cinema," *The Living Age,* translated from le Crappuillot, 343, January 1933: 441-444.

Davy, Charles. "The Old King and the Young King." *The Spectator* 154 (May 10, 1935), p.780.

Delahaye, Michael, ed. "Interview with Leni Riefenstahl." *Interviews with Film Directors.* ed. Andrew Sarris. New York: Avon-Discus, 1969.

Dreher, Carl, "Parade-Ground Art, the German Film Under Hitler." *New Theatre,* (June, 1936), pp.10-12.

Doob, L.W. "Goebbels' Principles of Propaganda." *Public Opinion Quarterly,* Fall 1950, pp.419-42.

Eisenstein, Sergei M. "Open Letter to Dr. Goebbels." *Film Art,* 2 (Winter, 1934), pp.7-11.

Eisner, L. *The Haunted Screen.* Berkeley and Los Angeles: University of California Press, 1969.

Fielding, Raymond. "The Nazi-German Newsreel." *Journal of the University Film Producers Association,* (Spring, 1960), pp.3-5.

Friedlander, Saul. *Reflections on Nazism; An Essay on Kitsch and Death.* New York: Harper and Row, 1984.

Funk, A. *Film und Jugend. Eine Untersuchung über die psychischen Wirkungen des Films im Leben Jugendlichen.* Munich, 1934.

Furhammar, Leif and Folke Isaksson. *Politics and Film.* London: Studio Vista, 1971.

Gardner, Robert. "Can the Will Triumph?" *Film Comment* 3 (Winter, 1965), pp.28-31.

Goebbels, J. *The Goebbels Diaries.* L.P. Lochner, ed., London: The Firnside Press, 1948.

Gombrich, E.H. *Myth and Reality in German War-time Broadcasts.* (The Creighton Lecture in History, 1969) London: 1970.

Griffith, Richard. "The German Film," in *The Film Till Now,* by Richard Griffith and Paul Rotha. London: Spring Books, 1967. pp.580-595.

Hale, O.H. *The Captive Press in the Third Reich.* Princeton: Princeton University Press, 1964.

Harlan, V., *Im Schatten meiner Filme. Selbstbiographie* (Gütersloh, 1966), translated into French as *Souvenirs; ou le cinéma allemand selon Goebbels.* (Paris, 1974).

Herma, H., "Goebbels' Conception of Propaganda." *Social Research,* vol. 10, no. 2, May, 1943, pp.200-18.

Hitchens, Gordon, ed. "An Interview with a Legend; Leni Riefenstahl."

Film Comment 3 (Winter, 1965), pp.4-10.

Hitler, A. *Mein Kampf.* Translated by R. Manheim. Boston: Houghton Mifflin Company, 1943.

Hollstien, Dorothea. *Antisemitische Filmporpaganda.* Berlin: Verlag Dokumentation München-Pulloch, 1971.

Hübl, Dr. Adolf. "The German Film Academy." *The Living Age* (from the Neues Wiener Tageblatt), June, 1934. pp.360-361.

Hull, D.S. *Film in the Third Reich.* Berkeley, Cal., 1969.

------. *"Forbidden Fruit: The Harvest of the German Cinema, 1939-1945."* Film Quarterly 14 (Summer, 1961), pp.16-30.

Kalbus, Oscar. *Vom Werden Deutscher Filmkunst.* 2 vols. Altona: Behrenfeld, 1935.

Kelman, K. "Propaganda as Vision: *Triumph of the Will." Film Culture* Spring 1973. pp.162-67.

Klimsch, G.W. *Die Entwicklung des National-Sozialistischen Film-Monopols von 1933-40.* München, 1954.

Kochenrath, H.P. ed. *Der Film im Dritten Reich.* Cologne, 1963.

Kracauer, S. *From Caligari to Hitler. A Psychological History of the German Film.* Princeton University, 1947.

------"The Conquest of Europe on the Screen. The Nazi Newsreel 1939-40." *Social Research* vol. 10, no. 3, September, 1943, pp.337-57.

Leiser, E. *Deutschland erwache! Propaganda im Film des Dritten Reiches.* (Reinbek, 1968). Translated as *Nazi Cinema.* London, 1974.

Lochner, Louis P. ed. *The Goebbels Diaries, 1942-1943.* Garden City: Doubleday, 1948.

Lydir, Waldemar, "Schatzkammer der Vergangenheit." *Film Woche* Berlin, 17. (August 30, 1939), pp.1093-1094.

Madsen, Axel. "Interview With Fritz Lang." *Sight and Sound 36* Summer, 1967. pp.108-112.

Manvell, Roger and Heinrich Fraenkel. *Dr. Goebbels, His Life and Death.* New York: Pyramid, 1961.

Manvell, R. and Fraenkel, H. *The German Cinema.* London, 1971.

Marcorelles, Louis "The Nazi Cinema, 1933-1945." *Sight and Sound, 25,* (Autumn, 1955), pp.65-69.

Mosse, G.L. *The Nationalization of the Masses. Political Symbolism and Mass Movements in Germany From the Napoleanic Wars through the Third Reich.* New York, 1971.

Neumann, C., Belling, C., and Betz, H.W. *Film-Kunst, Film-Kohn, Film-Korruption, Ein Streifzug durch vier Jahrzehnte.* Berlin, 1938.

Olimsky, Fritz and Padover S.K. "The German Motion Picture Today." *Public Opinion Quarterly,* 3 (January, 1939), pp.142-146.

Pardo, H. and Schiffner, S. *Jud Süss Historisches und juristisches Material zum Fall Veit Harlan.* Hamburg, 1949.

Patalas, Enro "Der 30. Januar 1945-Kolberg." *Filmkritik* 9 (December, 1965), pp.689-691.

------"The Kolberg Case." *Sight and Sound.* (Winter 1965-66), pp.22-23.

Phillips, M.S. "The German Film Industry and the New Order." in Stachura, P.D. ed. *The Shaping of the Nazi State.* London, 1978, pp.257-81.

Platt, David. "The Swastika Over German Film." *Daily Worker* (New York) 4 May 1939.

Regal, Helmut. "Zur Topographie des NS Films." *Filmkritik* 10 (January, 1966), pp.5-18.

Reiss, Curt. *Joseph Goebbels.* New York: Ballantine, 1960.

Riefenstahl, Leni. *Hinter den Kulissen des Reichsparteitagfilms.*

------. *Schönheit im Olympischen Kampf.* Berlin: Im Deutschen Verlag, 1937.

Robson, Mary M. "From Caligari to Hitler Letter." *Sight and Sound.* 16, (Autumn, 1947), p.117.

Ruehl, Raimond "Harlan über Kolberg." (Excerpt of a television interview with Veit Harlan), *Filmkritik* (December, 1965), p.697.

Rutenberg, Joachim K. "German Industry Completing Transition to Show 195 Films." *Motion Picture Herald* October 2, 1937.

------."Studios in Germany Facing Difficulties." *Motion Picture Herald* October 31, 1936.

Sander, A.U., *Jugend und Film.* Berlin, 1944.

Semmler, Rudolf. *Goebbels: The Man Next to Hitler.* London: Westhouse, 1947.

Schenzinger, K.A., *Der Hitlerjunge Quex.* Berlin, 1932.

Sington, D., and Weindenfeld, A. *The Goebbels Experiment. A study of the Nazi Propaganda Machine.* London, 1942.

Speer, A. *Inside the Third Reich.* London, 1970.

Speier, H. "Nazi Propaganda and its Decline." *Social Research,* vol. 10. no. 3. September 1943, pp.358-77.

Taylor, Richard. *Film Propaganda – Soviet Russia and Nazi Germany.* London: Croom Helm, 1979.

Trenker, Luis. "Ich filme in meinen Bergen." *Die Film Woche* 11 (November 8, 1933), pp.1418-1419.

Tyler, Parker. *Classics of the Foreign Film.* New York: Bonanza, 1952.

Vas, Robert. "Sorcerers or Apprentices: Some Aspects of Propaganda Films. *Sight and Sound* 32 (Autumn, 1963), pp.199-204.

Winge, John Hans. "Brecht and the Cinema." *Sight and Sound* 26 (Winter, 1956-57), pp.144-147.

270

Wollenberg, H.H. "The Strange Story of the Titanic." *Sight and Sound* 19, (August, 1950), pp.239-240.

Wulf, J. ed. *Theater und Film im Dritten Reich. Eine Dokumentation.* Ringbek, 1966.

Zeman, Z.A.B. *Nazi Propaganda.* London and New York: Oxford University Press, 1965.

INDEX

"Address to the German People" 75

Ahasuerus 9, 83, 115, 116

Alexander, Karl (of Württemberg) 16, 143, 144, 146, 147, 148, 150

Arliss, George 131

Baarova, Lida 16

Ballad of the Jew Gernutus 101

Battleship Potemkin, The 48

Bauer, Max 92

Berning, Bishop 72

Blum, Leon 132

Bois, Curt 133

Camus, Albert 168

Chamberlain, Houston Stewart 71, 83, 84, 85 87

Chaplin, Charles 133

De Haan, Felix 80

Der Angriff 133

Der Stürmer 43, 90, 93

Dinter, Arthur 92

Disney, Walt 36

Doctor Faustus 73

Dühring, Karl Eugen 78

Eckard, Dietrich 84

Einstein, Albert 133

Eisenstein, Sergei M. 48

Eternal Jew, The 9, 12, 44, 96, 114, 115, 116, 117, 131, 137, 138, 139, 140, 142, 159, 164

Fassbender, Reiner Werner 166

Feder, Gotfred 24

Feuchtwanger, Leon 15, 143, 144, 145, 147

Feuchtwanger, Martha 15, 16

Fichte, Johan Gottlieb 75

Fiorentino, Giovanni 100

Frankfurter, David 132

Freitag, Gustav 80

Frietsche, Hans 17

George, Heinrich 143

Gesta Romanorum 100

Gobineau, Joseph Arthur, De 83, 84

Goebbels, Joseph 16, 17, 23, 24, 33, 39, 40, 41, 42, 43, 44, 48, 57, 58, 59, 62, 91, 104, 109, 141, 144, 157, 164, 166

Godsche, Herman 98

Goldman, Emma 132

Grass, Gunther 166

Greenspan, David 132

Grierson, John 31, 113

Hans Westmar 62, 63

Harlan, Veit 16, 17, 44, 147, 148

House of Rothschild, The 115, 131

Hauff, Wilhelm 143, 145

Hegel, Wilhelm Friedrich 75, 76

Heimaker 66

Helwig, Herbert 111

Himmler, Heinrich 158

Hippler, Fritz 116, 117, 118, 131, 140, 141, 142, 164

Hitler, Adolf 16, 23, 24, 41, 42, 43, 44, 45, 48, 57, 71, 72, 73, 74, 76, 83, 86, 87, 91, 93, 98, 105, 111, 135, 141

Hitlerjunge Quex 59, 61, 62, 67

Hofjuden 102

Huxley, Aldous 71, 72, 86

Jew Süss (Jud Süss) 12, 15, 16, 17, 116, 143, 155, 157, 158, 159, 167

Joly, Maurice 98

Judaism in Music 82

Kar Peters 68
Kortner, Fritz 133
Krauss, Werner 143, 150, 153
Kristallnacht (The night of broken glass) 65, 74, 133
Lagarde, Paul De 71, 78
Lang, Fritz 133
Lenin, Vladimir Ilyich 33
Linen from Ireland 65
Lorentz, Pare 114
Lorre, Peter 133
Luther, Martin 72, 73, 74, 76
Luxemburg, Rosa 132
Mann, Thomas 72, 73
Marian, Ferdinand 143
Marr, Wilhelm 79
Marx, Karl 86, 132
Mein Kampf 12, 41, 44, 91
Mendes, Lothar 144, 147
Metzger, Ludwig 16, 147
Merchant of Venice, The 100, 101
Möller, Eberhard Wollfgang 95, 147
Momsen, Theodor 87
Murnau, Friedrich Willhelm 130
Niebelungen Ring 48, 83
Nietzsche, Friedrich 42, 76, 77
Nisan, Levin 132
Nosferatu 130
Ohm Kruger 66
Oppenheimer, Josef Süss 144, 145, 146, 147, 148, 149, 150, 151, 155, 156
Ostjuden 95
Petterson and Bendel 65
Protocols of the Elders of Zion The, 97, 98
Raab, William 80
Radcliffe, John 98

Rathenau, Walter 132, 145, 146, 147
Reinhardt, Max 133
Reliques of Ancient Poetry 101
Rembrandt 70
"Rembrandt Movement" 92
Riefenstahl, Leni 45, 57, 61, 71
Ritter, Karl 60
Robert and Bertram 65
Rosenberg Alfred 76, 84, 87, 93, 95
Rousseau, Jean Jacques 80
Rothschilds, The 116, 138, 139, 159
S.A. Man Brand 59
Seitz, Franz 59
Shylock 100, 101, 152
Soderbaum, Kristina 143
Sombart, Werner 85, 103
Streicher, Julius 17, 93
Stocker, Adolph 94
Steinhoff, Hans 60, 66
Taubert, Eberhard 116
Thus spake Zarathustra 76
Treitschke, Heinrich Von 77, 87
Togger 64
Triumph of the Will 45, 57, 61, 71, 139
Trotsky, Leon 104, 105
Um Das Munshenrecht 64
Van Leers, Johon 98
Veidt, Conrat 144
Wagner, Richard 8, 47, 71, 82, 83
Wandering Jew, The 9, 12, 45, 96, 101
Waschneck, Erick 161
Wessel, Horst 42, 62
Wenzler, Franz 62
Weller, Tudel 95
Wien 1910 69
Zerlett, Hans Heinz 109